STUDIES IN ECONOMICS
Edited by Charles Carter

14

Macroeconomic Planning

STUDIES IN ECONOMICS

Macroeconomic Planning

ROGER A. BOWLES

Lecturer in Industrial Economics, University of Nottingham, and Visiting Research Associate, SSRC Centre for Socio-Legal Studies, Wolfson College, Oxford

AND

DAVID K. WHYNES

Lecturer in Economics, University of Nottingham

London
GEORGE ALLEN & UNWIN
Boston   Sydney

First published in 1979

GEORGE ALLEN & UNWIN LTD
40 Museum Street, London WC1A 1LU

British Library Cataloguing in Publication Data

Bowles, Roger A
    Macroeconomic planning. — (Studies in economics: 14).
    1. Economic policy
    I. Title   II. Whynes, David K   III. Series
    338.9   HD82   78–40623

ISBN 0–04–330294–7
ISBN 0–04–330295–5 Pbk

Typeset in 10 on 11 point Times by George Over Limited and printed in Great Britain by Unwin Brothers Ltd, Old Woking, Surrey.

PREFACE

This books fails to satisfy two criteria which texts are normally supposed to obey. First, it is not the outcome of many years of careful working and reworking of some well-known theme and, secondly, the actual writing was most enjoyable from our own, possibly solipsistic, point of view. Lest our endeavours be thought worthless, may we offer a few words of explanation?

At the time of our first meeting, at the University of York in 1973, our research interests were somewhat disparate—labour mobility, law and welfare economics on the one hand and health, defence and econometrics on the other. By 1976, we found ourselves working together again, this time at the University of Nottingham, but now with teaching interests in macroeconomics and planning, respectively. Having approached these two areas from a common, essentially microeconomic, background, we found much of the conventional literature unsatisfactory for a number of reasons.

First, traditional macroeconomics texts tend to be mechanistic, abstract and (of particular importance from the practical point of view) lacking in any explicit treatment of the appropriate objectives of economic policy. Secondly, texts on planning tend to the opposite extreme, pursuing description of particular planning experiences at the expense of analysis. Thirdly, little account seems to be taken of the likely structure of the political process and thus of how the objectives of, and the constraints on, economic policy come to be specified. Fourthly, recent theoretical work on the microeconomic foundations of the macroeconomy has led to insights which cannot be ignored when discussing macroeconomics and planning in general. Fifthly, the distinctions made between different types of planning problems seem to us to be artificial and, in many cases, unhelpful.

With these points in mind, the prospect of a unified treatment of the central issues of both macroeconomics and planning came to suggest itself. We were concerned to develop a theoretical and applied framework which embraced both macroeconomics and planning and, in particular, which demonstrated the essential unity of all forms of macroeconomic planning by the consistent application of basic economic principles. We might note, incidentally, that, just as microeconomics normally sets out to establish an objective function, an opportunity set and thence an optimal decision in the partial sense, so we have taken macroeconomic planning to comprise a similar set of operations in a general context.

The book has been designed for an audience of third-year undergraduates and first-year postgraduates, who have taken courses in basic micro- and macro-theory. In addition, some knowledge of mathematics and statistics has been assumed, although any deficiencies on the part of the reader in this respect should not constitute too serious an obstacle to understanding. We also believe that certain sections of the text might be accessible to second- or even first-year undergraduates.

A simple 'thank-you' seems insufficient to repay the enormous intellectual debts which we have accumulated. Nevertheless, it must suffice and we extend our grateful thanks to the following:

friends and colleagues at the University of York for a stimulating environment which has had a lasting influence. In particular, we should like to single out and express our sincere thanks to our respective mentors, Alan Williams and Jack Wiseman;

colleagues and students of both the Economics and Industrial Economics Departments at Nottingham, for providing the fertile atmosphere necessary to produce a book of this nature;

Professors Charles Carter and Jack Parkinson for invaluable comments and encouragement during the preparation of the manuscript, and Paul Godwin for helpful comments on Chapter 5;

Yvonne Rogers for the efficient translation of our unintelligible drafts into a neat typescript;

Sue and Yvonne, for their extraordinary capacity for patience and understanding, and for generally being nice.

At the beginning of the Preface, we observed that the writing of this book was, in itself, an enjoyable experience. With this in mind, we should like to thank each other. Joint authorship is particularly susceptible to breakdown, especially when one author finds his favourite phrase has been censored by the other. In spite of this, or perhaps paradoxically because of it, we find our friendship unimpaired and we are willing to accept collective responsibility for all parts of the book, as long as we are both in the room at the same time.

CONTENTS

To our parents

CHAPTER 1

Macroeconomics and Planning

From the point of view of economic organisation, Robinson Crusoe must have been fairly happy on his desert island. His world was a simple agricultural one and was therefore, to a large extent, under the control of the elements and divine providence. Furthermore, at least until the arrival of Friday, he had only himself to please.

Compare this situation with that of present-day industrial society. First, whilst Crusoe's economy was restricted to the output of corn and goats, modern economies are capable of producing an enormous variety of consumption and production goods and services. Secondly, with the establishment of legal systems and methods of economic policy, extensive facilities for the control of the economic system came into existence, independently of Crusoe's more natural controls. Thirdly — and possibly of the greatest significance — societies now comprise, not one (or two) members, but many millions of individuals, each with their own particular views regarding the appropriate allocation of resources, distribution of rewards and so forth. The fundamental economic problem of relating commodity demands to supplies is therefore immeasurably more complex; in that the system is more complicated, it is also presumably more prone to chaos.

With the development of large-scale industrial societies, mankind has employed a number of organisational forms and economic techniques in an effort to ensure that order is maintained. In this book, we shall be concerned with just one particular method — macroeconomic planning — which we feel is of great relevance to the provision of a solution to the economic problems of the contemporary world. Starting from first principles, let us establish a few definitions.

We take the term 'planning' to refer to a purposive, means – ends process and we may define it as the deliberate manipulation of the parameters of a system in order to bring about a desired and specified alteration in the operation of the system.[1] The implications of this definition may be demonstrated by a simple, if slightly facetious, example.

Consider a mechanic on the forecourt of his garage; in front of him stands a motor-car (a mechanical system) with its engine running. Let us now persuade our mechanic to plan some action to influence the functioning of this system and follow his line of reasoning.

In the first place, to borrow some sociological terminology, the mechanic will 'define the situation'; that is, he will observe the system as it currently functions. In our case, he will presumably say: 'I observe a car with its engine running.' The mechanic's second step is to compare his observations of the prevailing situation with the way in which he would like to see it develop. Let us suppose that he now says: 'I want the engine to stop,' and we now have a state of affairs in which the operation of the system conflicts with the wishes of the mechanic. At this stage, our hero might well retire from the forecourt to engage in a spot of thinking. 'What strategies could I pursue', he might ask, 'to influence the system according to my wishes? As an initial option, I could ignore the engine and hope it stops by itself, although experience suggests that this is unlikely to happen. Alternatively, I could drive the car into a brick wall. All things considered, I believe that the best approach, in terms of the highest probability of success, would be to throw a spanner into the works.' Thus convinced, our mechanic returns to the car, wields his spanner and, lo and behold, the engine stops.

Let us summarise the main points of the mechanic's approach. First, he observed and understood the situation confronting him and, secondly, decided that its likely progress did not accord with his wishes. Thirdly, he used his knowledge of the system's functioning to design a strategy which could realise the state of affairs which he desired and, finally, he perpetrated the required action. These principles are, as we shall see, inherent in the planning of the macroeconomy.

[1] To make this definition crystal-clear, we may define a 'system' as a set of inter-related elements. As regards the definition of 'parameter', consider the derivation of a demand curve. When constructing price—quantity relationships, it is customary, for example, to hold income levels constant on a particular occasion, allowing a unique demand curve to be derived. However, on a different occasion we may permit income to be constant at a different level, thereby producing a new demand relationship. This specifically constant but generally variable entity is termed a 'parameter'.

Three complications may now be added to our simple model. In the first place, what could be inferred if the engine did not in fact stop? We should be forced to conclude that some unforeseen factor had come into play, or even remind ourselves that spanners do not necessarily have any effect when thrown into works. In other words, our mechanic either (1) had an inadequate knowledge of the operation of the system with which he was concerned or (2) the implement used to manipulate the parameters was innappropriate; the implications of both are the same. The plan was therefore unsuccessful but, given the *ex ante* specification of objectives and the deliberate perpetration of the action, we should still call it a plan *per se*. It is, incidentally, likely that the failure of this plan will contribute to the knowledge of the mechanic for use in future plans.

Secondly, suppose that the car's owner now appears on the scene and remonstrates with our spanner-throwing mechanic regarding the mistreatment of his engine. The former makes it clear that all he really required was that the engine be slowed down and not actually stopped. We should therefore deduce that the mechanic had mis-specified the objective of the exercise; he had interpreted it as 'stop the engine' whereas the correct desire on the part of the owner was 'slow the engine down'. In this case, that which succeeded was a plan, but it was the wrong plan!

Finally, we should note that the occurence of an action does not, of itself, constitute grounds for the belief that it was planned. In our case, we can only be sure that the violent insertion of the spanner was a planned action if our mechanic specified his objective *ex ante* and if he believed his deliberate actions to be potentially influential upon the attainment of his objectives. These two provisions clearly constitute the necessary conditions for 'planning'.

Turning now to a consideration of 'macroeconomics', the economist's conception is traditionally of the following form:

' "Macroeconomics" is, of course, to be distinguished from "microeconomics". Macroeconomics deals with economic affairs "in the large". It concerns the overall dimensions of economic life. It looks at the total size and shape and functioning of the "elephant" of economic experience, rather than the working or articulation or dimensions of the individual parts. To alter the metaphor, it studies the character of the forest, independently of the trees which compose it.' (Ackley, 1961)

Macroeconomics, in other words, is about aggregates. According to this definition, the macroeconomist is concerned, for example, with the economy's, rather than the individual's, consumption levels or with national, rather than individual, labour power.

Although this text will be dealing primarily with economic activities 'in the large', we should not lose sight of the means by which macrovariables are generated; as we shall see, this means is of great importance to the construction of economic plans. Macrovariables do not exist as autonomous entities; they are, in reality, the aggregation of all the economy's microvariables. Whilst, in certain instances, we might find it expedient to consider these macrovariables as quasi-autonomous, on the justification of some 'law of large numbers', we must not forget that such an aggregate is really the net result of individual, microeconomic actions. If we were to devise a plan for the steel industry, for example, we should have to consider the output of steel both as an entity in itself and as the sum of the outputs of the individual steel plants — outputs which clearly influence the total. Given that causality runs from the micro- to the macroeconomy, we accordingly think of the latter as an inter-relationship of microeconomic elements. To borrow the Ackley metaphor, the felling of just one tree in the forest does not destroy the essential characteristic of 'forestness'. However, it does make our forest a different forest, with the result that it will be necessary to treat the macroeconomy both as a 'forest' and as a 'collection of individual trees'.

Having examined both components of our title, we are now in a position to produce a definition of 'macroeconomic planning', namely, the deliberate manipulation of the parameters of the economic system to bring about a desired alteration in the functioning of the economy. Our general discussion has also indicated the sorts of areas to which aspirant planners must pay attention. More specifically, the economic-planning process must come to terms with five basic requirements and, during the course of this book, we shall be dealing with each in some detail.

Intervention requirement. Can the desired alteration to the economy be brought about by the 'natural' or inherent processes within it, or is some external influence required to determine our result? Is there, in other words, a 'need' for planning?

Political requirement. How do we, as members of society, come to decide upon and specify the aims of the plan? To return to our earlier example, how do the car owner and the mechanic come to agree upon, and clarify, the objective of the exercise?

Technical requirement. How do we obtain the necessary knowledge of the economy in order to (1) observe the relevant features of the current situation, (2) understand the overall workings of the system, and (3) select the appropriate policy instrument or operational technique for the realisation of our objective? Again, in terms of our example, is a spanner the 'best' tool to use under the circumstances and, if so, where into the works should it be thrown? In the real world, this requirement will involve us in the theoretical simulation of practicable alternative strategies which describe a number of possible results, in order to provide us with an *ex ante* estimate of the likely outcomes of the planning decision. These may then be related to our stated aims to provide a guide to the appropriate choice of action.

Implementation requirement. How is the chosen theoretical strategy actually applied in practice? What institutional decisions are necessary for its implementation?

Feedback requirement. How does that which has been achieved relate to our original specified objective or, did the engine stop and, if not, why not?

In spite of the increasing attention currently being paid to the methods of economic planning, it is clearly untrue to say that the latter has always been at the forefront of man's mundane activities. In reality, its importance has been dictated by historical circumstance, in terms of the particular epistomological views of the societies concerned. To illustrate this point, and in order to demonstrate the nature of the ideologies involved, a return to the Ancient World should prove instructive.

The writings of the Socratic School — essentially Plato and Aristotle — are amongst the earliest systematic views on economics with which history has endowed us. Economics for the Socratics was a 'teleological' process, in that it concerned itself equally with the means of attaining a particular end and also with the nature of that end itself. Plato's *Republic* is amenable to interpretation in this way, for it consists of a discussion of the appropriate objective of society ('justice'), followed by an analysis of the form of political and economic organisation necessary for the achievement of this end. Clearly, an approach of this kind could be construed as 'planning' in our sense of the word, and it is indeed Aristotle who first provides us with a clear and succinct planning methodology:

'All men seek one goal: success or happiness. The only way to

5

achieve true success is to express yourself completely in service to society. First, have a definite, clear, practical ideal — a goal, an objective. Second, have the necessary means to achieve your ends — wisdom, money, materials, and methods. Third, adjust your means to that end.' (Quoted in Thomas, 1970)

As the student of the Socratic dialogues will recall, this school of thought did not possess a monopoly on interpretation in the Ancient World. Of its many rivals, the most interesting from our point of view is the Sophist school:

'The manner in which economics was taught by the Sophists has a strong affinity with the approach which has come to be dominant in the twentieth century. In fact, their approach is much closer to that of the majority of modern professional economists than are those adopted by Plato, Aristotle and the Scholastics. For the Sophists, economics is a technology. Its techniques can be taught and mastered without reference to the desirability or lack of desirability attached to the ends or purposes which the technique can be made to serve. The discipline can be applied, for example, to increase the affluence of a particular household or a particular state. However, the question as to whether the form of affluence is worth acquiring is not a question with which economics is concerned.' (Gordon, 1975)

An important distinction between these two methodologies clearly lies in the status of the objective function; in the former approach, the search for the appropriate objective is an integral part of economic analysis whilst, in the latter, this is not deemed to be a question to which the subject may legitimately address itself. As we shall see, these two opposing views are inherent in the planning debate of the present time.

With the eclipse of the Ancient World, political economy — the relationship between human society and its material wealth — began to develop in new directions, as a reaction to man's changing perception of his social and economic environment. The actual causes and mechanisms of this evolution need not detain us here but, suffice it to say, we find that seventeenth-century Western philosophers such as Hobbes, Spinoza, Grotius and Locke, produced very different analyses from those developed by the Socratic school. At the risk of overgeneralisation, the orientation of these scholars was less towards 'social man' in the manner in which he had been conceived by Aristotle; rather, society was seen as an aggregation of individuals and existed solely to maximise the potential for personal liberty. In terms of the evolution of mainstream economics, the interpretations of Hume, Smith, the Mills, Bentham and the like, provided all that was necessary for a theoretical justification of the then-evolving capitalist system. In such an environment, the ideas behind the planning methodology were really nonstarters, as the famous 'invisible hand' was seen to be in perpetual operation to ensure that social welfare was maximised by individual behaviour.

The interest in economic planning which twentieth-century man now displays may be ascribed to two alternative causes, namely, (1) the view that planning is a logical corollary of increasing state intervention within the capitalist economy, and (2) the view that the capitalist system is inherently incapable of adequately meeting the requirements of social preferences. We shall now review each of these alternatives in turn.

Although the nineteenth-century socialist writers such as Marx generally regarded the United Kingdom as the most 'capitalist' of capitalist nations, a total reliance had never really been placed upon the free-market economy managed by its 'invisible hand'. Indeed, throughout its history, the UK economy has been the subject of a variety of forms of state intervention, the purpose of which has been to modify or supplant the functioning of such markets. When wars became too expensive for the purse of the individual monarch for example, kings were obliged to raise funds in a number of ways, such as taxation and borrowing, and this is one of the reasons for Wilson's reference to the seventeenth century as 'an age of debts and taxes' (Wilson, 1965). Regulations regarding the remuneration and employment of the labour force were certainly in existence long before our 'capitalist' theorists ever wrote, examples being the numerous Statutes of Labourers during the 1350s to 1370s which attempted to fix wages and restrict labour mobility. Even the nineteenth century, the so-called 'Age of *Laissez-Faire*' which supposedly represented a total divorce between political and economic activities, saw a considerable amount of intervention in, particularly, social matters on the part of the State (Taylor, 1972).

The degree of state intervention has progressively increased over time although, until the twentieth century, such growth had in fact been brought about by the accumulation of piecemeal legislation. Intervention took place on an *ad hoc* basis, when a particular emergency arose or when a particular interest group found itself threatened; examples of such forms of intervention include the introduction of the income tax in 1799 in order to finance the Napoleonic Wars, and the 1624 Monopolies Act which established the existence of patent rights to protect inventors. By and large, the other nations of the West were simultaneously experiencing similar forms of state intervention.

'The defenders of competitive capitalism had always argued that by the rational pursuit of self-interest the general good would be most effectively attained; that the laws of supply and demand in a free-market world would ensure the maximum production of wealth.' (Thomson, 1957)

This truth was taken to be self-evident, even allowing for state intervention to iron out the occasional market imperfection. By 1945, however, the faith of all but the most stalwart had been shattered as the capitalist world had by then been shaken by a number of crises of a far greater magnitude than had been previously experienced. First, the West had involved itself in two major wars which had necessitated the centralisation of command over resources to efficiently direct the war effort. These war-inspired interventions left their marks on the peacetime economies in many ways, including greatly enlarged public sectors and greater numbers of formal government controls. Secondly, it was clear that the free-market system had in no way prevented the serious interwar depression and, furthermore, might even have precipitated it; rather, it was only positive government action which seemed to provide any solutions to the obvious disequilibrium. As Thomson has concluded:

'Trust could no longer be placed in the capacity of any providential mechanism to regulate itself. Deliberate acts of policy and assertion of moral purpose seemed the only alternatives to anarchy in politics and chaos in economic life.' (ibid.)

To many observers, planning appeared to be the natural successor to interventionist capitalism; all that was necessary was a systematic rationalisation of the various *ad hoc* arrangements which the state had already made, arrangements which now existed in sufficient number and strength to serve as an effective force for economic control. The manifest failures of capitalism in the 1930s also led many to believe that it was the state, and not the entrepreneur, which had the superior notion as to the proper constituents of social welfare. With these points in mind, France formally instituted a planning system in 1946, whilst a number of other European nations including the United Kingdom began to experiment with a variety of planning procedures at both a macro- and a microlevel. Amongst the countries of the 'Third World', India drew up its first plan in 1950.

Our second alternative cause, the view that the capitalist (or, in some cases, the prevailing feudal) system is inimical to the appropriate development of social welfare, has recently found favour in such countries as the Soviet Union, China, the nations of Eastern Europe as well as a substantial part of the 'Third World'. In these cases, political and economic revolutions have paved the way for the establishment of 'socialist' societies, whose principal characteristic is the social ownership of the means of production (capital, land etc.). Societies of this persuasion are a twentieth-century phenomenon and, as we shall see, their commitment to economic planning is explicit. As they appear anxious to reinstate a form of the Socratic 'social man', we should expect Aristotle's dictum to be well received in both Moscow and Peking.

The Modern World is therefore displaying an increasing interest in planning. The process will, however, assume a particular degree of significance in a given economy, depending upon the degree of alteration to the system required and the number and range of parameters to be controlled.

'... some would-be planners envisage 'planning' primarily as a conferment of regulative power over each industry on some organisation representing the capitalist businesses engaged in it, under no more than a very general control exercised by the state in the general interest; while others insist that planning involves not merely the separate organisation of each industry into a co-operating group, but a right adjustment between industries and a social direction of the distribution of labour and capital between alternative uses. One set of planners, again, regards planning as a means of so reorganising capitalism as to give it a new lease of life; while another looks to it as a means of replacing capitalism by social ownership and operation of industry.' (Cole, 1937)

The conclusion to be drawn from this historical review is that most modern societies appear to have generated a 'need' for planning; the next chapter serves to prove that this is indeed the case.

CHAPTER 2

The Need for Planning

THE CAPITALIST MODEL

The following sections establish a simple model of the manner in which capitalist markets operate. The main reason for setting about such a task is not purely to devise a means by which (any) capitalist economy may be characterised, but to go further and show that the central workings of market mechanisms may be susceptible to imperfections of various kinds. The importance of such a demonstration lies in the implications for government intervention generally, and for economic planning in particular. If it can be shown that there are properties intrinsic to certain markets or classes of markets that impede the achievement of an appropriate equilibrium, we have *prima facie* grounds for supposing that government has an important role to play in the operation of the economy. Before investigating the forms that any such actions should take, it is necessary to demonstrate that action of some kind is, in fact, essential.

Prices constitute the device through which offers to buy and sell goods are mediated. The first task, then, is to examine how prices are set, how they are adjusted and whether their adjustment might be expected to lead to an equilibrium between supply and demand. This is done in two stages, the first being to describe the basic Walrasian model in which an Auctioneer is introduced. The second stage is to examine ways in which this fictional Auctioneer can be eliminated. An understanding of both stages is a prerequisite of a thorough understanding of why capitalist markets may not, without active guidance, constitute the most effective means of allocating resources.

THE BASIC MODEL

Let us consider an economy comprising z goods and services $(j = 1, \ldots, m; m + 1, \ldots, z)$ and n individuals $(i = 1, \ldots, n)$. The first m items of goods and services are used as consumption items,

10

whilst the remaining $(z - m)$ refer to services provided by the consumers for use in production. The quantity of the jth good or service bought or sold by the ith individual is denoted by q_{ij}, amounts supplied having a negative sign and amounts bought a positive sign. If we think of goods $(m + 1)$ to z as being amounts of different sorts of labour, then q_{ij} $(j = m + 1, \ldots, z)$ will represent the amount of labour of type j supplied by individual i, whilst q_{ij} $(j = 1, \ldots, m)$ will represent the amount of the jth consumption good that he buys.

A barter system in such an economy would be unwieldy if the number of individuals and/or the number of goods were large owing to the number of potential transactions. We normally find that such societies introduce money in order to facilitate exchange, since this device enables citizens to economise on the number of contacts (and contracts) they have to make when buying or selling a good. Thus, we shall assume that money is used as a medium of exchange in our models, enabling all price ratios to be expressed in a common unit of account. Money will not be allowed to function as an asset in our scheme, even if it is sometimes regarded as so doing in most monetary economies (Laidler, 1969).

The standard economic problem now is to find a price for each good that will ensure equality between supply and demand. We are looking for a price vector that will just clear all markets simultaneously, that is, a set of prices p^*_1 to p^*_z, more conveniently written in the formal notation p^*. In general, any of the many possible sets of prices may be denoted as a vector p. In the formative work on this problem in the nineteenth century, Walras (1874) invented a fictional character, the Auctioneer, who is put in charge of co-ordinating the economy's efforts to find an appropriate price vector. This Auctioneer proceeds by calling out alternative price vectors within earshot of all members of the economy until he finds one at which everyone's plans mesh.

Each member of the economy, when he hears a price vector called out by the Auctioneer, chooses how much of each good and service to demand or supply. At a given set of prices, a person may have too much of some goods (such as their own labour time) and will offer the excess to the market. Similarly, they will make offers to the market for those goods of which they have insufficient at current prices. These activities may be analysed within the conventional utility-maximising model.

An individual is assumed to be able to assign a real number to all possible combinations of labour supply and product consumption.

11

At any given set of prices, they will choose that combination open to them which gives the highest value for this utility index. If we suppose that the ith individual faces a price vector $\mathbf{p}$, we may write their problem as:

$$\text{maximise } \ U_i = U_i \ (q_{il}, \ \ldots \ , \ q_{iz}) = U_i \ (\mathbf{q}_i) \tag{2.1}$$

$$\text{subject to } \sum_{j \,=\, 1}^{z} p_j \ q_{ij} = 0$$

The utility function in equation 2.1 is thus defined over both the amounts of goods consumed and the amount(s) of labour supplied. We will expect higher consumption to be associated with higher utility and a greater supply of labour with lower utility *ceteris paribus*. This assumption is important since without it, the existence of a solution to our problem is jeopardised. The further assumption normally made is that the marginal utility of consumption will be decreasing and the marginal utility of labour supply increasing. Thus equation 2.1 will, typically, display the following characteristics:

$$\frac{\delta U_i}{\delta q_{ij}} > 0 \text{ and } \frac{\delta^2 U_i}{\delta q_{ij}^2} < 0 \text{ for } j = 1, \ \ldots \ , m$$

$$\tag{2.2}$$

$$\frac{\delta U_i}{\delta q_{ij}} < 0 \text{ and } \frac{\delta^2 U_i}{\delta q_{ij}^2} > 0 \text{ for } j = m + 1, \ \ldots \ , z$$

These conditions are illustrated in Figure 2.1, in which diminishing marginal utility of consumption is shown in the upper-right quadrant and increasing marginal disutility of labour supply in the lower-right quadrant.

The constraint in equation 2.1 refers to the requirement that the individual's income must equal his expenditure. Income is given by the product of the hourly wage and the number of hours worked. Thus, if the wage rate for particular labour services of type 3 is p_{m+3} and $q_{i\,(m+3)}$ hours are worked, then total spending on consumer goods will have to total $p_{m+3} \, q_{i\,(m+3)}$ exactly. The solution of equation 2.1 will appear as a vector of quantities $\mathbf{q}_i$ for the ith individual, several elements of which may well be zero.

We might note that our examples so far have been confined to an

12

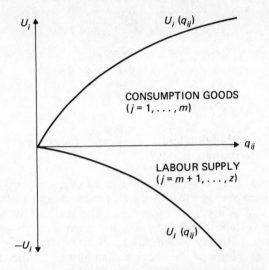

Figure 2.1 *Assumed form of utility functions.*

individual who supplies labour and buys goods. Some or all of the individuals will however, be 'entrepreneurs', that is to say they will hire certain types of labour as well as supplying their own, and supply certain sorts of goods to the market. They will also buy some intermediate goods for use in production and some consumption goods for their own private use.

Having established how the individual is acting, we may now return to our Walrasian Auctioneer and see how he behaves. So far, we know that when he calls out a price vector p, each individual will compute a solution to equation 2.1 and make it known to the Auctioneer. The latter may now assemble a matrix, that is, a set of vectors q_i, denoted q, of the demand and supply of each good by each individual.

This matrix gives us a complete description of how the economy would look if the price vector p were to be actually adopted. Each row indicates the demand and supply decisions of a single individual, whilst each column indicates the total demand and supply of a particular good by consumers and producers.

13

$$q = \begin{bmatrix} q_{11}, & q_{12}, & \ldots, & q_{1m}; & q_{1(m+1)}, & q_{1(m+2)}, & \ldots, & q_{1z} \\ q_{21}, & q_{22}, & \ldots, & q_{2m}; & q_{2(m+1)}, & q_{2(m+2)}, & \ldots, & q_{2z} \\ \cdot & \cdot & & \cdot & \cdot & \cdot & & \cdot \\ \cdot & \cdot & & \cdot & \cdot & \cdot & & \cdot \\ q_{i1}, & q_{i2}, & \ldots, & q_{im}; & q_{i(m+1)}, & q_{i(m+2)}, & \ldots, & q_{iz} \\ \cdot & \cdot & & \cdot & \cdot & \cdot & & \cdot \\ \cdot & \cdot & & \cdot & \cdot & \cdot & & \cdot \\ q_{n1}, & q_{n2}, & \ldots, & q_{nm}; & q_{n(m+1)}, & q_{n(m+2)}, & \ldots, & q_{nz} \end{bmatrix}$$

consumption and   factor inputs
intermediate goods

The Auctioneer's job is to find a price vector p^* at which individuals' plans are such that the total of each column is zero, that is, that demand is just met by supply. The method by which the Auctioneer establishes this equilibrium price vector is known as a *tâtonnement*. Having called out a randomly chosen first experimental price vector p^1, he adds up each of the z columns, each of which corresponds to a single element in the price vector. If for good or service j he finds that demand exceeds supply, he raises the price p_j^1, whilst if supply exceeds demand he lowers it. After adjusting all prices up or down by some amount that is likely to be proportional to the degree of excess demand, he calls out a second price vector. Again he notes the (quantity) responses and again makes (price) adjustments in the indicated direction. This action is repeated until a probably rather tired Auctioneer will declare that an equilibrium has been reached. At this stage the amounts demanded and offered will be written down in the form of contracts, after which the individuals leave the marketplace where the auction has taken place and go about their daily life, given the set of contractual obligations that they have acquired in the interim.

To summarise, we have introduced into our economy an Auctioneer who in a once-for-all experiment has uncovered an equilibrium price vector p^*. We have reached an equilibrium which may be characterised by four conditions:

$$p = p^* \tag{2.3}$$

Zero excess demand: $\displaystyle\sum_{i=1}^{n} q_{ij}^* = 0$ for $j = 1, \ldots, z$ (2.4)

14

Budgets balance: $\sum_{j=1}^{m} p_j^* q_{ij}^* = \sum_{j=m+1}^{z} p_j^* q_{ij}^*$ for $i = 1, \ldots, n$ (2.5)

Maximise utility: $U_i(q_i^*) = \max U_i(q_i)$ for $i = 1, \ldots, n$ (2.6)

Equation 2.4 summarises the constraint that demand and supply of each good and service be equal; equation 2.5 is the budget constraint to which each individual is subject and equation 2.6 ensures that all individuals obey the assumption of utility maximisation, given the ruling prices of equation 2.3.

The range of our analysis may now be extended very significantly by a change in the interpretation of the nature of the goods and services with which we are concerned. At least implicitly, time has not entered our model; the Auctioneer has been considering only demand and supply for the duration (which has remained unspecified) of the market period.

This shortcoming can be avoided by giving different labels to goods that are similar except in the date at which they become available. For example, wheat this year and wheat in twenty years' time are therefore now to be regarded as quite distinct goods; that is, they will occupy different columns of our matrix q. In other respects, things are just as before. At a given pair of prices for these two goods, the Auctioneer will still compare demand and supply and adjust prices accordingly. Distinguishing goods and services in this way corresponds to having a series of 'futures' markets as well as 'spot' markets. By allowing the 'market period' to comprise a number of different occasions upon which transactions may take place, this ingenious device enables us to regard each individual as going to an auction at the 'beginning' of his life and negotiating, via the Auctioneer, all the exchanges that he will ever want to make. Thus, all the citizens having gathered for the auction disperse when it is over, each having acquired a set of contracts completely determining all their future actions. There will normally be no scope for subsequent renegotiation of any contract.

One final improvement that we may make to our basic model in order to give it increased applicability, is to allow for the effects of uncertainty. Since many features of the world, such as weather, cannot be predicted far ahead and yet have important effects on economic activity, we need some means by which to account for such uncertainty. Suppose, for example, that we are farmers, considering whether to offer wheat for sale in twenty years' time. If we live in a country that enjoys great climatic variety, then it is likely that the total yield from planting a given acreage with the same crop will vary widely from season to season. The consequence of this is that we will be unable to firmly offer a particular level of supply to the market. Rather, we will have to make an offer that is contingent upon the weather conditions that will actually prevail during the growing season. Provided that people in the economy can guess the probabilities that the weather will be favourable or unfavourable, we may instruct the Auctioneer to regard wheat as a different product under different weather conditions. Individuals therefore now have to make offers to buy or sell that will only have to be honoured if certain specified conditions hold true. We will, of course, expect that the price of wheat in good times, in relation to the price in adverse times, will be determined by the relative likelihood of times being good or bad and the extent to which the crop yield is sensitive to the weather conditions, and possibly also by the attitude towards risk taken by the bidders. (For a more detailed discussion of the general problem of behaviour under uncertainty, see Chapter 5 and the references cited therein.) If the Auctioneer follows these instructions, he will still be able to devise an equilibrium price vector, although it will now have more elements than before since a wider variety of 'goods' is now involved.

SHORTCOMINGS OF THE BASIC MODEL

In the previous section, we developed a relatively sophisticated model of a market economy in which all individuals made privately optimal decisions that were co-ordinated by an Auctioneer who had a price system at his disposal. We suggested, rather than proved, that if the demand and supply functions conformed with a number of relatively weak conditions, then the Auctioneer would be able to derive the unique vector of prices at which all individual intentions could be carried out. The existence of such a general equilibrium — and the fact that our Auctioneer will be able to grope his way towards it — is in many ways most impressive. The fact is, however, that the Auctioneer is a hypothetical figure: we know that real-world economies do not have the wherewithal to enable all decisions to be made in concert in this way. We may also object that a matrix of quantities and a vector of prices do not, in themselves, embody a complete description of an economy. The present section is devoted to identifying some of the more significant discrepancies between the Walrasian world and the imperfectly functioning real-world counterparts it may have. This is done by referring to a number of particular types of failure to which markets may be susceptible, and then discussing whether the best solution is to introduce some form of additional guidance from outside or to allow any internal forces to try and correct matters of their own accord.

The first type of difficulty is the possibility that there may be goods that are not traded on the market — this embraces a large number of different phenomena. That which is common to all the situations we include here, is that the actions of one individual are affecting the well-being of another individual, in the absence of any contractual relationship between them. The simplest example of effects of this kind is where my consumption of a commodity, determined by me in the light of my utility function and the price called out by the Auctioneer, affects others' utility as well. If they benefit from such consumption then they would be prepared to pay me to consume at a higher level than I, on my own, would find appropriate. In many cases, however, there will be no mechanism through which such encouragement can be channelled. In the auction, we all have to bid simultaneously at each set of prices, so they never have sufficient information upon which to act. In any particular economy, the pattern of institutions will determine which goods are traded and which are not. Whilst our model does not imply that there will be gaps of this kind, the important point is that if such gaps can be shown to exist, then our Auctioneer will be unable to bring about an allocation that is socially optimal.

Some care is, however, needed with this concept. It is not suggested that the very existence of such interdependencies is a barrier to social optimality but rather that there may be no mechanism through which they are being adequately reflected. Since the mechanism involved is price, we are interested in those instances in which an action is not priced at all. In most economies, we find that 'rights' of various kinds can be traded just as can items that appear to be 'goods' in the more normal sense. Labour contracts, for example, are rarely completely specific in their stipulation about what is required of the labourer. Rather, they are likely to say that the worker will have to obey orders within limits of some kind. The disutility suffered by the worker involved will accordingly depend upon the demands actually made on the worker. Legislative controls on the form that such contracts may take may be such that some aspects of labour power may not be traded. Employers may not, for example, be allowed to hire a labourer for less than some specified period or to hire non-union labour for particular jobs. The net result is that 'property rights' will be attenuated, that is to say, that various goods or aspects of goods may no longer be bought and sold.

Conversely, the legal system may embody rules that effectively constitute prices by creating tradeable 'goods'. Consider the example of a producer of crocodile-skin handbags. If he allows his crocodiles to escape, he is imposing costs on other consumers or producers in that his creatures may attack people or domestic animals. Provided that the legal system specifies that damage caused by escaped crocodiles is the responsibility *either* of their careless owner *or* of those careless enough to get injured by them, then there exist the appropriate incentives for trade between the parties to take place. A social optimum will be reached provided that liability rules are specified before the trading period, as demonstrated by Coase (1960). Thus, in the case of the people going to the auction, the legislation governing who pays for the consequences of escaped crocodiles will be one of the factors determining the offers made for the appropriate safety devices at different price levels. A popular example of a situation where property rights are not fully defined is that of a beekeeper who operates near an orchard. The beekeeper will rarely be able to charge the orchard owner a fee for the improved pollination of the fruit trees which results from the presence of his bees. Similarly, however, the beekeeper will not have to pay the orchard owner for the food the bees get from the orchard. Effects of this kind are normally referred to as 'externalities'.

Having said that property rights may not be completely defined, and having deduced that this impedes the Auctioneer's search for a full social optimum, we have now to ask why we often find such gaps. The simple answer is that the creation of rights is in itself a costly business. The costs arise partly from the fact that an inconceivably large volume of research and legislation would be needed to create the rights at all, and partly from the likelihood that the existence of more rights would lead to an increased volume of litigation over esoteric points of detail. A perfectly functioning market system would accordingly give rise to certain sorts of cost that might be avoided if some resources were to be allocated by nonmarket means. A debate that encompasses some of these issues is the controversy about the most effective means of controlling pollution.

A firm discharging effluent into a river may either be sued by those who are affected, offer compensation to those affected before the event, or be subject to some publicly set upper limit on its pollution output. Some economists have argued that the third of these possible means of control is most desirable because it comes closest to minimising the total social cost, whilst there are, of course, other methods of control available, such as the imposition of taxes.

Another problem arising from the property-right characteristics of certain goods is that of excludability. Samuelson (1954, 1955) identified what he termed 'public goods', a characteristic of these goods being that they are available to all once they are available to any single individual. For example, if an individual pays, via the government, for the purchase of aircraft to be used for national defence, then all members of the society who benefit from a heightened sense of security as a result will be better off, just as will the benefactor himself. The latter cannot prevent others from benefiting because national defence is, by definition, a good that is collectively, rather than individually, used. An important corollary of the inability to exclude others from use of the good is that it will be very difficult to encourage citizens to reveal the true value they place on the provision of additional units. In a large society, the overall level of provision will be very insensitive to the amount an individual is prepared to contribute, and thus when asked for his marginal valuation of the good (on which we may assume will be based the contribution he makes to its cost), he will find it optimal to take a 'free ride' on the service already being provided at the expense of others. The Auctioneer will find it impossible to deduce the socially optimal level of provision and pattern of charges for goods of this kind and there will accordingly be a need for some alternative mechanism, such as a political system, through which decisions of this kind are made.

A most important class of externalities that has until recently been rather neglected, involves interdependencies between generations. Many decisions taken today have significant implications for consumers, and sometimes producers, many years hence. Since many of these consumers may not even have been born when current decisions are being taken, they cannot possibly be brought into a trading relationship with today's generation. The absence from the auction of future generations inevitably implies that the future consequences of actions will be inadequately

19

reflected whether they be beneficial or detrimental. If current production plans entail using a natural resource such as a forest, an oil deposit or a species of crocodile at a very high rate, then the availability of these depletable resources to future generations will be reduced. Selfishness on the part of the current generation is, for example, likely to deprive those born in the future. A similar problem arises with the disposal of waste. To present future generations with a legacy of nuclear waste that has a strictly finite — even if very long — half-life is to impose costs on future citizens. The Auctioneer is powerless to prevent effects of this kind, and again it will be necessary to invoke the political process as the means by which appropriate adjustments can be made.

In addition to the problems of dependencies between the decisions of today's citizen and the well-being of tomorrow's citizen, there is the problem that individuals may make decisions that lay an irrationally small emphasis on their own future well-being. This tendency to take a myopic view of the importance of tomorrow's consumption relative to today's was called the 'defective telescopic faculty' by Pigou (1920). The major thrust of the argument is that if someone were to intercede on behalf of the individual, and adjust the decisions he makes today in such a way as to give more weight to future pleasures, at the end of his life the individual would say: 'Thank you. Your actions made my life as a whole more enjoyable than it would have been had my own earlier foolish ideas held sway.' A considerable literature has developed in the search for conditions that we might expect an individual's 'life plan' to meet. Some of the more sophisticated models of the consumption function such as Friedman (1957) and Modigliani and Brumberg (1954) set out to demostrate that, at any time in his life, a consumer will relate current (and expected future) consumption decisions to the stream of income receipts expected over the rest of his life. The general problem can be thought of as devising an optimal sequence of consumption (or saving) levels. Philosophers such as Ramsey (1928) and Fried (1970) have been interested in these problems, just as have economists such as Strotz (1955/6) and Pollack (1968). Discussion of some of these points will be resumed when we look at the problem of determining the optimal growth rate of the economy (Chapter 5); for the moment, it is sufficient to note that individuals at the auction may make bids that lack consistency in the rate at which future utility is implicitly being discounted.

In order to ensure that the Auctioneer would be able to generate a unique market-clearing price vector p^*, we made a number of assumptions, some of which were left implicit. One of the most important of these was that there be no increasing returns in production. If average costs continue to decline as the scale of production increases, we are no longer likely to get a determinate solution. Several firms may be prepared to supply a high volume of output at certain prices, but the cost conditions will suggest that one firm ought to supply the whole market (Arrow, 1971; Arrow and Hahn, 1971).

A second area that may be troublesome is that of uncertainty. Although our model allows for the possibility of specifying prices that are contingent upon the occurence of certain specified events, this may not be sufficient to remove the effects of all forms of uncertainty. There are certain sorts of risks that cannot be adequately handled by individual agents. When the same risk, or type of risk, is faced by many agents, specialised institutions such as insurance companies find it possible to accept responsibility in return for a fee or premium. This is possible because, provided that the number of separate risks are statistically independent and large, the insurer can rely on the 'law of large numbers' to keep the amount of loss close to the computed expected loss. As the number of risks involved falls, the likelihood of a serious loss or ruin rises, with the consequence that the premium that the insurance company must charge rises very rapidly. In the case of certain forms of economic activity, risks may be insufficiently frequent to be of interest to private insurance companies and it has been argued that, in situations of this kind, the inability to insure will lead to an underinvestment in the riskier forms of enterprise. A singularly good example of this is the 'research and development' expenditure decision of a firm. Inevitably, it is difficult for the small or medium-sized firm to spread the risk of such investment because the budget is simply not large enough to permit much diversification. Accordingly, even if the *expected* return from such expenditure is relatively large, the high degree of variation to which this expected return is subject may deter the firm from going ahead. In aggregate, however, such variation will be much lower and the net result will depend upon the size distribution of firms in the economy. Especially where there is a large number of small firms, we may expect to observe low expenditure on risky ventures. Some authors have concluded that the only means of avoiding underinvestment in such fields is to finance such work collectively; that others dispute this view is clear from the work of

21

Demsetz (1969) in which the arguments of Arrow (1962) are challenged.

Since the central thrust of this chapter is to argue that some forms of economic planning may have a role to play in capitalist economies, we only show the more likely types of failure to which markets are subject. It is as well to note, however, that once a failure has occurred somewhere in the economy, the difficulties of correcting any subsequent failures will be enormous. The Second-Best Theorem of Lipsey and Lancaster (1956/57) tells us that, if any deviation from the equalities between marginal rates of substitution and marginal rates of transformation should occur in a single market, then action to correct this problem offers no guarantee of an improvement if the equalities do not hold in other markets. Thus, if the Auctioneer is impeded by problems in one market, the derivation of optimal solutions is complicated.

Having shown that our hypothetical Auctioneer is capable of reaching an equilibrium under an impressively wide variety of conditions, the next stage is to ask whether this ability disappears if we adapt the form that the marketplace itself takes. In real economies, we rarely find that all citizens meet together and simultaneously communicate all their offers to an impartial referee. Rather, we find that the price adjustments occur slowly in different markets, with the result that we may suspect that equilibrium is, in fact, rather elusive. Over the last decade, this has proved to be a fruitful field of enquiry, both in terms of our understanding of the way that individual markets may work and perhaps, even more important, in terms of our understanding of the forms of macrodisequilibria. The depression of the 1930s and the associated writings of Keynes (most particularly in *The General Theory of Employment, Interest and Money,* 1936) gave rise to a tradition of economics in which the existence of disequilibria, such as unemployment, was implied to be a consequence of aggregates and the way in which these aggregates interacted. More recent writings, as typified by Phelps (1971), however, analyse such problems by reference to the more traditional methods of microeconomics. The methods of general equilibrium have been applied to problems that, for many years, had largely been thought of as lying in the domain of the macroeconomist. An understanding of modern macroeconomics is thus helped by a more specific discussion of general equilibrium analysis. However, it is clear that models in which the services of an Auctioneer are used will be a relatively fruitless source in understanding the kinds of problem that are of interest, even if they do provide a necessary starting point. Thus, we now move on to see the consequences of progressively removing the theoretical devices which were an essential basis for the equilibrium discussed in the previous two sections.

IMPROVED MODELS OF PRICE FORMATION

The way in which we will change the form of our model is to relax the assumption that only one auction ever takes place. There are two main alternatives which we may consider, the first being to allow a series of auctions — one in each market period — to take place, and the second being to allow prices to be adjusted continuously. In this way, we can allow for the overlapping of different generations, changes in tastes and preferences not predicted in advance, and so on.

If we decide to hold regular auctions, we have first to fix the frequency with which they are to be held. Once this has been established, we simply ask the Auctioneer to find an equilibrium price vector in each period. Although the basic working of the system appears to remain much the same, a number of differences may be noted. We shall find that people may now speculate in those goods or claims to goods which have a useful life of more than one period. For example, if I think that the price of some particular work of art is likely to rise more rapidly than the price of the other goods in the economy, I may choose to buy it now in the hope of making a gain subsequently. Of course, its present price will, to some extent, reflect the expectations of other potential speculators, and thus I will make a gain only if I outguess my competitors. If we allow people to lend or borrow cash through the sale and purchase of financial claims of some kind, we may run into a particular sort of problem. An individual is likely to borrow money early in life when times are hard against the prospect of future income, thus incurring an ongoing financial obligation of a size that is related to the rate of interest. Since we might expect the rate of interest to vary as the demand and supply of borrowing varies, we may find that the individual who has borrowed heavily goes bankrupt. In other words, if the rate of interest rises above a certain level, the individual may no longer be able to meet his debt. Clearly, if this happens on a large scale, then we encounter some form of disequilibrium.

A related problem of considerable significance is that there may be occasions on which the gap existing between the transactions that an individual makes means, effectively, that the individual offers labour at an auction for the price that prevails at the time, and yet does not actually receive his income until some later date, by which time the prices of goods have changed. This is most likely to result in mistakes, since the decision about how much labour to supply can only be made rationally once the terms upon which labour power can be traded for consumer goods have been specified. Similarly, firms may have to decide how many workers to hire before they know how many units of the good they will be able to sell, since the product will be ready to go to market until the following auction. Returning to the problem of the worker, the point is made very clear as follows:

'For if realized current receipts are considered to impose any kind of constraint on current consumption plans, planned consumption as expressed in effective market offers to buy will necessarily be less than desired consumption as given by the demand functions of orthodox analysis.' (Clower, 1965)

If we decide to allow prices to adjust continuously, rather than to have a series of auctions, then we may pension off the Auctioneer. The consequence of this is that we allow each market to feel its own way towards equilibrium, so that price is atomistically forced upwards or downwards as those in the market perceive that the *rate* of demand exceeds the *rate* of supply or vice versa. One important side effect may accompany processes of this kind: If we suppose that sellers set an initial price and then adjust it as they find their inventories growing larger or becoming depleted, there will be many cases in which the seller is selling at the 'wrong' price. It is likely that if some change takes place in demand it will be some time before this is unambiguously signalled to the seller through his stock levels, and in the interim consumers will be paying rather more or less than if they deferred their purchase. It has been shown that, provided the parameters underlying the demand and supply functions remain stable for a sufficiently long period, we may expect an equilibrium to finally emerge. Samuelson (1947) and Arrow (1959) have suggested a formal treatment of this problem that proceeds by assuming that the rate and direction of price adjustment depends on the proportion of excess demand. If we denote demand at time t and price p_j as $D(p_j(t))$ and supply as $S(p_j(t))$ and denote derivatives with respect to time by a superior dot, the hypothesis may be written as:

$$\dot{p}_j(t) = k \left(\frac{D(p_j(t)) - S(p_j(t))}{S(p_j(t))} \right) \qquad (2.7)$$

where k is a positive constant.

At the equilibrium price p_j^*, demand will be equal to supply and hence there will be no tendency for price to change; that is, $\dot{p}_j(t) = 0$. Whilst this is in some ways reassuring, it is clear that the market will take some finite time to return to equilibrium if ever disturbed. Stabilisation policy, in fact, is frequently aimed at speeding up the process of the return to equilibrium.

To summarise, we have shown so far that the basic capitalist model, even in the idealised Walrasian form, may suffer from shortcomings. The incompleteness of the specification of property rights for example, is likely to mean that the price vector which emerges does not necessarily coincide with the maximisation of welfare. Specifically, in addition to the problem of choosing where on the consumption-possibility frontier we are to operate, we may find ourselves somewhere *inside* the frontier. It was proposed that we could use alternative models of price adjustment that worked less perfectly than the Auctioneer but did predict that we may observe phenomena such as unemployment. The implications of this latter finding are, first, that there seem to be grounds for arguing that active government planning may be used to avoid or lessen the impact of market disequilibria, and secondly, that, when analysing the form planning is to take, we will be well advised to see whether we can learn any lessons from our heightened understanding of disequilibria in the capitalist economy.

THE SOCIALIST MODEL

In the previous section, we saw that there are a number of significant reasons for believing that the unrestricted operations of the market might give rise to a suboptimal set of values for the parameters of the economic system. It was also intimated that, even if the market mechanism did, in fact, best serve the interests of society, the adjustment process might be sufficiently slow to warrant intervention by the planning authorities. Unless we give an unrealistically large weighting to the personal-freedom component of the individual's utility function, some form of macroeconomic planning is inevitable even under a capitalist system of production. We now move on to an examination of the planning requirements of an alternative form of economy – one in which the desirability of planning is explicitly recognised. This model may be conveniently labelled the 'socialist' system of production.

Socialist states have been seen, by the majority of economic theorists of this particular political persuasion, to be the result of the supercession, violent or otherwise, of capitalist, imperialist or feudal regimes. Another common feature of this style of argument is the lack of an *ex ante* specification of the nature of the socialist or communist state to be developed after the transition in the mode of production. As Myrdal observes in the case of Marx:

'There is ... throughout Marx's writings, very little thought given to the actual organisation of that end-product of the natural development of the capitalist society — the free and classless communist society where the rule is: "from each according to his ability, to each according to his need". Neither was he interested in clarifying the techniques of policy which the temporary dictatorial government in power after the revolution would employ to transfer the old class state into the new egalitarian one.' (Myrdal, 1960)

Whilst we should not wish to criticise these writers for failing to specify the end to which they are working— the immediate operations of the new society would possibly be determined pragmatically by historical circumstances and are beyond the range of present-day forecasting techniques — we can, even so, conceive of how such a society might appear in the abstract. Presumably, it will be a society in which the economic problem of equilibrium has been solved by either (1) an increase in output to match demand, or (2) a fall in demand to match supply. In mathematical terms, such a 'Utopia' might be presented as follows:

The society under consideration will possess two fundamental properties which serve to distinguish it from the capitalist model. First, there will be the basic socialist requirement of communal ownership of the means of production, that is, the absence of individual command over particular productive resources. Secondly, in this particular economic system, money will only fulfil the role of a medium of exchange. It simply possesses the characteristics of any other commodity and, as will be seen, need not in fact appear in the arguments of the basic model at all— the same is also true for prices.

Let us first of all consider the production or supply side. Commodities will be produced by technologically determined production relationships involving labour inputs and also the inputs of other produced commodities. Given that our economy consists of K industrial sectors producing K commodities, we can express the output of any industry i as:

$$q_i = L_i + \sum_{j=1}^{K} q_{ij} \qquad (2.8)$$

where q_i is the total output of industry i ($i = 1, \ldots, K$), L_i is the number of workers employed in industry i (assumed constant through time) and q_{ij} represents the commodity input from industry j going into industry i. In some cases q_{ij} may be zero, depending upon the nature of the production relationship.

The total output of industry i will be allocated for two different purposes, namely, consumption and investment. For convenience, let us examine the course of the economy over a number of time periods. Taking a starting point (time superscript $= 0$) with an initial endowment of: $\sum_{j=1}^{K} q_{ij}^0$ (the set of inputs available to industry i in period 1) and applying labour inputs of L_i, we may express the output of industry i in period 1 as:

$$q_i^1 = L_i + \sum_{j=1}^{K} q_{ij}^0 \qquad (2.9)$$

Denoting total consumption of good i in period 1 as C_i^1, we may derive the following identity:

$$C_i^1 + \sum_{j=1}^{K} q_{ji}^1 \equiv q_i^1 \qquad (2.10)$$

where q_{ji} is that part of the output of industry i to be used as an input to industry j, that is, investment. Similarly, in the second period, we may derive two analogous relationships:

$$q_i^2 \equiv L_i + \sum_{j=1}^{K} q_{ji}^1 \qquad (2.11)$$

27

and

$$C_i^2 + \sum_{j+1}^{K} q_{ji}^2 \equiv q_i^2 \qquad (2.12)$$

If, for the sake of simplicity, we assume that the economy is in a 'steady state', that is, the net consumption level is both constant through time and just feasible in the light of the initial endowment, the investment requirements will be exactly equal to the quantity of commodities used up in the original production process of period 1; that is,

$$C_i \equiv q_i - \sum_{j=1}^{K} q_{ji} \qquad (2.13)$$

for all time periods.

Having discovered the relationship of consumption to output, the members of our society are now in a position to specify the production decisions consistent with their particular consumption requirements; that is, once the consumption vector in period 0 is determined, producers may be instructed to act accordingly. The level of aggregate-derived consumption would be established by summing the individuals' desired consumption levels; that is,

$$C_i^* \equiv \sum_{m=1}^{n} c_{im}^* \qquad (2.14)$$

where c_{im}^* represents the mth (of n) individual's requirement of the ith commodity. It clearly follows that 'social bliss' will be attained if C^* is feasible in terms of the practical production possibilities summarised in equation 2.13.

The internal logic of the Utopian economy in a situation where all equations and identities hold is therefore extremely simple: All goods and services are publicly owned and society, by means of the appropriate social preference function, can easily equate production and consumption. Money and prices are irrelevant to our system because, in equilibrium, demand will match supply for all commodities and exchange between individuals need never occur. To describe this in a more concrete fashion, we may think of the results of an entire day's output being laid out in the national supermarket and the labour force, returning from the factories, simply entering the store and taking that which it requires, according to the previously specified consumption level of each individual. The equations of Utopia dictate that the last individual, who happens to demand a loaf of bread and a pot of jam, finds these – and only these – two items remaining on the shelves.

As in the capitalist model, the existence of such a perfect equilibrium in Utopia precludes any need for regulation — any such need will only manifest itself when certain of the equations become inequalities. In our socialist model, however, the type of adjustment will be different, owing to our *ex ante* decision to exclude the individual ownership of the means of production and the price mechanism from the argument.

Let us examine what would happen if, for example, population grew or a change in taste occurred. If these changes were not anticipated when the initial production decisions were made, we might now find that the sum of individuals' desired consumption of a certain commodity exceeded the quantity actually produced. In the capitalist model, regulation would take place via the price mechanism, but this option is not open in Utopia as no prices have been defined. Consumption would presumably have to be rationed between the members of the population, possibly as a proportion of the consumption desires they originally expressed; alternatively, a 'first-come, first-served' principle could operate. The same would be true if it was felt that additional investment resources were required, as these can only be obtained by the restriction of consumption.

We could also envisage a case where the inequality was reversed, that is, when supply exceeded demand, resulting in overproduction. What should be done with these surplus resources? They certainly would not be required for investment purposes as this would simply serve to generate an even greater surplus in the next time period. However, the most likely occurrence in Utopia is to have both of these problems occurring simultaneously — shortages of some commodities accompanied by surpluses of others.

Although we have decided that commodities will be produced on the basis of technologically determined production functions, where is the incentive in our Utopian model to ensure that the individual firm produces efficiently and economises on commodity inputs — an implicit assumption of equation 2.13? Because of the requirement of the social ownership of the means of production, no concept of individual profit exists and it is just this factor which is employed by the capitalist model as an indicator of the appropriate way in which resources should be allocated.

Incentives from the consumers' point of view are also lacking. If, for example, resources are allocated to me on the basis of my previously specified consumption statement, I, as a rational individual, should naturally exaggerate my requirements in the hope of being provided with a greater quantity than I really 'need': for would I not usually prefer more to less? Is it not also likely that I should understate my assessment of society's investment requirements, hoping that some other, more far-sighted individual would compensate for my myopia?

Given that demand exceeds supply in industry X and the converse in industry Y, how can Utopia be organised so as to achieve a more effective system of allocation? One obvious method would to increase the output of industry X and decrease the output of industry Y, the decision to do this having been reached on the basis of the observation of a shortage and a surplus in the respective industries' production. Let us assume that this decision is brought about by government *fiat*, resources being shuffled around the economy accordingly. The potentially disastrous effects of this are obvious: Any alterations in industrial outputs will have substantial implications for other industries because of our specified interrelationships; for example, if industry Y's output is cut, industries A, B, C and D might suffer from a shortfall in inputs. Consumption too will be influenced, depending upon the quantities of products offered, and, as we might reasonably expect real-life consumption patterns to change over time, the planned alteration in the output mix might still not accord with the new set of individual requirements. Therefore, unless the planners possess a virtually complete knowledge of production functions and the range of individuals' requirements, bottlenecks, shortages, surpluses and other forms of disequilibria are bound to result.

The problems of control in the absence of prices and private ownership faced by our utopian model are analogous to those encountered by the form of national economic planning undertaken by the Soviet Union during the early Stalinist period (the late 1920s and the 1930s). In this particular case, the objectives set by the planners included a massive capital-investment drive, and the resulting sacrifices from consumption were enormous. As this form of planning represented the first major attempt at economic engineering, it is perhaps worth considering it in more detail.

In his important study of the economic development of the

USSR, Nove (1972) outlines a number of central features of Stalinist planning, or what has come to be known as the 'command' economy.

(1) With the introduction of the command economy, all major industrial enterprises came under the direct control of centralised ministries.

(2) The national objective function was manifested as direct instructions to individual firms and plants, in the form of regulations as to the quantity and quality of output, quantity and sources of inputs, wages, prices, size and composition of the labour force, and so on. Note that, in the Stalinist case, prices had been reintroduced to bring about the familiar reconciliation of supply and demand, as in the capitalist model. However, as consumption and investment decisions were *politically* determined by the central authorities rather than derived from the market process, these prices generally bore little resemblance to the notional market equilibrium as they were not necessarily reflecting either scarcity or input costs. This being so, their influences on the motion of the economy towards equilibrium was hardly likely to prove helpful.

(3) Plans were developed by a consideration of the interaction of feasibility and requirements, on the parts of both the individual enterprises and the national planning body, *Gosplan*.

(4) Plans were drawn up in the form of 'material balances'; that is, the annual national accounts were expressed in terms of the actual quantities of the commodities produced. From this information, the allocation between consumption and investment could be decided but, owing to the complexity and sheer size of the Soviet Union's aggregate output, any alterations to production planning involved wholesale modifications to the structure of the overall plan.[1]

'Any change in the plan required hundreds, even thousands, of changes in material balances. Thus a decision to make more tanks calls for more steel; more steel requires more iron ore and coking coal, in quantities which can be estimated from technical norms and past experience; these in turn may

---

[1] A 'material balance' simply consists of an audit of physical quantities, subdivided into sources of inputs and distribution of output (market, reserves, exports etc.) for the current period, with physical targets for future periods. This form of planning is discussed in more detail in Chapter 6.

require more mining operations and transport; but these need more machinery, power, construction, wagons, rails, and to provide them still more steel is needed and many other things too.' (Nove, 1972)

Given that the world is an uncertain place, any unforeseen divergences between production targets and realised output would produce similar disturbances throughout the entire system. The capitalist model deals with such occurrences by the automatic mechanism of the market; this being effectively absent in the command economy, the alternative is again to recompute the entire plan on the basis of the new figures for realised output.

(5) Under the Stalinist system, individual firms were encouraged to make profits although this was almost impossible to do deliberately, owing to the all-too-visible hand of the central planners and also to the irrationality of prices. In any case, any profits produced were not for use by the members of the particular enterprise, but were liable for appropriation by the central planning body. Any incentive effect on enterprise managers to ensure the efficient allocation of resources was therefore lost.

(6) The 'material balances' approach required the collection of, and reconciliation between, a vast number of data sets. For the sake of consistency, it was attempting to obtain detailed production decisions for every plant producing every commodity in the Soviet Union. The magnitude of this task, coupled with the proliferation of bureaucracy, inevitably made the planning process more cumbersome and ponderous, and progressively less receptive to changes in technology and consumption patterns.

The problems of the command economy, a modification of our utopian example, therefore centre on two of the fundamental planning issues which we shall be examining at later stages of this book. These are (1) the accumulation of sufficient data on all aspects of the economy in order to derive the matrices of production possibilities and consumer preferences, and (2) the absence of any automatic stabilisation mechanisms in the system, such as prices and profits, which mitigate against incentive and flexibility.

The early critics of the Soviet system of central planning — and, indeed, the principle of planning in general — were not slow in recognising these problems. Von Mises and Von Hayek (1935) pointed out these basic deficiencies and went on to suggest that a socialist economy could not possibly continue to function without the reintroduction of private property, prices and profits as a means to achieve the efficient allocation of economic resources. Even at its very inception, however, the command economy, both in theory and in practice, was undergoing changes which divorced it even more from its utopian antecedant. One significant feature of the historical development of the socialist systems was indeed the rapid reintroduction of the price mechanism, although its purpose was seen as something different from that it served in the capitalist model. In the sense that exchange appeared inevitable in a socialist system, as our utopian equations could never be guaranteed to hold at any one point in time, the reintroduction of money as a medium of exchange was also inevitable.[2] Lange and Taylor (1938), following the important work of Barone (in von Hayek, 1935), justified this point theoretically by stipulating that the prices at which commodities were to be exchanged for money were not to be left to the free market. On the contrary, the price machanism was to provide the required policy variable to bring about the equilibrium specified in our utopian equations. Socialist prices were to be derived by the 'trial-and-error' method; that is, an arbitrary commodity price would be fixed and the resulting supply and demand observed to provide indications of individual preferences and also a guide for the appropriate level of prices for equilibrium. Moreover, such arbitrary prices also serve to *modify* the perceived demand to meet the prevailing supply conditions. It would therefore appear that the planning body was coming to the Walrasian equilibrium from a different direction, and this feature led Lange to remark that:

' ... the accounting prices in a socialist ecomony, far from being arbitrary, have quite the same objective character as the market prices in a regime of competition ... As there is generally only one set of prices which satisfies the objective equilibrium condition, both the prices of products and costs are uniquely determined.' (Lange and Taylor, 1938)

In parallel with the trend of the reintroduction of a form of the price mechanism was the belief that some form of 'profit' or surplus

---

[2] It is pertinent to reflect also that, even if our utopian equation does hold, the existence of 'second-hand' markets would give rise to a role for a price mechanism.

might indeed be permissible as a guideline in the search for allocative efficiency.

The gradual readoption of such market mechanisms by socialist economies during the periods of their economic evolution has led some observers to put forward a 'convergence hypothesis', suggesting that the two polar models which we have discussed are, in fact, merging to generate a composite general system which, in the long run, will become the prevalent economic form. First advanced by Tinbergen (1961), this hypothesis points to a wide range of areas in which such convergence has taken place. With respect to the socialist countries, examples are the reinstatement of private property rights, the profitability criterion and the extension of the role of market prices. The capitalist nations, on the other hand, now pay more attention to social issues, by the nationalisation of industries, price controls, income redistribution measures, and so on. Whilst our present purpose is not to discuss the merits of this particular argument, it is manifest that one aspect of the convergence which is substantiated is the ubiquity of macroeconomic planning and, in the next section, we attempt to show that the nature of the planning process is fundamentally common to all forms of economic structure.

PLANNING METHODOLOGY

In the previous two sections we developed two models of economic organisation, both of which, for all practical purposes, will generate a need for planning. However, it might appear at first sight that the form of planning required by each is totally different, and this was the view of some of the earlier protagonists in the planning debate.

Anxious to contrast Soviet planning with the interventionism of the capitalist economies, Kuibyshev addressed a 1927 Central Executive Committee meeting in the USSR in the following terms: 'In America and elsewhere, plans are usually an attempt to foresee how the further development of the economy is blindly forming itself as a result of the business management of economic units which are not interconnected by a unified will and leadership. With us it is quite a different matter. We can construct plans based not only on forecasting what will happen but also on a definite will to achieve specific tasks and purposes.' (Quoted in Carr and Davies, 1974)

Some years later, Durbin found it necessary to distinguish between two types of planning, between what might be termed 'macroeconomic policy' and 'planning proper'. This distinction was as follows:

'(a) Planning meaning simply the *intervention of the Government in a particular industry* at a time when the greater part of the economy still remains in private hands, and

(b) Planning which results in the *general supercession of individual enterprise* as a source of economic decision.

This distinction is of importance, because the basis of authority and the probable results of the two types of planning are quite different.' (Durbin, 1949)

Modern planning theorists, however, tend not to make such fine distinctions. As we saw in the opening chapter, the process of planning can be conceived of in the most general of terms, and the particular instances and applications of planning techniques appropriate to the capitalist and socialist nations now form special cases within a unified planning methodology. Planning, in other words, possesses a fundamental unity and this can be seen by formalising the general planning framework presented in Chapter 1.

We originally referred to planning as the deliberate manipulation of the parameters of the economic system in order to bring about a desired and specified alteration in the functioning or the results of that system. What are the components of this definition?

First, there will exist a vector of 'data variables', D, which describes, so to speak, the economic system as it currently exists. The nature of the individual elements within this data vector will naturally be specific to the particular economy being analysed, but we might typically consider them to include values for the present levels of consumption and production of the economy's industries, the size and composition of the current labour force, present wage levels and so forth. The essential feature of this data vector is that it describes the economy as it *is* and the elements are therefore beyond the control of the planners. If we assume that the economy possesses i of these data variables, the vector D is given as:

$$D = \begin{bmatrix} D_1 \\ D_2 \\ D_3 \\ . \\ . \\ . \\ D_i \end{bmatrix} \qquad (2.15)$$

In order to influence the system described by D, there must exist a class of variables which are exogenous to the data variables. This is the set of 'policy instrument variables' P, and it is this that, being determined outside the system, the planners may employ to bring about the alterations in D. Again, the individual elements of P will be economy—specific, although we might cite as examples the marginal rate of income tax, the interest rate, the money supply, and so on. In considerating P, however, an extra dimension will come into play because, not only will there be elements within P representing each possible policy instrument, but each element may take on a range of values. We could think, for example, of the tax rate as varying between zero and 100 per cent, or the interest rate varying between zero and 1000 per cent. If we suppose that our economy possesses j policy instruments, each of which can take on any one of k values, then there will be k^j possible permutations of the policy instrument vector, the class of which we represent as P. To take a simple example, suppose we had five instruments ($j = 5$) with three possible values for each ($k = 3$). Of these five instruments, V, W, X, Y, Z, the first can take on values of v_1, v_2, v_3, the second can take on values of w_1, w_2, w_3, and so on. If we take the variables, X, Y, Z, we see that, when $X = x_1$, there are nine (or k^2) possible ways of arranging the values of Y and Z, namely, $y_1z_1, y_1z_2, y_1z_3, y_2z_1, y_2z_2$, and so on up to y_3z_3. By now permitting X to take on any one of *its* three possible values, we shall have twenty-seven (or k^3) permutations. In expanding the system to allow for the three possible values of W, we gain a total of k^4 permutations, whilst the inclusion of the V variable gives us our k^5, that is, k^j possible variations for the class of vectors P. We may now describe P formally as

$$P = \left[P_1^a, P_2^a, P_3^a, \ldots, P_j^{\overline{a}} \right] \qquad (2.16)$$

where the superscript, a, indicates that each of j elements can take on any value in the range one to k. Our description does, of course, assume that the number of possible values for each instrument is identical — in reality, this is unlikely to be the case, with the result that k^j will not be the true figure for the number of variations. The same principle of permutations will, nevertheless, hold in all cases so that the appropriate size of the P class is always identifiable.

The only additional information which we require is an understanding of how each element of P and D interacts; what change for example, in the level of steel production, will be induced by setting the rate of interest at a particular level? Given that these empirically based functional relationships are identifiable, we can include in our model an operator, F, which describes how the row vectors of P and the column vector, D, should be combined to produce a column vector of possible end states. This latter class of column vectors represents the set of transformed values for D after the implementation of the appropriate policies. Because the nature of the functional relationships remains unspecified, it is not necessary at this stage for P and D to be conformable; that is, i need not equal j. It could be, for example, that F demands that a number of elements of P be multiplied with one of D, or vice versa.

This set of end-state vectors which correspond to the functional influence of P and D may now be written:

$$E = \begin{bmatrix} E_1^1, E_1^2, E_1^3, \ldots, E_1^{k^j} \\ E_2^1, E_2^2, E_2^3, \ldots, E_2^{k^j} \\ \cdot \quad \cdot \quad \cdot \quad \quad \cdot \\ \cdot \quad \cdot \quad \cdot \quad \quad \cdot \\ \cdot \quad \cdot \quad \cdot \quad \quad \cdot \\ E_i^1, E_i^2, E_i^3, \ldots, E_i^{k^j} \end{bmatrix} \tag{2.17}$$

The first stage of the planning process can therefore be described as establishing the functional inter-relationships of exogenous policies and data which determine, on the basis of the system's parameters, a set of possible end-states. More formally,

$$F(P, D) = E \tag{2.18}$$

In his important contribution, Tinbergen (1952) uses a similar type of framework to construct a methodology for the analysis of economic policy. Whilst he recognises the importance of the P and D exogenous vectors, he chooses to partition the E matrix into two classes, as he believes that the policy makers will not be interested in *all* the end-state variables for planning purposes. Those which are important are labelled 'policy target variables', whilst those which, for one reason or another the planners are content to ignore, are termed 'irrelevant variables'. Seen in this light, we can now interpret a possible distinction between our capitalist and socialist models from the point of view of planning — typically, the capitalist model will contain a higher proportion of irrelevant variables relative to target variables as more economic activity will be left to the individual, rather than the social, decision maker. We should also anticipate that the elements of the P vectors display less variety, as capitalist planners are generally given less parameters to control. What is important, however, is to appreciate that our two models simply reflect different cases of the same approach.

We now have a situation where society can generate a number of hypothetical end states from a variety of possible policy options. How do we determine which of the columns of E is, in fact, the best? In Tinbergen's terms, which of the possible targets is *the* target?

If any one column of E contained consistently higher values for all elements than any other, the choice problem would clearly be trivial. In reality, however, this is seldom the case. Central to economics is the concept of 'trade off', and this idea of the commitment of resources in one area precluding their uses in another is the point at issue here. An end state which contains high levels of present consumption for example, will generally only permit a small volume of investment, whilst an end state which allows for high economic growth will usually include limitations on consumption. The appropriate target for the economy must therefore be determined by presenting the alternatives to the social decision maker for an indication as to just which target should be pursued. This being done, the appropriate target vector of E, namely E^*, can be pursued by choosing a particular policy vector, P^*, which gives rise to it.

In this approach, therefore, the planners will simulate a number of possible end states which can *ex post* be submitted for social approval. An alternative formulation, however, is to establish a social preference function for trade offs *ex ante* and to use this as a second operator in the calculation of E. This is the approach favoured by Theil (1964).

Instead of giving society a choice between possible end states, a social-welfare function will have been established previously to give preferential weight to the particular variables which society has come to consider important; for example, society might favour policies which produce higher investment rather than high consumption. By applying such a weighting function to $F(P, D)$, simple maximisation should then produce E^* as the optimal result, with P^* as the necessary instrument vector. We may observe that both of these approaches require specification of a set of social preferences, although, given consistency in the welfare function applied, we should anticipate that both methods yield the same result. Conceptually, the Theil approach is less satisfactory as it involves society making decisions before the subject for discussion has actually been raised! We should also be interested to know whether the welfare function changes over time: in terms of social preferences, are planned decisions to be consistent indefinitely? These issues are important and we shall return to them subsequently.

The Theil–Tinbergen planning methodology serves to demonstrate the unity of planning by formulising the basic treatment of our opening chapter. This methodology embodies a knowledge of the nature of the economy, permissible policy variables, functional relationships and also the derivation of the rules for social choice. As we have seen, this latter factor is implicit in all formulations, whether *ex ante* or *ex post*, and these mechanisms of social decision making form the subject for the next chapter.

CHAPTER 3

The Derivation of Planning Objectives

In Chapter 2 it was suggested that in market economies we might expect some form of government action to be employed to counteract any failures to which such economies might be prone. It was further proposed that socialist economies will, by definition, provide a large role for the government to play. The form that such government action takes is referred to as a 'plan'. In order to formulate a plan, the society has to establish both the objectives to which action is to be directed and the parameters that will govern the way in which any set of actions taken by the government will alter the course of the economy. It is to the derivation of these objectives that we now turn.

Objectives may be expressed in different ways, and will often not be explicitly presented in a form that is of direct use when plans are being designed. In some cases, they may take the familiar form of a function that is to be maximised. Thus, a plan that simply entails a transfer of £x from individual 1 to individual 2 can be easily evaluated *if* the objective is to maximise a specified utility function defined over the wealth of the two people. Clearly, the size of the transfer is chosen so as to bring about the greatest possible increase in total welfare. In other cases, such information about objectives may not be available. If society does not regard the concept of a welfare function of this kind as legitimate, or has not specified the form that the function is to take, it will no longer be possible to say unambiguously whether any specific transfer would be a good thing or not. In such instances it will be necessary to devise some means by which society's views of its merits may be articulated. A wide variety of methods is available for this purpose; the society's political structure may, for example, be such that problems of this kind are resolved by referring the decision to a body of elected representatives or to the whole electorate for voting.

40

THE DERIVATION OF PLANNING OBJECTIVES

The function of the economic planner will be quite different under different political regimes, and this will have important consequences for the mechanism by which objectives are established. His function may be simply to produce for society a description of the consequences of adopting alternative plans, the choice of an optimal plan from amongst these alternatives being made at a later stage by some political body. In other countries, his role may be broader and entail establishing for himself what social preferences are and designing a plan that is optimal in the light of them. We will be discussing in later chapters the different sorts of techniques that are applied by the planner in these different contexts. In all instances, however, it is a necessary condition for planning that objectives be established. For the moment we concentrate on the nature of social preferences — how they may be derived and how they may become translated into a plan or into decisions about what actions come to be taken. There is, however, one very important topic that we must discuss before looking at the more technical details that surround the search for a means of deriving social preferences from individual preferences, namely, why do governments exist at all?

Without some basic model of why governments exist or of how the 'proper' extent of government activity is determined, we have no basis on which to establish the more detailed information that will be expressed as planning objectives. The planner in a socialist economy will be working on a set of premises that is likely to be quite different from that on which the planner in a mixed economy is working, and consequently we will expect planning objectives to differ between the two economies. It is, for example, crucial that the planner knows whether nationalisation of the steel industry is (1) itself an objective (for ideological reasons), (2) an admissible policy (that is to be adopted if it can be shown to have more desirable consequences than other available policies) or (3) an inadmissible policy (again for ideological reasons). The next section examines the fundamental question of why collective action, which is a necessary condition for the existence of government, may be found desirable, and how such analyses can set the scene for the derivation of planning objectives.

If we are to be concerned with deducing the appropriate form of government action, it is useful first to investigate the role that society has designed government to fulfil. One way in which we might approach the problem of the rationale for the creation of a government would be to go back to the basic capitalist and socialist

41

models of the earlier chapters. This would lead us to argue, in the case of the capitalist economy, that the need for a clear definition of property rights and the enforcement of these rights creates a *prima facie* need for government. The next stage would be to look at the more technical problems such as how to smooth out any violent fluctuations or disequilibria to which the economy in question may be subject. There is, however, a quite different way of looking at this area that makes it possible to avoid treating the capitalist and socialist cases separately. This alternative has the further advantage of allowing a discussion of social-choice problems in more general terms.

The theory of games draws a distinction between games in which the players may co-operate with one another and those in which they may not (Weintraub, 1975; Taylor, 1976). A particular type of game, normally referred to as the 'Prisoners' Dilemma', has a structure that illustrates very clearly the advantages that may be associated with a change in the conditions under which the game is played. Consider the game in which the pay-off matrix is given by the following:

		B's action	
		I	II
A's action	I	3,3	1,5
	II	4,1	2,2

Each player may pursue either action I or action II. The four possible combinations of actions each yield a pay-off to each player, the amount received by A appearing as the first figure in each pair and the amount received by B as the second. In this situation each player will find that by pursuing action II he does better, irrespective of the action of his opponent. For example, if A adopts II he makes 4 rather than 3 if B employs action I, and 2 rather than 1 if B employs action II. The solution that emerges, therefore, is that they both employ action II and both make a gain of 2. Neither has any incentive to move away from this point, since, if either were to switch to action I, he would lose one unit. Clearly, however, if they *both* changed to action I at the same time, they would each gain an additional unit, and thus the move would represent an unambiguous improvement. This can, however, only be brought about if the two players co-operate, since, in the absence of an agreement to this end, they will both continue to employ action II.

What implications do the 'Prisoners' Dilemma' have for the existence of government? The straightforward answer is that we have demonstrated that in a particular type of situation, the participants may all become better off as a result of an agreement between them to act in co-operation with one another. We might then predict that if such situations are widespread then individuals, sensing the gains to be made, will organise collective agreements over a range of activities. For example, they might all agree not to take more than a specified maximum number of fish each per year from the lake around which they live, because the exercise of such restraint will be of benefit to them all over the next few years.

The next stage is to examine whether there are any particular sorts of activity into which our rudimentary government (which so far consists solely of a fishery-protection agency) is likely to move. A most plausible target, for reasons that will become clear shortly, is the provision of defence of our lakeside community from marauders coming to steal catches of fish. It may well be that the community will decide to form an army to ward off attacks of this kind — and this may be something that a collective agency is best equipped to arrange. The basic reason for suggesting that collective action will be appropriate in cases of this kind is to be found in the 'public' characteristics of the good in question. The important aspect of goods in this category is that a unit of the good can be consumed by several (sometimes all) consumers at the same time: consumption of the good by one individual in no way excludes the possibility of it also being consumed by another individual. Thus, if one citizen makes it known that he will be searching for and annihilating intruders, outsiders will presumably be discouraged from entering the village and, as a consequence, all of the inhabitants will enjoy a higher level of security.

In principle, what we have just established is that an individual member of the community will be unable to appropriate all the gains flowing from his action, a corollary of which is that the good will be undersupplied. The citizens may, however, be able to act in concert. If we suppose that they do so, we meet next the question of how they decide on the size of the army to be formed. The difficulty now is that the citizens may be tempted to understate the value of different levels of provision, because the obvious method of financing the army would be to tax citizens at a rate determined by their individual valuation. This understatement will result from the fact that the difference in the overall level of provision will be relatively insensitive (especially in a large community) to the contribution of the marginal citizen we are quizzing. A large sacrifice on the citizen's part will increase the size of the whole army only by a small fraction, and thus, even if the person is very security-conscious, he will not feel disposed to make a high valuation. Since we may assume that all citizens will behave in this essentially nonco-operative way, the result will be (as suggested by Olson, 1965, amongst others) that too small an army will be formed. This is precisely analogous to the 'dilemma' faced by the 'prisoners'; what is needed is some medium through which the co-operative solution may be reached. The government that we introduced earlier may now be asked to set up some means of voting in order that the relevant information about preferences may be gathered.

We have now reached a stage at which we may pose some very general questions. The choice between a large army in conjunction with a large tax bill and a small army in conjunction with a small tax bill may be approached directly, as indeed may almost any choice between two conflicting alternatives. The government may either, after consultation with the citizens, devise criteria that it can mechanically apply itself in choice situations or it may, again after consultation, devise a means by which a choice may be subjected to arbitration on a collective basis. For example, we may either (1) decide to mandate the government to adopt an investment project provided that it has a positive net present value (having first set the discount rate to be used) or we may (2) insist that elected representatives have a vote whenever a significant adjustment of the tax system is felt necessary, and thus have a delegated decision about defence provision, or we may finally (3) have a direct referendum on whether the level of defence provision should be high or low.

It might be useful to pause for a moment to note that there do exist schools of thought that regard the problems of public goods and nonco-operation as relatively unimportant. *Laissez-faire* economists and minimalist political philosophers argue that only a narrow range of activities fall within these categories, with the implication that the 'proper' extent of government is very limited. A corollary of this view is that economic planning is, at best, redundant and, at worst, something that reduces very considerably the level of social welfare. Rowley and Peacock are amongst the most recent critics of this tendency to overstate the benefits likely to result from employing nonmarket methods of choice:

'. . . liberals have a preference for a system that encourages voluntary exchange through market processes, and they share a

44

belief that some form of competitive capitalism provides the strongest safeguard for such a system.' (Rowley and Peacock, 1975)

Among the political philosophers of recent times, Nozick has argued that there are few areas of state action that can be regarded as legitimate:

'Our main conclusions about the state are that a minimal state, limited to the narrow functions of protection against force, theft, fraud, enforcement of contracts, and so on, is justified: that any more extensive state will violate persons' rights not to be forced to do certain things, and is unjustified; and that the minimal state is inspiring as well as right.' (Nozick, 1974)

Having drawn attention to the fact that there exists controversy about whether extensive collective action really constitutes a 'good thing', we return to our policy-choice problem. We may regard ourselves as searching for a way in which alternative social states may be evaluated or at least put into a ranking from which we may derive the most preferred state. In the case of the defence example, a social state would consist of a level of defence provision and a tax bill of some particular size for each citizen. Our next concern is to examine some of the ways in which alternative social states may be evaluated — for in the final analysis, it is this evaluation that will be expressed in the criterion that we apply when deciding which of the set of possible plans is the best.

SOCIAL DECISION MAKING

It will be recalled that, via the actions of the central planning authority or the Walrasian Auctioneer, we established a matrix q^* giving the amounts of each good and service demanded and supplied by each individual. The fact that the central authority used a material-balance approach and the Auctioneer a price *tâtonnement* approach is for the moment of no significance. Each individual i may be thought of as having a utility function $U_i = U_i(q_{il}, \ldots, q_{i(m+z)})$ from which we may derive the level of utility associated with any row vector q_i taken from a matrix q. In the case of the matrix q^*, this means that we may assemble a vector containing the utility levels of all individuals that we may denote as U^*. For example, if the matrix q^* is established, the first individual enjoys a utility level U^*_1, where $U^*_1 = U^*_1(q^*_{11}, \ldots, q^*_{1(m+z)})$, the second a utility level U^*_2 and so on.

We know that this equilibrium constitutes an optimum, because any subsequent changes would reduce the level of well-being of at least one person. Could we not, however, use some quite different process to allocate resources? If we did, and found that by doing so we arrived at a new situation characterised by a consumption — supply matrix, say $\bar{q}$, might it not be that individuals taken as a whole are better off? Associated with this new matrix would be a new set of utility levels for all individuals that we may denote $\bar{U}$. This, too, will represent an optimum since any further adjustment would entail a loss to at least one person. What we need, therefore, is some stronger means by which we can decide whether or not $\bar{U}$ is superior to U^*. Of course, if every single individual fares worse under our new scheme (which we denote by $\bar{U} < U^*$) then no-one would advocate it. Suppose, however, that under this scheme some people are made better off and some worse off; what should we do then? There are no longer any *a priori* grounds on which we can argue that one is manifestly preferable. The derivation of rules to be applied when resolving conflicts of this kind is a branch of study with a very long history. Ethical postulates of one kind or another have to be made in order to escape the *impasse* which would otherwise make any choice between the $\bar{U}$ and U^* situations impossible. In most of the following, we will be concerned with cases where a choice is only being made between two alternatives. We may for example, be deciding whether expenditure should be 50 units or 100 units or else we might be deciding whether the last 50 units should be spent on defence or education. The following sections examine, in turn, three strands of thought which, whilst they have certain overlapping elements, are distinctive enough, both in their origin and implications, to repay separate examination.

THE UTILITARIAN APPROACH

Perhaps the best-known attempt during the eighteenth and nineteenth centuries to develop criteria for choosing between the options open to a society is the work of Bentham (1789). The essence of his argument is that the choice criterion should be the pursuit of 'the greatest good of the greatest number'. He was suggesting that, in deciding whether to move from situation q^* to situation $\bar{q}$, the key question was whether the sum of individual welfare levels increased. He was thus proposing that in a society of n individuals, the move should be recommended if, and only if,

$$\sum_{i=1}^{n} \bar{U}_i > \sum_{i=1}^{n} U_i^* \tag{3.1}$$

This suggestion lies at the heart of the political theory of Utilitarianism. Its central assertion is that the impact of alternative policies on the total well-being of all the individual citizens is the only proper concern of government.

Perhaps predictably, Bentham's rather naïve suggestion came under strong attack, most particularly in the early part of this century. The central thrust of the attack was the implausibility of arguing that interpersonal comparisons of utility had any meaning. This is crucial in any policy context, since if we are to conclude whether an action is in the social interest, then we need to be able to add up the gains and losses of different individuals. As this cardinal utility concept fell into disrepute, statements about the extent of a change in an individual's well-being and, *a fortiori*, about changes in the level of total well-being, became invalid. It was at this stage that the Paretian School advanced their weaker criterion, namely, the familiar one that we only regard a change as being preferred if it makes no-one any worse off and at least one person better off. Reluctance to accept any stronger value judgments has meant that the Pareto criterion is still very widely employed in economic analysis.

In the 1930s it was suggested by Hicks (1939) and Kaldor (1939) that the Paretian criterion was too stringent. They argued that it gave a bias towards conservatism and that in many cases we could use a better criterion that yielded a more balanced view of suggested changes without necessarily introducing any further ethical notions. They proposed that, if it could be shown that a potential change would generate benefits to such an extent that the gainers were able to fully compensate the losers, then the change should be endorsed. For example, if the change involves me gaining £100 and you losing £80, we should proceed with it, since, potentially I could give you £80 (thus restoring you to your original position) leaving myself a net gain of £20. This principle is still widely used, notably in the sphere of cost–benefit analysis. The latter sets out to measure explicitly in commensurable, financial terms the costs and benefits (that is, the gains and losses) of a proposal, in order that we may see whether it would potentially offer a *net* gain to society (Pearce, 1971).

A rather different suggestion, yet one that seems to lie within the mainstream of utilitarian thought, was put forward by Bergson (1938) at around the same time as Hicks and Kaldor were writing. The basis of this approach is to argue that we may define a social-welfare function that depends upon the levels of utility enjoyed by each citizen. In our terminology, this amounts to setting up a function that relates social welfare W to the vector of individual utilities U. Thus, in our example, the criterion we apply is to recommend the change provided that

$$W(\bar{U}_1, \bar{U}_2, \ldots, U_n) > W(U_1^*, U_2^*, \ldots, U_n^*) \qquad (3.2)$$

Note that we have, as yet, said absolutely nothing about the nature of this function although, in line with convention, we normally add the restriction that it increases as any element U_i increases *ceteris paribus*.

The difficulty with this approach is, however, that in order to determine whether a change would constitute an improvement, we would have to specify both the changes in the utility level enjoyed by each individual and the precise form taken by the welfare function. This problem has not deterred the more resolute economists, who have become familiar with such setbacks. We might feel, for example, that everyone's well-being should be accorded equal importance — in which case each argument in (that is, element of) the social-welfare function is given equal weight. In this particular case, we will find that recommendations are the same as those we obtain from an application of the Hicks–Kaldor method, provided that the utility functions obey certain conditions such as constant marginal utility of wealth. Another suggestion about the nature of the social-welfare function has been put forward by Weisbrod (1968). He proposed that a study of past decisions made by government could be used to derive the implicit weight being assigned to different individuals or groups of individuals. If one then argues that social judgements are to be consistent with one another in the importance they attach to the welfare of individuals, then the weights implicit in past decisions can be used for subsequent decision-making purposes, until some explicit decision to alter these weights is taken. Others have argued that such an approach will run into difficulties, either because it will be found that governments have not applied a consistent set of weights in the past or because, even if they have, there is no *a priori* evidence that such weights have any significance, since by assumption, they had not been the result of rational discussion.

To summarise, utilitarians of whatever persuasion take the basic view that the only appropriate determinants of whether a change is for the better or worse are the changes in the levels of well-being of all the affected individuals. The possibilities for making different assumptions about the conditions that must be met before the change may be sanctioned, or the admissible ways of adding up the utility levels of different individuals, do not alter the basic approach.

THE CONTRACTARIAN APPROACH

A quite separate tradition of thought about the criteria for evaluating alternative policies is based on the concept of the individual as being a signatory of a hypothetical social contract. The important difference between the contractarian and utilitarian approaches is that the former is based on the premise that all individuals possess certain rights that the state guarantees to uphold, but that they also have a series of obligations to their fellow citizens. An immediate and most important consequence is that there may well be a wide variety of policies that cannot be considered simply because they would not be consonant with the rights and obligations that constrain the possible actions of the state or the individual. For example, all individuals might be guaranteed protection from external aggression but, in turn, might have agreed to do military service. In such a situation, it would not be possible to examine the suggestion that labour resources be freed from defence activity and used in some different way if this threatened the ability of the state to keep its promise of protection. Once the rights and duties have been established, it is inconceivable that the state allows them to be ignored because it would mean that society in effect was being dissolved.

In some ways, the most important part of this problem is how the contract is to be drawn up in the first instance. The way in which this is done is to start from an 'original position' in which no society as such exists, and then to ask what arrangements individuals in such a situation would make amongst themselves. Although some of the earlier works by writers such as Locke and Rousseau are of considerable importance, attention here will be focused on the more recent major contribution by Rawls (1973).

49

Rawls proceeds by starting with an abstraction in which all the future members of society are faced with the problem of defining a set of rules governing a great variety of institutions. In order to achieve some degree of fairness in his society, Rawls deprives the individuals of many important pieces of information about the characteristics with which they will be born. Thus, when discussing whether income tax is to be strongly progressive or not, individuals will not know whether they will be born with many talents enabling them to earn high (pre-tax) incomes or not. By application of the theory of decision making under uncertainty, and the assumption that individuals are averse to risk, it can be shown that people will opt for relatively egalitarian institutions. Thus, in our tax example, people will prefer a strongly progressive tax because they think it more important to ensure themselves a reasonable income should they be born with a low-income earning capacity, rather than that they earn very large sums even after tax, should they be born with a high-income earning capacity. A slightly simpler example of the same problem is the so-called 'cake-cutting problem' (Pattanaik, 1968). In this individual A is asked to cut a cake into two pieces having been told that individual B will have first choice of slice. We should expect individual A to cut the smaller slice as large as possible, on the assumption that B will always choose the bigger; that is, he will cut the cake in half. This basic idea of making people choose, behind a 'veil of ignorance', is applied to a whole series of situations. The conclusions reached by Rawls are various. One of the more interesting is that there will be a category of goods that we might label 'primary', of such basic importance to survival (such as the basic means of subsistence) that they will be made available to everyone, financed from tax revenue. Another finding of relevance to the question of policy evaluation is that, in the situation described, people will establish the rule that policy changes should be made only if they improve the position of the least advantaged member of the community, irrespective of the benefits accruing to those higher up the scale.

The contractarian approach has been the subject of criticism for a wide variety of reasons. Many, for example, argue that discussion of how individuals might react in some purely hypothetical situation is of no interest. Even if the rules were to be established in this way, people, upon discovering the position that they actually occupy, might exert pressure to change policies to favour their own position. Others of a more anarchist persuasion (such as

Nozick) argue that individuals will only agree to the barest minimum of institutions being established, and thus that protracted discussion of such issues is of no relevance in most instances.

THE SOCIAL DECISION RULE APPROACH

The third type of approach to be examined here is one that bears a close superficial resemblance to the idea of a social-welfare function but is, in fact, a rather more general formulation. Social-welfare functions define the terms upon which we, as a society, are prepared to trade a loss of welfare of person A against a gain of welfare of person B. Thus, if A's claims receive more weight, then policies favouring A will stand a better chance of being adopted than if the reverse were true. The idea of social decision rules, on the other hand, is the derivation of a procedure governing the way in which individual preferences may influence collective decisions. The search for decision rules that obey certain axioms, and which may be derived from individual preferences, has attracted considerable attention in recent years. Following the initial work of Arrow (1951), many authors, such as Sen (1970), have examined whether a re-specification of the axioms increases or reduces the likelihood of the existence of consistent social decision rules. Arrow had shown that the imposition of apparently mild restrictions on properties that decision rules should possess was sufficient to make it impossible to derive a consistent set of social preferences from individual preferences.

The general strategy of work in this area is to establish whether a social ordering over a set of alternatives would obey certain conditions, given that the orderings of the individuals trying to generate the social ordering could take any form. The economic analysis of consumer behaviour makes certain assumptions about what we term 'rationality'. For example, we assume that choices are *transitive*; that is, if I prefer x to y and y to z, then it is reasonable to expect that I will also prefer x to z. We also normally assume that choices are *consistent*; that is, confronted with a choice between two alternatives on different occasions, the consumer will always choose the same one. Similarly, in the analysis of social choice we set certain requirements, many of which are directly analogous to those made in the analysis of individual choice. For example, we will expect social choices to be transitive: if, in the social ranking, alternative x beats alternative y and y beats z, then we will expect x

51

to beat z. If it fails this test, we are prepared to argue that the decision rule producing the result is unacceptable.

Put more simply, we are trying to devise standards to which all reasonable constitutions, or sets of social rules, must conform. For example, if a constitution demands that all decisions be made on the basis of the majority of votes cast by the electorate, we will be concerned to discover whether there are occasions on which inconsistencies may result. If there are, we may go on to examine other possible methods, examining, in each case, whether the method fails any of our tests. A possible alternative to the majority-vote method would be a system in which a straw is issued to each citizen, one straw being shorter than all the others. The person who draws the short straw is then allowed to implement whatever policies he likes. This method we would reject on the grounds that any system in which one person's ordering uniquely determines the social ordering fails a criterion normally referred to as the 'nondictatorship' condition, discussed below.

In order to demonstrate the approach systematically, we may follow the seminal contribution of Arrow (1951, 1967). Four conditions are put forward, all of which any acceptable constitution will be expected to fulfil. They are as follows:

(1) *Collective rationality:* It is assumed that the rule for making a social choice can be derived from an ordering of all the possible alternatives open to society. This ordering is itself expected to obey two conditions that individuals' orderings also obey: These two conditions are those of *completeness* and *transitivity*. Completeness refers to the requirement that individuals have preferences that are fully defined; that is, every alternative is ranked *vis-à-vis* every other. It is also assumed that the social choice is derived from an ordering in the sense that the alternative preferred to all others in the ordering is the alternative that the decision rule instructs us to adopt.

(2) *Pareto principle:* If, in every individual ordering, x is preferred to y, then in the social ordering, we require that x be preferred to y.

(3) *Independence of irrelevant alternatives:* It is assumed that the resulting social choice is unaffected by any alternatives that are not genuinely available to society at the time the decision is made. Thus, whilst citizens may have preferences that relate to holidays on the moon in five-star hotels, the social ordering

should be completely insensitive to this fact, at least for the time being.

(4) *Non-dictatorship:* The set of social choices must not be invariably based on any single individual's ordering (unless all individuals have the same ordering). In other words, no individual's ordering is accorded special status.

Using relatively straightforward methods, it is possible to demonstrate that no constitution can satisfy all these conditions at once. Thus, we speak of this finding as Arrow's 'Impossibility Theorem'. As an example of how an apparently sensible decision rule or constitution may fail, consider the so-called 'Condorcet Paradox'. We employ majority voting in a situation in which we have three voters and three alternatives to consider, that we may call x, y and z. If voter 1 prefers x to y and y to z, voter 2 prefers y to z and z to x and the third voter prefers z to x and x to y, then we see that our transitivity assumption is violated. This is because, whilst a majority (that is, two voters) prefer x to y and a majority prefer y to z, a majority also prefer z to x.

Amongst the important implications of the 'Impossibility Theorem' is that the kinds of constitution actually in use give rise to various inconsistencies. For example, it will be impossible to devise a constitution that will enable decisions to be made in the way suggested by Bergson; the fact that a welfare function may be consulted to produce an unambiguous guide as to whether a policy represents an improvement, is not to say that there is any operational way in which such information may be elicited from society.

It is important at this stage to draw a distinction between the preferences of a society and the corresponding objective function to be used in the planning model. Preferences, as we have seen, may be derived from various sorts of voting procedures, but will rarely themselves provide the planner with sufficient detail to embody directly in the form of an objective function. Thus, whilst planning problems are most often regarded as being soluble by using the ordinary mathematical optimisation techniques, it is crucial to be aware of the difficulties that arise when any attempt is made to articulate the objective function itself. It will normally be necessary either for society to delegate representatives whose task is to inform the planner of the missing links or for the planner himself to be instructed to deduce the relevant information.

In contrast to the lines of inquiry pursued by Arrow and subsequent writers in the 'social-choice' vein, an alternative has been suggested by Downs (1957) in which much more significance is ascribed to the political process itself. The social-choice model, in essence, is concerned with the relation between individual preferences and social preferences, the latter forming the basis for policy decisions. The Downs model, on the other hand, is aimed at an understanding of how two-party democracies with elections at fixed intervals work. It is postulated that government consists of parties that are concerned to gain and retain power in the face of voters who back the party they believe to be most conducive to their own individual well-being. In most so-called 'democratic' countries, the citizen's preferences are signalled to government largely in the very limited form of a vote in favour of party x or party y. The analysis of voting behaviour and its relation to individual preferences therefore becomes the central concern, with the implication that the search for social preferences is something of a wild-goose-chase. Using this approach, another question of importance is how parties choose packages of policies to offer the electorate, and how the policies adopted by party x differ from those adopted by party y. These issues are pursued further, later in this chapter.

The model suggested by Downs has important implications for the derivation of planning objectives. In the social-choice model, changes in individual preferences affect the social ordering, and thus presumably can be immediately incorporated into the objectives to be used in planning, whilst in the Downs model, periodic elections are the source of any change — any changes in individual preferences, and hence possible changes in voting intentions, being of little significance in the interim. This may give rise to pressures to adopt myopic policies, a possibility examined in more detail in the discussion of planning for stabilisation in Chapter 5. Another difficulty suggested by the Downs model is that the planner will need much more in the way of supplementary information and help than in the case where he is completely informed of social preferences.

The voting system used by society is unlikely to be sophisticated enough to permit direct derivation of the very detailed information needed by the planner, so it will often be helpful to think of a figure who acts as 'broker' between the austere world of results of votes and the extensive detail that the planner will require. Although this intermediary will be neglected when we talk about the two basic ways in which the structure of the plan may be derived, we may find that, in practice, certain bodies are established specifically to facilitate such interaction. We may note, however, that the choice of method (either simulation or direct optimisation) will affect the role of the intermediary. To anticipate part of the next chapter, we may argue that, in the case of simulation, the planner will devise a number of alternative plans that seem, on the basis of limited knowledge, to lie in the right sort of area and then analyse the implications of each in detail. The findings may then be relayed by our intermediary back to the political process proper for a decision about (1) whether any further possible plans be explored by the planners and (2) which of those that have been examined yields the most attractive consequences. In the case of direct optimisation, the intermediary has the more difficult task of interpreting for the planner just how to construct an objective function from fragmentary information about social preferences. It should be stressed that the intermediary is performing the function of 'reading between the lines' but is not—or should not be—applying his or her own preferences, because this would contravene the non-dictatorship axiom and tend to make the acquisition of any information about social preferences redundant.

Nevertheless, we must bear in mind that our intermediary is not simply a theoretical convenience and that, in the real world, we will expect considerable interaction between the planner and the political process to take place. In a complex economy in which a wide range of policy instruments is available, it is not realistic to suggest that, working on his own, the planner will be able to devise a means of isolating a small number of relevant policies for analysis. Neither is it really plausible to argue that he will ever be given all the information he needs in order to compute an optimum directly.

OBJECTIVES AND INSTRUMENTS

In the first half of this chapter, we have examined a number of theoretical models for the derivation of social preferences which were, in general, to be articulated via the medium of an entity variously termed 'government' or 'the state'. We now turn to an examination of the two major areas where such collective decisions are of the greatest significance for the planning process. First, society will make choices regarding its preferred policy instruments or methods of economic control; it will be defining that set of tools which it finds acceptable to permit the planners to employ in order to bring about the desired end state. Secondly, society will also have predispositions towards certain of the entire range of end states that an economy could possibly produce, and this information will form the basis of the plan's objective function. We shall accordingly review these two areas and conclude with an analysis of how contemporary political processes cope with these planning requirements.

CONTROLLING THE ECONOMY

In our earlier discussion of planning methodology, we discovered that the variables of the economy could be divided into two distinct classes, namely, 'data' and 'policy instruments'. The central difference between the two was expressed in terms of control; whilst the level of the latter could be set by the planners, the level of the former could not. Using this methodology, our end states are brought about by setting the values of the policy instruments and confronting them with the data vector, the outcome being determined by the functional relationships. However, as an example will show, a different form of control is also possible.

Let us assume that the level of labour migration into a region is some increasing function of the wage differential between that region and its neighbours (the estimation of such functions being the concern of the next chapter). If one element of our desired end-state vector was a certain level of migration, then we could compute and then set an appropriate wage differential (assuming that society gave us the power) sufficient to encourage the required volume of movement. This technique would be an *indirect* policy, as we are simply inserting one (policy) variable, that is, wage differential, into the 'black box' of the function, in order to induce the required level of the second (end state), that is, migration. It will be appreciated, however, that the same result could have been brought about in a *direct* manner. In the case of our example, we could simply order the labourers to move into the region (again, assuming that society gave us the power), with the threat of dire penalties for refusal. In this second situation, we have modified our assumptions about migration; that is, outcomes are no longer to be determined by the spontaneous actions of individuals described by our previous functions, but rather by a set of commands issued by the central authority.

A key piece of information for the planners is therefore the permissible number and range of the values for the policy instruments and the acceptable number and nature of direct controls. In general, the larger the number of controls a society permits, then the larger the range of end states that will be attainable, although this is not to say that all societies will attempt to maximise the range of planning controls. Societies of a liberal persuasion might argue, for example, that extensions of central control impose *per se*, progressively more disutility and, all other things being equal, the number of policy instruments should be minimised. At the opposite extreme is the proposition that virtually all macro- and microeconomic variables *are* capable of being controlled, either directly or indirectly, the only major exception being the weather; the planners in this society will be provided with the maximum possible scope for their operations.

In practice, no contemporary society operates at either of these extremes; in fact, the range of socially acceptable controls displays a remarkable uniformity throughout the world, as we shall now see.

Indirect controls
The two sets of policy instruments which can make some claim to universality are termed monetary and fiscal policy, and we shall review each in turn.

Monetary policy refers to any action which effects an alteration in the quantity, availability or cost of money. In capitalist economies, the traditional methods of monetary control are the supply of money, credit arrangements, government borrowing and debt management, and the interest rate. Although the theory of money in relation to the real, physical economy was well established early on in the development of economic thought, monetary policy has only recently come more into prominence. Classical economics saw money largely as a transactions veneer superimposed upon an economy determined by real productive forces. As real investment and real savings were the 'prime movers' in this economy, the interest rate merely performed the marginal adjustment necessary to equilibrate demand and supply of loanable funds at the 'natural' rate. Money supply during the Classical period was not really, in any case, an effective policy variable, as it was conditioned by the machinations of the international gold standard. The innovations of the Keynesian School furthermore, suggested that monetary policy might be ineffective in economic control under certain conditions.

Since the Second World War, however, capitalist economies have been looking at monetary policy with renewed interest. On the one hand, the War had required state borrowing via the public debt on a much higher scale than ever before, and it appeared that variations in interest rates and funding procedures could determine the rate at which state-held monies could be reintroduced into the system to influence aggregate demand. Again, economic research conducted since the War (Friedman, 1956 and 1970) was beginning to suggest that there existed a significant correlation between inflationary pressures and the expansion of the effective money supply.

In classical socialist theory, money has no role to play in the direction of a socialist economy as, in the long run, it will be superceded by transfers in kind. As we have seen, money and prices did indeed have little relevance to the command economy, but the post-Stalin economic reforms have meant that socialist planners too have begun to take notice of the potential of policies of this form. Under the reformed Soviet system (Chapter 6), individual enterprises have been given considerably more freedom in deciding upon methods of fulfilling plan targets, to the extent that a form of capital market has been established. In this context, the interest rate is becoming increasingly significant in allocating funds to producers and is accordingly serving as a criterion for productive efficiency. With the gradual reintroduction of wages and prices into socialist economies, it is clear that the control of the money supply is essential to prevent distortions between allocation in the money and real sectors.

Fiscal policy refers to any action which effects an alteration in the level or composition of government expenditure or the structure or burden of taxation. It seems fair to say that the realisation of the potential for fiscal policy in capitalist economies only developed by accident. At an early date, certain commodities and services came, on the basis of social choice, to be provided publicly, with the result that public payment as taxation became inevitable. Government expenditure in such economies takes the form of defence, education, public health, administration, social security, and so forth, although the relative emphasis of particular types of spending naturally differs from country to country, as does the overall size of the government sector. The ideas of the Keynesian School simply implied that such expenditure could be used as a policy variable to regulate the level of aggregate demand in the economy. Similarly, taxation (and such particular facets as the balance between direct and indirect taxation and its incidence upon particular commodities) came to be seen as a possible control mechanism, in addition to a source of revenue.

Fiscal policy has always played a dominant role in the operations of socialist economies. State expenditure provides the finance for centrally determined investments and also the 'socio-cultural programme', the socialist equivalent of publicly provided goods and services. Such expenditure is financed by deductions from surplus enterprise profits (a source of increasing income, as enterprises are now encouraged to overfulfil their targets), turn-over taxes (the difference between the producer's price and the centrally determined retail price) and income taxes. In particular, it is the setting of the level of turnover tax, and hence the retail price level, which is the most important fiscal determinant in ensuring equilibrium between supply and demand conditions across the economy.

Although, as we have seen, both socialist and capitalist economies possess a wide range of similar forms of indirect controls, it is the 'Third-World' planner who is faced with the greatest problems. Because of the nature of these economic systems, planning in such situations will be obliged to function within a much narrower range of policy instruments. Owing to the problems of income asessment, for example, taxation will generally be of the indirect form (such as trade taxes and duties, or sales taxes) and variations in this may not be particularly influential on the overall income level. Monetary policy might be similarly constrained owing to the lack of developed financial institutions and the comparatively small size of the monetary, as distinct from the subsistence and barter, sector. Uncertainty may surround the level and pattern of employment and unemployment and, indeed, the applicability of standard economic models in general. In such situations, we should expect the 'Third World' planner to place much less reliance upon indirect forms of control.

Irrespective of the type of indirect control applied, an important consideration must be timing. Indirect policies work by effecting changes in other variables, rather than by directly changing these latter variables themselves, and planners must accordingly be aware of the length of time ensuing between the alterations in the policy variable and the change in the appropriate element of the end-state vector. Friedman (1961, 1964) suggests that the time taken for monetary policy to exert its effects in the money, and, eventually, the real, economy is of the order of one year. In a similar manner, the total impact of the multiplier effects of fiscal policy might not be felt until some years after the initial injection or withdrawal; Prest (1968) suggests a time lag of one to two years for the UK economy. Reliance on indirect policies therefore implies that the planners must take a longer-term view, with a realistic assessment of the likely course of events during the time in which their policies begin to take effect.

Direct controls

In the capitalist economies, reliance is typically placed on indirect controls which exploit market forces to bring about the desired end state. In certain cases, however, we have observed the imposition of direct measures which either modify the normal functional relationships of the market or even attempt to supercede them. Given the ideology of free-market systems, we tend to find such direct controls imposed only in periods of war and economic crisis. In fact, we have here the basic distinction, which is frequently made, between 'indicative' and 'imperative' planning systems. *In extremis*, under the latter regime, end states are brought about directly by what might be termed coercion, whilst, in the former case, an attempt is made to induce required end states by, primarily, indirect methods.

There are numerous instances of direct controls to be found in the experience of the United Kingdom. Import and export licencing has occurred to control the international allocation of scarce resources, and also to support the balance of payments. In the context of regional planning, a whole range of directives have been issued, governing the location of industry and the possible uses of land. However, the most contentious direct controls during recent years have been the prices and incomes policies which successive governments have attempted to apply since 1948. The policies have been aimed at solving the inflation problem which has been endemic since the end of the Second World War, and some have been more successful than others. This issue need not concern us here but it seems that, to date, none of these policies has succeeded in containing inflation for long and we can possibly ascribe this to the fact that price controls and income restraint have rarely been applied with equal effect; labour is reluctant to curb its income when it observes profit increases, in the same way as firms are reluctant to keep prices down in the face of increasing labour costs.

Direct controls form the central policy instrument of the command economy and were therefore the predominant type of direction of economic activity in the early Soviet system. In the absence of any market mechanism and with only notional wages and prices, all the inputs and outputs of the economy had to be directly allocated rather than indirectly induced. This preponderance of direct control has now diminished somewhat owing to the selective decentralisation of socialist economies but major items such as the overall balance of production may still be enforced in this manner. Producers, in other words, will still be told what to produce, if not precisely how it is to be produced. An additional major area for the direct control, as in the capitalist economy, will be the provision of public goods. In such a case, resources will be directed into the required area on the basis of some established social-choice criteria.

We see, in conclusion, that the range of instruments available is similar in most modern economies, although each nation naturally retains its own peculiar features. Typically, social preferences in socialist economies have endowed planners with much more scope for employing direct controls and, in such systems, it is this form of policy which has become the more sophisticated, the converse being largely true for the capitalist world. This has an important corollary for the planner. Whilst we might be aware that a certain desired end state could be simply brought about by a particular policy, we might, in fact, be precluded from using it owing to the preferences specified by society; an alternative — and possibly less direct — policy must be employed instead. To give a rather extreme example, few societies would permit their planners to produce the desirable end state of increases in per capita income by the literal decimation of the population. More plausibly, it is doubtful whether Western societies would sanction an increase in industrial output at the expense of slave labour.

POLICY GOALS

If we examine the historical experiences of contemporary societies, we discover that divergences in society's preferences regarding economic evolution occur, not with respect to the overall direction of progress, but rather with respect to the particular route to be taken and, to continue the metaphor, the mode of transport. There seems, in other words, to be substantial agreement at the present time as to the basic long-term goals of economic policy.

The fundamental objectives fall into three major categories. First, the full employment of economic resources — land, labour, capital and raw materials — is indeed regarded by many observers as the primary goal of economic development. Its desirability is almost axiomatic to the 'economic problem'; given the economist's standard assumption of more being preferred to less, we clearly require the full use of all available inputs in order to achieve maximum output, all other things remaining equal. Employment is also important from an individual, as well as from a collective, point of view. Modern societies tend to provide rewards to members as some function of the individual's contribution to national output, with the result that personal employment is a *sine qua non* of the simple business of living.

A second agreed objective is price stability, whether in monetary- or in physical-exchange terms. Increases in prices may have a number of undesirable consequences, such as reducing disproportionately the living standards of citizens with fixed incomes or reducing the competitiveness of exports. Finally, our third area of consensus is some progressive growth in real living standards for the mass of the population over time.

We could be reasonably certain, therefore, that an economic program which stimulated employment, stability and growth, would be welcomed in any corner of the world. However, the peculiarities of individual plans arise from (1) the wide range of additional, particular goals which any one nation might espouse, and (2) the possibility that the achievement of one set of goals might preclude the achievement of another.

Clearly, the range of particular objectives can be very wide indeed and we shall therefore only consider a sample. Possibly the most significant in the capitalist world, of a similar status to the three mentioned above, is the requirement to maintain a satisfactory balance of payments equilibrium. It is important to appreciate that the idea of a balance of payments disequilibrium is simply an institutional problem which stems from the accepted conventions of international trade. These dictate that any economy which imports commodities must pay for such items by means of export earnings or else be obliged to incur a debt which will eventually require repayment. The long-run equilibrium, given that such repayment must occur, is clearly equality between the values of imports and exports. As the demand for imported commodities, and therefore the volume of trade between capitalist nations, has risen substantially over the past few decades, the balance of payments goal has become more significant. The Soviet bloc, on the other hand, pursues a much more autarkic (self-sufficient) economic policy, with the result that this goal appears much lower down its list of priorities.

A more equal distribution of income and wealth is another commonly accepted goal, as is evidenced by the fact that most countries apply a progressive form of income taxation; some also have wealth taxes (for example, death duties) applicable to the rich, complemented by state allocations to the poorer members of society. Generalisations on this issue may not be particularly valid, however, as there exist great divergences in the degree of income disparities throughout the world.

Those economies with substantial public sectors will be concerned, as one of their policy goals, to maintain an 'adequate' balance between the different sectors of the economy. Along with the growth of manufacturing industry, most economies seem keen to expand the 'social goods' sectors, such as transport, health and education, as all these are important determinants of the quality of lifestyle which eventually results from the planning decision. In parallel with sectoral balance, societies may also be concerned with the regional balance, that is, with appropriate geographical distribution of economic activity.

In recent years, a number of additional goals have been gathering support and now appear in the economic calculus of most nations. The preservation of the natural environment is being seen as increasingly important as is, as far as the developing countries are concerned, the control of population growth. With the establishment of high-consumption societies, thoughts are also turning towards the possibility of decreasing the labour effort in favour of increasing leisure time, accompanied by the provision of the necessary facilities for its enjoyment.

As we observed in our discussion of planning methodology, the planning decision would be trivial if any one particular policy vector scored consistently higher in terms of *all* the goals of our economy — growth, full employment, the protection of the environment, and so forth. In practice, this is not the case, however, as by and large the objectives which we have established as universal tend to be mutually exclusive. This fact is, of course, the basis of economic science as, if it were not true, the study of the subject would have little meaning as a purposeful exercise. At a microlevel, we clearly cannot use the same resources to produce both guns and butter. At a macrolevel, conflicts also occur. Suppose, for example, we decide to inflate the economy in order to stimulate the employment of resources. Amongst the possible consequences of this policy are price inflation caused by an excess of purchasing power, and an imbalance of international trade caused by an increasing demand for imports necessary for the production process. Again, if we relocate industry to provide a more even geographical balance within the economy, we may reduce growth by moving resources from more productive regions, and even destroy the environment in the newly industrialised area. High taxation of the rich, it is also argued, might improve income equality but could discourage this class of individuals from undertaking growth-generating investment. As a final example, and one to which we shall return at a later stage, it is, by definition, impossible to obtain maximum present consumption and the maximum possible future consumption with finite resources — we can have our national cake now or eat it later but, unfortunately, we cannot do both!

Social choice, as far as the planner is concerned, will therefore present substantial problems. Whilst we can be fairly certain of the relative importance of the elements within the end states — in the same way as we can be fairly certain of the general range and nature of the policy instruments which are considered acceptable — we still possess an enormous set of possible candidates, each of which describes particular national goals reflecting different trade offs between the individual objectives. Fortunately, the political processes of modern societies go a long way towards solving our problem of narrowing down this wide range of possibilities.

THE POLITICAL PROCESS

From the point of view of the planner, the problem of social choice is as follows: how do we derive a unique objective function to be maximised, or a unique set of targets to be attained, given the existence of millions of individuals who have a variety of preferences regarding an enormous number of possible social and economic issues? In this section, we shall consider a number of ways in which modern polities have sought answers to this fundamental problem of government.

The simplest political regime, as far as the planner is concerned, is dictatorship. In this case, the views of individuals are, by definition, ignored and the objective function explicitly stated by the ruler or the ruling elite: social preferences are the ruler's preferences. There is no reason to believe that such situations must always be tyrannical — the Leviathan in Hobbes's society was governing with the active consent of the people — but this attitude of *l'état, c'est moi* usually only prevails in a small number of countries whose rulers possess messianic tendencies. It seems to be felt generally that the objective function with which the planner works should, in some sense, reflect individual choices which have been manifested democratically. Turning therefore from the intellectually trivial solution of dictatorship, how do democratic systems generate social preferences?

Let us assume first of all that the constituent members of our society participate in a referendum to determine the socially preferred level of present consumption, which can range between 0 and 100 per cent of current national output. We could expect, for example, a distribution of votes of the form presented in Figure 3.1. Given that society is to be governed by the axiom of simple

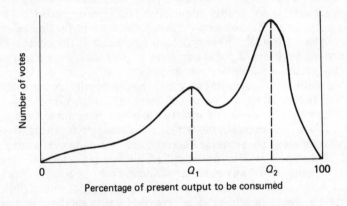

Figure 3.1

democracy — one person, one vote — it is clearly the modal value, Q_2, which 'best' reflects social preferences. Such simple democracy rests upon the tacit assumption that all those who did not choose Q_2 are willing to abide by the modal decision, and it is therefore the social preference Q_2 which forms the criterion for the planning authorities. Note that in this simple model we have not recorded the strength of preferences, that is, how passionately individuals hold their particular beliefs, but we could in principle allow for this by devising transferable or preference-intensity vot-

65

ing systems; irrespective of this, however, we shall clearly be able to generate a unique solution for our planners.[1]

Again, in principle, we could conduct additional referenda for all other instances where a social choice is to be made, such as the optimum output of steel, the appropriate length of the working day, the acceptable levels of inflation and unemployment, and so forth, and all these results would serve as additional planning criteria in the same manner. Finally, we could also poll the members of society as to their preferred trade off between goals which might possibly come into conflict, and this information would serve to generate the ultimate objective function for the planners to maximise, or a set of targets at which to aim.

In reality, we are unlikely to find such a system of 'one person, one vote, one issue' in operation for a variety of reasons. The process of voting on each particular issue, for example, is extremely costly in terms of time and effort. Some members of society might not consider themselves sufficiently informed to make a rational decision and certain areas may in fact be of no concern to them at all. These problems may be set in the context of the general problem of polling millions of persons for each marginal change in social and economic policy.

The method of government which has generally come to be adopted is termed *representative democracy* and, under this system, individual members of society elect to a national governing body those representatives whose declared preferences best reflect their own. These elected persons are then endowed with the right of decision making on behalf of the society which elected them. Assuming that any member of society may become a candidate for election, any individual who chose Q_2 consumption in Figure 3.1 would clearly be an appropriate representative; in general, any person from the modal class is the 'correct' choice.

Even so, this state of affairs is still not appropriate to reality. In practice, only a few individuals will be willing, or even permitted, to stand for election. Let us suppose that, in our model, we have just two, one who chose Q_2 and also one who chose Q_1. In this case, the choice of the elected representative is unclear. The Q_2 candidate may again be elected but, if all those who chose levels below Q_2 regard the levels which they chose as the absolute maximum they would wish to consume, it follows that all their votes

[1] If the voting suggested that society was truly indifferent between a number of levels of consumption, the planners would, by definition, be at liberty to choose any one of these.

will go to the Q_1 representative, and he will be the person selected. Naturally, the problem of the split in voting will be exacerbated by the introduction of willing candidates who stand on a platform of different consumption levels (Q_3, Q_4 etc.) but again, in principle, one single candidate can be elected. This model is similar to the familiar auction situation — we can envisage candidates in the political marketplace declaring preferences, the person receiving the most votes being the victor. Obviously, the candidates will be encouraged to make marginal alterations in their platform to ensure the necessary majority.

If this particular strategy of representative democracy were to be followed, we should clearly have as many representatives as there are elements in the end-state vector which, as we have suggested, could possibly exceed the number of individuals in society. Naturally, this will not do. To make the system workable, the solution adopted is (1) to amalgamate a number of elements of the end-state vector into a particular electoral 'package', and (2) to eliminate some decisions from social choice altogether and to simply talk in generalities.

Our social-preference process now becomes much simpler. Each candidate will present an end-state matrix, E, for popular approval, the element E_{ij} representing the candidate's position, j, on any particular issue, i. With three candidates for election, we might see electoral 'packages' as follows:

$$\left. \begin{array}{l} \text{Candidate 1 } E_{1,6}, E_{2,8}, O, E_{4,9}, \ldots, E_{i,6} \\ \text{Candidate 2 } E_{1,3}, E_{2,3}, E_{3,1}, O, \ldots, E_{i,4} \\ \text{Candidate 3 } E_{1,2}, O, E_{3,4}, E_{4,7}, \ldots, E_{i,8} \end{array} \right\} \qquad (3.3)$$

where a zero indicates that the candidate has no view on this particular issue, be it inflation, or the growth of population. Each member of society is now obliged to vote for that 'package', and therefore that candidate, which 'best' matches his or her own preferences. Note that in this society, we will be implicitly choosing the content of the target vector, as well as the levels of the elements. The candidate elected has clearly proposed a package which, in aggregate, best represents popular preferences. It is clear that very few other individuals' personal choices will exactly match this package, but this discrepancy, it might be argued, is the price paid for a viable political system; in return for a representative democracy in which the majority of individuals do not wish, or are not permitted, to actively involve themselves, such individuals accept social choices which may be some way removed from their true preferences. As a means of defence, however, the electorate would still retain the right of 'hire and fire' and the opportunity of standing for election themselves.

For the sake of simplicity, we have contented ourselves with demonstrating the derivation of the required unique policy vector by describing the election of a single individual. Such a regime of democratic monarchy is not, however, the prevalent form of government but, as will be appreciated, the operations of political parties and other systems of voting which elect a larger number of representatives to form the government, are analogous to — if immeasurably more complex than — the simple model described above.

These, then, are the principal methods of practical decision making currently employed. Because of the impossibility of producing social choice from individual preferences with complete duplication unless there exists a total consensus amongst the members of the population, a political process is established in order to generate a range of socio-economic policy goals and instruments. Preferences could be implemented by force, as in the case of a tyrannical dictator, or we could see some popularly supported government in operation. In the latter case, a monarch could be elected to enforce his own preferences, or we could see the democratic election of a group of individuals who present to the electorate a 'package' which best duplicates social preferences over the end-state vectors. The final social decision will best approximate individual choices when there exists a degree of consensus in society; in cases where consensus is low, we could see what many regard as the worst facet of democracy — the imposition of the will of the majority on to the minority.[2] As this text is not designed as a treatise on political morality, we shall not dwell on these matters. It is sufficient to reaffirm the central point of this chapter — given the wide range of possible goals and policy instruments, contemporary societies have found it expedient to establish decision processes which substantially narrow down this variety to give their planners the required information about the general form of end states to be pursued. With some degree of certainty, therefore, the planner can specify his objective function.

[2] This leads us to the interesting proposition that the only true democracy, where social preference always reflects individual choices, is the 'one-party state', where individuals all willingly possess the same preference function.

CHAPTER 4

The Nature of the Economy

As we saw in the opening chapter, the primary technical requirement for macroeconomic planning is an understanding of the nature and the functioning of the economic system with which we are concerned. In practice, this will involve three lines of inquiry:

(1) The identification of the variables within the economy, for example, aggregate consumption, investment in coal mining, taxation on electrical goods, and so forth.
(2) The quantification of these variables, either in monetary or in physical terms.
(3) The development of the appropriate causal relationships between these variables; for example, why and by how much does the rate of interest affect the level of investment?

In a perfect planning world we should of course, possess a full knowledge of all these aspects. Every element of economic life could be identified and measured with precision, from the national output of steel down to the purchase of a packet of cigarettes at the corner shop, and all these pieces of information would be available to the planning body. The planners would also possess a complete understanding of the causal relationships operating within the economy and would be aware of all the arguments in each producer's and consumer's utility function to the extent that, for example, they could accurately estimate just how many visits to the corner shop might be precluded by an increase in the price of tobacco.

The world, alas, is not perfect. In the first place, national economic systems are exceedingly complex. Modern economies are composed of many millions of individual consumers with individual preference functions which are likely, moreover, to change unpredictably over time. The sophisticated systems of East and West produce countless types of consumption and production goods and services implying *in toto* that an enormous number of individual economic variables need to be identified at any one

69

point in time. Furthermore, in spite of the increasing expansion of economic research, many of the basic causal relationships in the economy still remain unclear—for example, is inflation generated by the increased wage pressure of labour or by an increase in the money supply or by neither or both? Again, if income tax is increased, does the individual choose to work less as leisure becomes relatively more attractive, or does he work more to maintain his post-tax income at the previous level?

A second reason for our comparative lack of knowledge revolves around the question of cost. The desired information about the working of the system is not a free good in that resources — manpower and capital equipment— must be expended in order to gather and collate data. The collection of economic data therefore involves an economic decision and it seems reasonable to suppose that, as with most commodities, the greater the volume of data required, then the greater will be the costs incurred. In other words, even if society could potentially understand all the complexities of its economy, it might not choose to do so for reasons of cost.

In terms of understanding the nature of the economy, society will therefore aim at obtaining an *adequate* rather than a perfect knowledge. This definition of adequacy is essentially pragmatic and we shall meet the problem again during the course of this chapter. However, in order to demonstrate the idea, let us return to the simple example given in our opening chapter. We saw that our mechanic had an adequate knowledge of the machine in that he appreciated that a spanner in the works would bring about his desired result of stopping the engine, presumably by jamming the mechanism. Clearly, however, he did not have a perfect knowledge of the system as, with a wider understanding of the engine's mechanism, he would have realised that he could have brought about his desired result by, say, disconnecting the ignition system, a safer and more certain method for achieving his aims. If we pointed this out to him, he could, however, reply that the acquisition of this additional knowledge was 'uneconomic' as he had obtained his desired result without incurring the expense of acquiring this information — such as time spent reading a book.

In the same way, the mechanics of the economic system might well decide that their knowledge is adequate for the purpose in hand; we might, for example, be content to appreciate how consumption in aggregate is affected by changes in household income, without an understanding of the influences on each individual's consumption. This notion of adequacy, combined with the problems of complexity and costs, explains the macroeconomic planners' preoccupation with *economic models*. In order to understand just what is meant by a model, let us return to our utopian economy of Chapter 2.

In this example, we possessed a complete knowledge of each individual's desired consumption level of different commodities. Aggregating these consumption levels over all consumers gives us a one-for-one mathematical representation of economic reality, in that everything which appeared in the real world possesses a single counterpart in our representation. We might say, however, that this formulation is inappropriate for our purposes because either (1) the real world is, in fact, too complex to be understood, or (2) it is unnecessary for us to totally understand reality, or (3) it is too expensive to understand the process, and we might therefore be content with a different version in which aggregate consumption is somehow related to household income. By identifying what to us represent the salient features of the real world, this new equation might approximately predict the behaviour of consumers but it does not, as it did before, exactly duplicate it. In that a number of the arguments have been ignored or subsumed into others, this is a many-to-one representation or, in short, a model.

A first step in the understanding of the nature of the economy therefore comes down to (1) the collection of suitable data with which to develop models of economic mechanisms and (2) the construction of models which adequately — as far as the planners are concerned — reflect economic reality. It is clear that these requirements are bound to be interactive — model development will be constrained by the availability of data to construct and test such models, whilst the types of data collected will reflect the varieties of models currently being constructed. It is accordingly important that any advances being made in the collection of data and the evolution of models be made with due regard for each area's needs. Let us first turn our attention to the question of economic data.

ECONOMIC DATA

It is difficult to generalise about the quantity and nature of the data required for planning. On the one hand, a simple plan in a capitalist economy aimed at lowering the personal consumption level of a particular commodity might only require time-series data for a few variables, such as the tax rate and the prices and output of the commodity concerned, and its complements and substitutes; on the other hand, a complete macro-plan for a command economy will require information on every conceivable economic variable, from the output of fountain pens to the number of ships in the navy, from the number of houses being built to the notional (or shadow) price of bread. Modern economies usually make provision for their economic agencies to produce official statistics within their own field of operation, in that such a system produces certain economies in information gathering. To take the example of the United Kingdom, each joint-stock firm is obliged by law to produce an annual report of business activity, involving sales, profits, investments, and so on. Superimposed upon this is the requirement for all firms and individuals to submit an account of their incomes for the purpose of taxation. The major public-sector areas, such as local government, education, defence and the nationalised industries, all submit statistical reports of activities, including figures for employment, throughput, breakdowns of costs and revenues, and so forth, On the basis of all these individual data sources, the government collects, collates, modifies and augments the data to produce the appropriate national accounts. The type of data collected will therefore be influenced by the nature of society's economic agencies and the particular form of the economic structure of the country in question.

It is, however, easier to generalise on some of the problems likely to occur when employing data of this type as the basis of our understanding of the nature of the economy. Statistical errors are likely to be prevalent for a number of reasons.

Sampling. As we have seen, one important requirement for comprehensive macroplanning is a knowledge of consumer and producer preferences. The strategy which would yield the greatest accuracy in this domain would be to ask each individual producer and consumer to specify their particular preference function. For a nation the size of the United Kingdom, this could involve the government in interviewing some 55 million individuals who would presumably have to be reinterviewed whenever their preferences altered. The cost in terms of resource commitment and time would clearly be astronomical and the only feasible technique would be to question a *sample* of the population and, on the basis of this information, make inferences regarding the preferences of the whole population.

Such a technique offers myriad possibilities for inaccuracy and error. How large should the sample be, for example? Should it be selected at random or should its composition reflect the composition of the population (quota sampling)? In any event, how certain can we be that the attitudes of the sampled accurately reflect the attitudes of the total? Can we ensure that the questions to be asked in the survey are unambiguous — to give a slightly exaggerated example, we might suppose that the two alternatives, 'Do you think that the government should increase taxes?' and, 'Do you not think that the Government ought not to not lower taxes?' would engender totally different responses! Sampling by questionnaire cannot guarantee a truthful response on the part of those being interviewed. It would be quite irrational, for example, for a competitive firm in a capitalist economy to reveal its production plans for the next few years in view of the advantages which this information would give to its rivals. Again, the plant manager in the command economy would have no incentive to fix a high production target if he could get away with a lower, and therefore a more easily attainable, one.

Inaccurate responses might also be brought about by ignorance rather than by deliberate fabrication, and this was one of the key problems of the 1965 National Plan in the United Kingdom (Brunner, 1965). The basis of the planning framework was an industrial survey in which producers were required to furnish information regarding their capacities and expansion possibilities and requirements. In general, the firms found this impossible. Demand forecasts over the next period were unavailable or unreliable and entrepreneurs had little prior knowledge of the likelihood of future innovations and input prices. Of particular importance was the fact that the government itself was unwilling to provide any guidelines regarding its own future policies towards industry, in terms of taxation, membership of the European Economic Community, and so forth, as it was felt that these could only be developed on the basis of the results of the industrial survey. In such a situation, where neither side can operate without a knowledge of the other's activities, the resulting data are bound to be inappropriate. Clearly, such a problem could potentially arise in all mixed economies unless special links between government and industry are developed.

Classification. As data systems evolve and become more complex, then the wider and more comprehensive does the data classification system become. It is therefore likely that the number of categories devised for classification will expand and, as a consequence, the nature of these categories might well alter. To give an example, if a nation is only allocating a minimum of its resources to environmental protection, these might well be initially classified under a 'miscellaneous expenditure' heading of central government. However, if progressively more spending is allocated, the environment might be seen to justify a category to itself and may then be taken out of its original classification. This implies that the time series of 'miscellaneous expenditure' is no longer internally consistent over the periods. Obviously, this type of reclassification problem can occur in any data area.

Even if consistency is achieved across categories, a number of changes might occur within the classes. To give just a few examples, it may now be decided, for administrative convenience, to base calculations on financial rather than on calendar years; in jobs where there is an amount of part-time employment, the figures for total employment may now be expressed as 'whole-time equivalents' rather than as the actual numbers; accounting may now take place under a new measurement system such as money rather than physical units; money values in a series will be influenced by inflation or exchange rates. Any of these possibilities will cause problems when examining variable trends over time.

Time. Data cannot be prepared instantaneously. It clearly takes time to assemble, collate and classify material with the result that the planners will always be working with information which is already out of date. This time lag can have an important effect in planning policy. If it is seen from the prepared data, for example, that the economy is inflating, the planners might decide to deflate the system although, in reality, the economy has already started on a deflationary path. The policy prescription is therefore likely to overcompensate for this inflation which, although it was prevalent when the data was collected, now no longer exists.

Immeasurables. We have so far assumed that all the variables within the economy are capable of objective measurement, but this is not necessarily the case. Whilst there is a certain unambiguous precision in recording the output of steel at x million tonnes, or the current output value of coal at £y million, many areas of economic activity produce almost intangible products. How, for example, do we value, in either monetary of physical terms, the increase in the levels of health and education produced by hospitals and schools? What costs, if any, are imposed upon the community by increases in atmospheric pollution? What is the social value of convenience and time saved by a faster rail service? If our plan is to be a complete guide to economic development, it seems essential that such factors as these should be included.

Contemporary planners do indeed attempt to account for these immeasurables which contribute a great deal to the overall standard of living although, in the early planning experiments, they were largely ignored, the emphasis being on the progress of the real, productive economy. Measurement clearly has to take the form of subjective (as distinct from objective) social valuations; in other words, it is the social decision process which decides what values to ascribe to particular pieces of 'immeasurable' data, such as the quantity of sulphur dioxide in the air or the number of patients treated by a hospital. One simple method of ascribing value is to measure outputs as inputs; that is £1 spent on defence produces £1 in defence output, although any such translation process could be employed in principle. In such ways, immeasurables like pollution can be subjectively quantified and included in the planning calculus, on a par with commodities of a more tangible nature (Victor, 1972). The planner therefore looks to the government for guidance as to the appropriate valuation rule for use with the immeasurables, and the planning of these is therefore only as good as the specification of values. Furthermore, the identification of these social valuations is a special case of social decision making in general, the nature and inherent problems of which we examined in the previous chapter.

A prerequisite of any form of macroplanning must be the development of information services providing consistent, comprehensive and reliable information in the shortest possible time. Data in isolation, however, are not appropriate to planning unless used to understand the inter-relationships between economic variables. Data, in other words, are important to the development of economic models and we now turn to a consideration of the two major forms of model currently employed in both capitalist and socialist systems.

INPUT–OUTPUT ANALYSIS

A central feature of economic systems is the interdependence between economic variables. One particular firm or industry may obtain its raw materials from another firm and may also direct its production to further industries or consumers. Steel mills, for example, will require inputs from the coal and iron industries and may sell their output to the motor-car firms which provide the commodities for household consumption. Furthermore, a large proportion of these consumers provides the labour force and, in the capitalist world at least, receives wages to finance such consumption. Similarly, the firm's profits will pay for the cost of inputs from other industries.

Input–output analysis explicitly recognises these fundamental interdependencies and, as the name suggests, is concerned with identifying and quantifying the origins of inputs into, and the destinations of outputs from, any particular economic agent. This quantification can take place in either physical or, as is more common in the West, monetary units.

The first concern of input–output analysis is with industrial production, or the 'processing' sector of the economy. The analyst subdivides industrial production into a number of different industrial categories for the purpose of understanding how the inputs and outputs of each interact. In the case of the United Kingdom, the 1968 analysis identified 35 distinct industrial sectors, whilst the Soviet Union and the USA have identified even larger numbers — in 1970, the USSR was believed to be operating with 125 sectors (Wilczynski, 1970), whilst as early as 1947, the USA possessed data for 500 industrial classes (Miernyk, 1965).

Figure 4.1 presents an aggregated and simplified version of the 1968 UK input–output matrix. Here we identify six industrial sectors which approximate to (1) agriculture and mining, (2) iron, steel and engineering, (3) shipbuilding, aerospace and motor vehicles, (4) other manufacturing, such as construction and textiles. (5) services, such as gas and electricity, (6) distributive trades, administration and miscellaneous.

The interdependencies of the processing sector are presented in the 'Industry Inputs – Industry Outputs' submatrix, in the upper-left section of the full table. Horizontal rows indicate the sales, or output, of each sector and their destinations; industry 4, for example, sold £681 m. of output to industry 1 and £428 m. to industry 2. Correspondingly, the vertical columns represent the purchases of inputs of each type of commodity from others in the table; industry 5, for example, purchased £637 m. in inputs from industry 1 and £233 m. from industry 2. This submatrix therefore describes all interindustry relationships in the domestic economy.

| | INDUSTRY INPUTS *Purchases by industrial sectors* | | | | | | FINAL DEMAND | | | | TOTAL OUTPUT |
	1	2	3	4	5	6	C	G	I	X	
INDUSTRY INPUTS											
1	2,155	393	104	904	637	242	4,829	439	172	1,364	11,239
2	314	1,219	1,222	655	233	189	331	356	1,872	1,929	8,320
3 Sales by	242	468	313	290	208	186	546	573	849	1,468	5,143
4 industrial sectors:	681	428	329	1,787	179	932	2,915	653	3,914	1,120	12,938
5	806	420	176	587	199	1,049	2,103	312	267	1,319	7,238
6	916	657	359	920	198	465	10,539	4,564	196	1,186	20,000
PAYMENTS											
Imports	1,849	929	361	1,334	948	118	2,013	446	662	446	9,126
Taxation on expenditure	–55	89	43	352	259	832	3,976	339	171	–36	5,970
Employment income	2,372	2,823	1,798	4,534	2,666	11,225					25,418
Gross profits	1,939	894	438	1,575	1,711	4,762					11,319
TOTAL INPUT	11,239	8,320	5,143	12,938	7,238	20,000	27,252	7,682	8,103	8,816	116,711

Figure 4.1 *Aggregated input – output table for the United Kingdom, 1968 (in £ million).* Source: Derived from the full summary matrix in *National Income and Expenditure 1971*, HMSO.

Clearly, not all industrial output will be reabsorbed as inputs to other industrial sectors; some will be taken up by household consumption and some will be exported to other regions of the world. These additional destinations are recorded in the 'Final Demand' section, on the upper-right of the matrix. In the case of industry 1, therefore, we see that £4,829 m. in output were consumed by households (C), £439 m. were consumed by the government sector (G), £172 m. were allocated to capital investment and the accumulation of stocks (I) and £1,364 m. in outputs were exported (X). The sum of the elements in each row of the table therefore produces the total sales or output of each industrial sector and these figures are presented in the final column.

In a similar manner, industrial sectors will need to purchase a wider range of factors of production, that is, more inputs, than simply those obtained from other industries; they will require, for instance, labour inputs and raw materials imported from abroad. These items are recorded in the 'Payments' section at the lower-left of the full table. In the case of industry 3, therefore, we see that £361 m. of inputs were imported from abroad and £43 m. were paid for government services such as defence and the publicly-provided infrastructure. It should be noted that the identification of taxation as a payment for such services is arbitrary and is employed for convenience. The valuation of these services is particularly difficult and the payment made need not necessarily reflect the quantity of services provided. This is particularly true of agriculture — sector 1 — which the UK government feel 'ought' to be subsidised. Sector 3 also required the services of labour and capital, to the value of £1,798 m. and £438 m. respectively. The sum of the elements of each column therefore produces the total purchases, or input, of each industrial sector and these figures are presented in the final row. As we have accounted for *all* inputs and outputs, the values of the two totals for each sector must be identical.

There will also be an interaction between 'Payments' and 'Final Demand', as is evidenced at the lower-right of the full matrix. Certain final-demand commodities will be imported directly from abroad and taxation as payment for public services will also be levied. The sum of the 'Payments' rows hortizontally, and the 'Final Demand' columns vertically, will accordingly provide totals for the nonprocessing sectors of the economy. Given that all inputs and outputs have been included, it is clear that 'Total Input' (the sum of the elements in the final row) must be equal to 'Total Output' (the summation of the final column), this figure being recorded at the bottom right of the table. This is, of course, true by definition, as the final total is simply the sum of all the individual elements in the complete matrix, excluding the two 'Total' vectors.

So far, input–output analysis is little more than a way of arranging economic data in a form of national accounts. However, because of the manner in which the data have been identified and presented, we may now use the final table to throw considerable light on the operations within our economy. We know, for example, that the total output of sector 1 was valued at £11,239 m. and, in order to create this production, it was obliged to purchase £681 m. in inputs from sector 4. In other words, for each £1 worth of output produced, it purchased £(681/11,239) or 6·1 pence worth of input from sector 4. Given that industrial production functions are likely to be fairly stable over time, and everywhere linear in all inputs, we can infer the important conclusion that the expansion of the output of sector 1 by £1 will necessitate the expansion of the output of sector 4 by 6·1 pence, and a similar inference can be made for all combinations of inputs and outputs in the processing sector.[1] From the basic input–output table we can therefore derive a new matrix of direct inputs — the amount of input which each industry must provide to generate £1 worth of output for any other particular sector. The table of direct inputs appropriate to the 1968 UK matrix, derived by dividing each element in the column of inputs for each industry by the total output of that industry, is presented in Figure 4.2.

		Purchases by industrial sectors:					
		1	2	3	4	5	6
	1	0·195	0·047	0·020	0·069	0·088	0·010
Sales by	2	0·028	0·146	0·235	0·050	0·032	0·010
industrial	3	0·022	0·056	0·060	0·022	0·029	0·010
sectors:	4	0·061	0·051	0·063	0·137	0·025	0·047
	5	0·073	0·050	0·034	0·045	0·027	0·052
	6	0·083	0·079	0·069	0·071	0·027	0·023

Figure 4.2 *Direct input coefficients per £1 of output (£).*

[1] In making these calculations, it is necessary to subtract from total output the accumulation of stocks, as these items have not in fact appeared as output in transactions. This subtraction has been performed for all calculations.

These direct purchases do not, however, convey the full impact of sectoral expansion as far as final demand is concerned. Because of the industrial interdependence which we know to exist, any expansion in one sector will set up a chain of sales and purchases throughout the entire system, and, so far, we have simply estimated the technical input coefficients, that is, the amount by which sectors need to expand to allow a unit increase in, say, sector 1. The total requirements for expansion, however, include both direct *and* indirect purchases, as follows: if sectors 2 to 6 are to expand to meet the needs of sector 1 (direct purchases), they too must purchase additional inputs from the other sectors; that is, sector 2 must have additional inputs from 1 and from 3 to 6, sector 3 must purchase from 1, 2 and from 4 to 6, and so on (indirect purchases). To return to our previous example, a unit increase in output by sector 1 requires the increase of 6·1 pence in input from sector 4. To facilitate this increase, sector 4 must accordingly increase its purchase of the output of sector 5 by £(0·061 × 0·045) or 0·3 pence. In other words, to allow sector 1 to expand its output by £1, sector 5 must not only increase its sales to sector 1 by 7·3 pence, but it must also increase its sales to sector 4 by 0·3 pence, and a similar accumulation of requirements will occur for all pairs of industrial interactions. By working through all such interactions, we can derive a matrix of total (direct and indirect) input requirements, as shown in Figure 4.3[2].

		Purchases by industrial sectors:					
		1	2	3	4	5	6
Sales by industrial sectors	1	1·124	0·049	0·020	0·074	0·096	0·010
	2	0·029	1·171	0·307	0·053	0·033	0·010
	3	0·022	0·059	1·064	0·022	0·030	0·010
	4	0·065	0·054	0·067	1·159	0·026	0·049
	5	0·079	0·053	0·035	0·047	1·028	0·055
	6	0·091	0·086	0·074	0·076	0·028	1·024

Figure 4.3 *Total indirect and direct input coefficients per £1 of output to final demand (£).*

[2] Although the system can clearly be solved by a continuation of the iterative process already begun, requirements are, in practice, calculated by using matrix algebra — the matrix required is the inverse of the difference between the identity matrix and the direct input coefficient matrix. This in turn approximates to a power-series expansion of each element.

Clearly, the development of the input–output table has thrown considerable light on the basic structural relationships of the economy, particularly if the matrix is as disaggregated as those which are in current use in the USA and the USSR. Not only can we see just what type of economy we are operating within, but we can also readily identify the areas which, as far as the planners are concerned, are in the greatest need of attention, such as deficient aggregate demand, excessive imports, and so forth.

Let us assume that an increase in final demand for a particular commodity in the next time period is forecast — just how these forecasts are made forms the subject matter of the next section. The planners will accordingly be concerned with how the economy might be adjusted to deal with this change. If the time period is reasonably short, say, two or three years, we could suppose quite fairly, that the technical coefficients specified by interindustry inputs and outputs will remain constant. Using the table, we are in a position to identify the industrial requirements of demand expansion and we could therefore take pre-emptive steps to ensure that bottlenecks, shortages and surpluses do not occur during the development of the economy. A projected input–output table, drawn up on the basis of predicted variations in final demand, can be estimated from the total input-requirements matrix (Figure 4.3). We may see, for example, that the expansion of 'Final Demand' by £1 for the output of sector 1 would require the expansion of output to the value of 2·9 pence by industry 2 and by 2·2 pence by industry 3. Similarly, an increased demand for the products of sector 2 by £1 would require the expansion of sector 1 by 4·9 pence and sector 3 by 5·9 pence. By multiplying these coefficients by the projected final demand, we clearly have the basis for a table which describes our new industrial requirements.

Whilst such an analysis is invaluable in predicting the complex needs of industries when demands change, there are a number of problems with which this form of analysis is obliged to cope. First, the assumptions of simple input–output analysis include fixed technical coefficients and the constancy of relative prices. However, in reality, there is likely to be some degree of substitutability between inputs and frequent changes in relative prices, both of which violate the model's assumptions and, hence, may cast doubt upon its predictions. Secondly, the dynamic applicability of the model will also be hampered by the emergence of new industrial sectors and by the presence of technological change in existing industries. The solutions to these problems involve the economist

81

in research outside the formal input–output field. In the first case, he will be concerned in attempting to evaluate the relative price shift and, in the second, he will try to estimate the effects of innovation, possibly by examining time-trend data or by deriving technical production functions for the most efficient industries at the present time, their practice being taken as a guide for the future. On the basis of this extra information, the original total input coefficient matrix can be modified and it is this refined matrix which will serve as the basis for the projected table.

A second area of importance is the calculation of multipliers, a knowledge of which is needed for the evaluation of the likely effects of a particular policy. The income multiplier can be conveniently calculated by considering the households as 'industries', to form an additional row and column in the processing sector submatrix: the inputs to the households are their consumption of the different commodities from other sectors, whilst the outputs are the labour services provided to industry. By including households, we may now perform precisely the same operations as above and the enlarged total coefficients matrix will now indicate the income generated by unit increases in final demand for the output of particular processing industries.[3].

We have seen, therefore, that the collection of economic data and their arrangement in the form of an input–output matrix can provide a useful insight into the nature of the economy, by demonstrating the technical linkages between industrial sectors. Using such data, the planners will immediately be aware of industrial requirements for demand or output expansion. However, we have also seen that input–output analysis often requires additional information to yield further predictions — it needs to have available forecasts of changes in certain variables and also functional relationships such as technical progress. In order to gain this form of knowledge about the economy, the planners must resort to a different form of analysis, and it is to an examination of this that we now turn.

ECONOMETRIC SIMULATION

Econometrics is concerned with the subjection of theories of economic relationships to testing, on the basis of statistical infer-

[3] The inclusion of the household sector into processing will require some reclassification of the basic data, as input and output must be equal as in the other industrial sectors — this clearly is not yet the case in Figure 4.1.

ence from empirical observations. Let us suppose that we believe that a functional relationship exists between two economic variables, X and Y — examples of such an hypothesis are commonplace in economics and may take the form of, for example, the relationship between aggregate consumption and disposable income through time (time series), or the influence of the outputs of a number of industries on employment requirements in those industries at any one point in time (cross-section observations). As we have seen, an important requirement for planning is some knowledge of how variable Y is likely to behave, given certain changes in another variable or policy instrument, X.

Pairs of data points for our variables may be derived from the appropriate statistical sources, but it is important to appreciate that these observations constitute *sample* values. Because of the complexities of economic reality, it is inevitable that far more factors than simply X will be operating on Y from one observation to the next and, furthermore, it is likely that these 'disturbance' factors will act in a different and *a priori* indeterminate manner for each pair of observations recorded.

'. . . figures for gross national product appear at first sight to be absolute (population results). Think of them, however, as the end product of a set of decisions which could have been taken in an infinite variety of ways; the universe or statistical population becomes all the possible sets of decisions which could lead to a figure for gross national product (GNP), the actual figure being one of these and therefore a sample.' (Yeomans, 1968)

For precision, we must therefore specify our functional relationship for any pair of n observations, i, as

$$Y_i = f(X_i) + e_i \tag{4.1}$$

where e_i measures the influence of all other factors operating when and where X_i and Y_i were recorded. Our task, therefore, is to infer the behaviour of the statistical population from the sample values of our variables, by deriving a relationship which is 'most likely' to be the true one. How is this to be done?

For the sake of simplicity, let us assume that the real population relationship is linear, that is,

$$Y = a + bX \tag{4.2}$$

where a and b are the population coefficients. Our values of Y, however, are only sample values and are related to the population values by the associated disturbance term; that is,

$$Y_i = \hat{Y}_i + e_i \qquad (4.3)$$

where a circumflex indicates sample values. It is clear, therefore, that, if we derive a function of the form

$$\hat{Y} = \hat{a} + \hat{b}X \qquad (4.4)$$

which *minimises* the sum of the disturbance terms, we can obtain coefficient estimates for $\hat{a}$ and $\hat{b}$ which best approximate their population values, a and b. Furthermore, this same principle will hold for a multiple relationship with a number of independent variables, each with its associated sample and population coefficient.

From the point of view of estimation, the simple minimisation of the sum of the disturbance terms,

$$\sum_{i=1}^{n} e_i,$$

will not always yield our required function. This can be seen from Figure 4.4. In the case of these three points, any line A will meet our criterion, as long as the positive disturbance, e_1 cancels out the negative disturbance, e_2,

$$\sum_{i=1}^{2} e_i$$

being zero. It is clear that the appropriate functional form is given by line B and this can be isolated by minimising, not the sum of the deviations from the line, but by minimising the sum of *squared* deviations. This process of squaring has the effect of treating all disturbances as positive and therefore significant, and the cancellation effect is eliminated. Under this criterion, only line B would pass the test. The technique of minimising the sum of squares of deviations from the estimated relationship is one of the major weapons in the econometrician's armoury and is referred to as *ordinary least-squares regression* (OLS).[4].

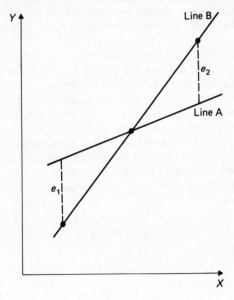

Figure 4.4

For the purpose of this example, we have assumed an *ex ante* knowledge of the appropriate functional form to be determined. In reality, this is unlikely to be the case; there will be a large number of potential influences and it is indeed the job of the econometrician to determine the population relationship by selecting those variables which consistently explain the behaviour of the dependent, both in terms of economic theory and statistical probability. In order to see how this is done, let us suppose that we have performed an OLS estimation on some economic data and have derived an equation as follows:

$$\hat{Y} = 10 \cdot 7 + 0 \cdot 36X_1 + 0 \cdot 47X_2 + 1 \cdot 72X_3 \qquad (4.5)$$

[4] There are also a number of substantive statistical reasons for preferring OLS estimations. As this section is designed simply as an introduction to the subject, the reader is referred to the further reading for specialist texts covering the precise estimation techniques.

Before we can categorically assert that this equation represents an accurate description and explanation of reality, we must examine a number of additional factors. One simple issue will be the number of observations — we should be more likely to trust inferences based on a dozen observations than inferences based on two!

Minimum variance. Although we have been concerned in deriving an equation which minimises the sum of squares of the disturbance factors, it is clearly better if the value for this minimum is as near to zero as possible. In other words, we require as little variation as can be attained between the recorded values for Y and the estimates of Y predicted by our functional form.

One method of expressing this idea is to compare the variation about the mean of our recorded values of Y with the variation about the mean of our predicted values. This comparison produces the *coefficient of determination* (R^2), given as:

$$R^2 = \frac{\sum\limits_{i=1}^{n} (\hat{Y}_i - \bar{Y})^2}{\sum\limits_{i=1}^{n} (Y_i - \bar{Y})^2} \tag{4.6}$$

where n is the number of data points being considered, $\hat{Y}_i$ is the predicted value from the derived equation, Y_i is the recorded value, and $\bar{Y}$ is the value of the mean. Clearly, the nearer the value of R^2 is to unity, then the better the functional form approximates to the behaviour of the dependent variable. In fact, R^2 measures the proportion of the total variation in Y explained by the functional form. One criterion for accepting a particular equation as a representation of reality is therefore to ensure that the value of R^2 is close to unity.

An alternative way of looking at this question of variation is to calculate the *F-ratio*, an expression which relates the variance of our predicted values for Y to the variance of their associated disturbance terms. The variance explained by the regression is divided by the 'unexplained' variance derived from the disturbances, and our 'best' equation will accordingly possess a high value for this *F-ratio*, up to an extreme value of infinity.

Significant coefficients. Although the calculated values of R^2 and the F-ratio might suggest to us that our formulation of the model could be correct, we have yet to examine the contributions of each individual independent variable within the equation, measured in terms of the estimated coefficient. As the process of OLS is, in principle, a sampling method, the coefficients calculated will not be precise values but will be represented as probability distributions about a, b, and so on. Now, sampling theory tells us that, given sufficiently large samples, we can be 95 per cent certain that the population coefficient lies within approximately two standard deviations about the coefficient mean, and so we can evaluate our hypothetical equation above as follows: suppose that the standard deviation or error of the coefficient of X_3 is $0 \cdot 12$. We can therefore be 95 per cent certain that the population value for the coefficient lies within the range $1 \cdot 72 \pm 0 \cdot 24$. However, if the value for the error was $1 \cdot 22$, our estimated coefficient would now give a possible range of $-0 \cdot 72$ to $4 \cdot 16$. A very high standard error relative to the coefficient implies that the relationship between X_3 and Y must be very tenuous, consistent with a wide variety of coefficient values. Moreover, this particular range includes the value of zero, which suggests that the interpretation is consistent with the existence of *no* relationship between X_3 and Y. In other words, we could safely omit X_3 from our estimation whilst losing hardly any explanatory power from our model. An additional requirement for our formulation is therefore that the estimated value of the coefficient relative to its standard error (a quotient known as the *T-ratio*) should be as high as possible: clearly, to eliminate zero from the range, it must take on the value of 2 or more.

Autocorrelation. When we formulate our projected equation, we are implicitly assigning to the disturbance term such factors as measurement errors and the net effect of unidentifiable additional influences. A fundamental assumption behind OLS is that the behaviour of these disturbances or residuals is random. However, we could find that, in our equation, these disturbances are related to one another; that is, at any one point in time, each disturbance is a function of the measured disturbances at points preceding it. Clearly, in this case, we have misunderstood the population relationship because we have not discovered the implicit interdependence between those entitites which make up the disturbance term. This form of problem is particularly prevalent in time-series data, where all macrovariables tend to display a recurrent cyclical pattern. In order to feel confident about our model, we must therefore examine the relationship between disturbances in the series to ensure that they are not correlated with one another. A class of tests exists which may be applied to detect the presence of autocorrelation known collectively as the *Durbin-Watson* tests.

Heteroscedasticity. In a similar fashion to autocorrelation, it would well be that our random disturbances do not share a common variance — again, there is an implicit functional relationship involving factors in the disturbance terms and this suggests that at least one other (as yet unspecified) variable is in operation. This problem of heteroscedasticity is most likely to occur in cross-section data where, for example, we are examining economic agents such as households or firms of widely differing income, output or scales of operation. Error variances could well increase as scale effects begin to play a part in our relationships, and our model must not possess any of these tendencies if it is to be a satisfactory representation of the population relationship.

Multicollinearity. If two or more of the independent variables, X_1, X_2 or X_3, are highly correlated with one another, it will be impossible for us to estimate just how our dependent variable is affected by either. At the limit, in the case of perfect correlation between X_1 and X_2, for instance, it will clearly be impossible to say which of the two brings about the changes in Y as the effects of each will be identical. When deriving our model, we must therefore ensure that the correlations between the independent variables are minimal, in the same way as we had to ensure minimal interaction between the disturbance terms.

Specification of the equation. The application of econometric techniques to basic data does not have the status of a formal science, nor does it permit us to determine the precise functional form immediately. Rather, trial and error, coupled with a knowledge of previously estimated relationships, is generally the method employed. Suppose, for example, we were attempting to estimate a time-series consumption function. Economic theory suggests that consumption could reasonably be expected to be a function of disposable profits, wage and nonwage income and, using data for these variables, we could in the first instance specify and estimate a linear function based on the OLS criterion. We should now pay particular attention to the additional factors outlined above — are the R^2 and F-test values high enough, are all the coefficients significant, and can we detect the presence of autocorrelation, heteroscedasticity or multicollinearity? If these criteria are not met, it will be necessary to respecify and re-estimate in order to improve the performance of our model on the basis of these tests. New variables might have to be added and old ones omitted, or we may wish to make the function nonlinear by including exponential or polynomial expressions. Similarly, for each equation which we derive, we can use our tests to provide guidelines for the next approximation towards the population relationship, and this process will continue until we are satisfied that no more improvement is possible.

In the context of the specification of time-series functions, an important consideration when determining the correct form of equation is the appropriate use of *time lags*. It could well be the case that the dependent variable is related, not to the current value of the independent, but to one or more of its past values. There are a number of examples of this in economics. Trades unions in capitalist economies often bargain for wages on the basis of the performance of the economy over the past few years, and also with a view to increasing the wage rate by some proportion of its former level. The equation for wages (w_t) might therefore contain terms for the previous year's wage level (w_{t-1}) and terms for the current and previous years' national output $(Y, Y_{t-1}, Y_{t-2}$ etc.); that is:

$$w_t = f(w_{t-1}, Y_t, Y_{t-1}, Y_{t-2}, \ldots) \tag{4.7}$$

Again, the accelerator theory of investment suggests that capital accumulation is a function of economic performance over time, so we could also formulate an investment function which is determined by the previous year's aggregate output. In all cases, the actual length of each time period will depend upon the time range of the data sample, which could be collected annually, quarterly or monthly — indeed any time period is conceptually possible, although the first two mentioned are most common in macroeconometric work. Which of the particular lagged terms are to be included in the specification is determined in the same way as for the nonlagged variables, namely, by recourse to economic theory and statistical significance.

Finally, two observations on the status of econometric relationships must be made. First, econometrics derives *statistical* models on the basis of the data available. Whether or not these estimated forms actually add to our understanding of reality is conditional upon whether they are coincident with reasonable propositions derived from economic theory. Secondly, it is most unlikely that our final equation will score 100 per cent on all our tests; the value of R^2 might be less than unity or some coefficients might not be particularly significant. The assessment of the adequacy of the model, in the same way as the assessment of the data, is a pragmatic decision. In general, we should argue that a model is adequate if it is capable of accurate predictions, coupled with our previous observation that we be able to interpret it in the light of economic theory. This ability to predict is therefore both the test and, as we shall see, the application of the estimated equation.

Let us suppose that we have derived an expression which suggests a constant proportionality between savings and income over the past ten years. If we believe that this functional form is an accurate description of economic affairs, we should be sufficiently confident to assert that next year's savings will form the same proportion of next year's income and, if this turns out to be true, our theory has been substantiated. However, not only have we tested our theory, but we have also applied it: we have said that, for example, if income rises to a certain level, savings will rise to a certain proportion of that level. In other words, given that certain events occur, we can forecast the occurence of other events. This possibility of predicting the likely outcomes of a system on the basis of its history, as modelled by an econometric relationship, provides the planners with a method of simulating different policies before they are actually implemented, and we shall return to this possibility at a later stage of the argument. In the meantime, however, let us look into the problems of econometric forecasting in a little more detail.

From the equations estimated by econometric techniques, our planners will be in a position to evaluate, for example, how data variables in the economy are likely to react when the level of a policy instrument is varied. What the planner is really doing, therefore, is *forecasting* future events within the economy from the functional form which uses the evidence collected to date. His line of reasoning might therefore run as follows: in previous years, consumption has always fallen by a certain amount when direct taxation is raised, so it is reasonable to assume that this tendency will continue into the next time period. Alternatively, I can include additional factors which might have a particular influence, and can modify the basic tendency accordingly.

The forecasting of economic activity is a vital ingredient of any plan and it usually forms the first step in plan construction. At the aggregate level, we can use our equations to predict aggregate demand and supply trends over the planning period as it will be a primary role of the plan to correct for any discrepancies between these two entities by the stimulation or depression of one or the other. In reality, these two macrovariables will have to be dis-aggregated so that forecasts can be made for component sectors.

From our earlier theoretical discussions, it might appear that the modelling of functional forms is a simple matter — it is just a question of feeding all the data into a computer and testing formulations by 'trial and error' until the 'perfect' model results. In practice, the world is not so simple and, because the identification of functional forms is such a vital ingredient of the planning process, it is as well to deal with some reservations regarding econometric forecasting which will serve as a review of empirical econometric problems in general.

Streissler (1970) opens his critique of econometric forecasting with a perceptive question:

'The potential snag of this logical framework is the supposition that it will be the *same phenomenon* that will repeat itself. Without repetition in society no stochastic equation describing it can be conceived; but does society repeat itself?'

In other words, just because varible X appears to have influenced variable Y in the past, there is no guarantee that it will continue to do so; nor, indeed, might there by any reason why it should not. The answer to Streissler's question therefore determines the relevance of forecasting, and simulation in general. We may be sure that this answer is not unrelated to the type of phenomenon which we are attempting to forecast: whilst we may be confident that houseowners will, in the short term at least, continue to buy glass for their windows according to certain economic and cultural 'laws', we might not be so sure that they would continue to prefer curtains to wooden shutters or venetian blinds!

In particular, Streissler outlines four stages of transition in the progress of the econometrician's observations of reality to his generation of an econometric model, each of which is a potential source of error. First, the analyst is obliged to simplify his observations into a narrow conceptual framework which includes only

91

those features which are regarded by him as relevant in explaining reality. There can be no guarantee, however, that the omitted influences are necessarily irrelevant: this is a function of the skill, and possibly the luck, of the analyst in question, and also of the type of problem on which he is working. For example, a model investigating household behaviour in general, might justifiably omit the influence of butter prices as they form an extremely small component of overall household expenditure, although this would hardly be conceptually satisfactory if the equation was then to be used in the analysis of the operations of the dairy industry.

Secondly, the conceptual framework must be respecified in a mathematical manner to facilitate estimation. The real-world proposition that 'smoking causes lung cancer' must therefore become 'the probability of contracting lung cancer is an increasing function of cigarette consumption'. In this transition, the problems are obvious: 'Smoking' and 'cigarette consumption' are not the same thing – different cigarettes have different chemical compositions; individuals might smoke the same cigarette in different ways (by inhaling less, for example) and health risks are also individual-specific. In addition, we have little evidence to suggest that nature operates in a manner describable by neat mathematical functions, such as linear or parabolic functions, although we shall be obliged to estimate the standard form which provides the closest, but not necessarily the perfect, approximation.

Thirdly, we must translate this precise, deterministic mathematical relationship into a stochastic or probabilistic one. As we have seen, this is only a reasonable course of action if we are confident of the independence of the variables and the disturbance factors. This will only occur if our variables have been judiciously selected as we observed above. Here we might encounter a conflict between the statistical and the economic justification for the inclusion or exclusion of a particular explanatory cause. Finally, the accuracy of the model, in terms of the explanation of reality, will be a function of our economic theories and the quality and quantity of the data available for calculation and testing — as we have seen, data are particularly prone to errors of diverse forms.

Models which purport to explain should also be able to predict, and their powers of explanation should therefore match their forecasting ability. However, there exists another class of forecasting methods which makes little attempt at explanation at all. If, it might be argued, the requirements of our plan are such that we need to forecast consumption demand over the next five years, we require *accurate* forecasts rather than *theoretically justified* ones; as long as the answer is correct, we are not particularly concerned with the method of derivation. It seems to be the case that, over time, a number of macroaggregates possess fairly stable growth trends, or at least growth paths such as cycles in which successive observations are autocorrelated; aggregate consumption, for example, is usually strongly influenced by the consumption patterns of previous time periods, and population growth is an additional instance. Starting from simple linear extrapolation, autoregressive forecasting (where future values are to be predicted on the basis of the past record of the variable under consideration) has now become extremely sophisticated with the development of the Box—Jenkins approach (Newbold, 1975) which allows for a substantial degree of individual discretion in modifying the time series in the light of available and complementary data.

Although often lacking any theoretical economic basis, such iterative forecasts do possess considerable usefulness for the planners. Where there exists intertemporal stability, they are capable of producing quite accurate forecasts, an accuracy which might often exceed the predictions derived from an inadequately specified econometric model. In addition, they obviously require much less data and they can be produced quickly at minimal resource cost. Autoregressive techniques were particularly popular in the earlier periods of Western planning (up to the mid-1960s) although now, with the developement of high speed computers and improved data collection, most capitalist countries are concentrating their forecasting efforts on explanatory models since

'The best forecasts should be made from the best estimate of the structure of the economic system.' (Klein, 1953)

As an illustration of the problems inherent in forecasting, it is instructive to consider the experience of the UK steel industry in the early 1960s (Burn *et al.*, 1965). The forecasting method employed was trend extrapolation, coupled with estimates based upon functional relationships between the use of steel and overall industrial development. During the early 1960s, the consumption of steel was significantly lower than that forecast, largely due to the fact that the assumptions on which the forecasts were based did not accord with the events that in fact occurred. National industrial output only grew at some 80 per cent of the assumed rate and it also became clear that the major purchasers of steel, such as the railways and the coal industry, had grossly overestimated their likely requirements. In addition, imports of steel and finished steel products were higher than anticipated, although these deficiencies were made up to some extent by the greater-than-expected expansion of the motor-car and building industries. Clearly, a forecast is only as good as its assumptions and the fact that these themselves might also be forecasts introduces further scope for error.

So far, we have considered econometric analysis of a number of individual and unrelated equations. However, given that our economic system is essentially integrated, as the input–output table suggests, an obvious next step after the calculation of separate equations is the combination of these into a larger model. For example, if we possess two independent expressions relating savings to income and savings to investment, we implicitly have a relation between investment and income. As the number of relationships and variables grows, we are now developing, not descriptions of particular aspects, but an integrated model of the entire economy — a macroeconomic model.

Econometricians have been calculating such models since the Second World War and these have become progressively more sophisticated with the development of large-scale data-processing systems and techniques. As an example, let us examine one of the earliest and simplest macromodels, the initial analysis of the US economy by Klein (1950).

Using data for the period 1921–41, Klein developed a Keynesian income – expenditure model, with three *behavioural* equations, estimated by econometric methods from the available data. First, Klein specifies aggregate consumption (C_t) as a function of the total wage bill in private industry (W_{1_t}) and in the government sector (W_{2_t}), and also as a function of profits (P_t). In the case of profits, however, Klein believes that consumption not only varied with current levels, but also with the previous year's level. An extra term for lagged profits (P_{t-1}) is therefore included, giving a final form estimated as:

$$C_t = 16 \cdot 79 + 0 \cdot 020P_t + 0 \cdot 235P_{t-1} + 0 \cdot 800(W_1 + W_2)_t \quad (4.8)$$

The level of net investment (I_t) is determined by the volume of corporate profits, both current and previous, and also by the size of the previous period's capital stock (K_{t-1}):

$$I_t = 17 \cdot 78 + 0 \cdot 231P_t + 0 \cdot 546P_{t-1} - 0 \cdot 146K_{t-1} \quad (4.9)$$

This equation quite reasonably asserts that the more capital that industries possess in any one year, then the less likely are they to acquire more.

Finally, labour demand is specified as the private wage bill (W_{1_t}) as a function of economic activity — defined as net national income (Y_t) plus corporate taxation (T_t) — less government sector wage payments (W_{2_t}). Also included is a time-trend variable, (Z), measured in calendar years, which indicates the influences of additional factors which might cause W_{1_t} to rise from year to year, institutional agreements with unions over wage levels being an example.

$$W_{1_t} = 1 \cdot 60 + 0 \cdot 420(Y + T - W_2)_t + 0 \cdot 164(Y + T - W_2)_{t-1}$$
$$+ 0 \cdot 135(Z - 1935) \qquad (4.10)$$

In addition to these behavioural estimates, there are also three *identities*. These are true by definition and are derived from the system of data classification. First, we define national income from the expenditure point of view:

$$Y_t \equiv C_t + I_t + G_t - T_t \qquad (4.11)$$

whilst from the income approach:

$$Y_t \equiv W_{1_t} + W_{2_t} + P_t \qquad (4.12)$$

Finally, the current level of the capital stock (K_t) is taken as current period additions to the stock of the previous year:

$$K_t \equiv I_t + K_{t-1} \qquad (4.13)$$

In this model, there exist nine *predetermined* variables whose values are fixed before the equation system is solved. Four of these are termed *exogenous* $(W_{2_t}, G_t, T_t$ and $Z)$, being determined by external factors such as government policy. The remaining five $(P_{t-1}, Y_{t-1}, K_{t-1}, W_{2_{t-1}}, T_{t-1})$ are lagged variables, their values being predetermined on the basis of the previous time period. There accordingly remain six variables $(C_t, I_t, W_{1_t}, Y_t, P_t, K_t)$ which are *endogenous*, determined by the functional relationships and the values of the predetermined variables. These six endogenous variables are inter-related in six different equations, so that the model can be finally determined by simultaneous solution.

At present, the model's equations are not clearly presented, as we have expressions for endogenous variables in terms of other endogenous variables. In order to examine the manner in which exogenous factors affect the values of the endogenous variables, we can rewrite the equation system in such a way that all the endogenous variables are expressed solely in terms of the pre-determined variables. Theil and Boot (1962) have estimated this so-called *reduced-form coefficient matrix* for the Klein model (Figure 4.5). This reduced form tells us, for example, that a unit increse in W_{2_t} produces a rise in C_t of $0 \cdot 666$, whilst a unit increase in T_t lowers Y_t by $1 \cdot 484$. These coefficients are termed the *impact multipliers* and they measure the change in the endogenous variables brought about by a unit change in the exogenous variables over one time period, in this case one year. These multipliers may be thought of as being analogous to the direct input coefficients of the input–output table which we discussed in the previous section. Similarly, they do not reveal the full impact of the changes which must occur in an interactive economy. When a unit change is made in an exogenous variable, the effects of this change will be felt over a number of time periods, during which the economy is returning to an equilibrium position at a similar or a different level.

$$
\begin{bmatrix} P \\ Y \\ K \\ C \\ W_1 \\ I \end{bmatrix}_t
=
\begin{bmatrix}
0 \cdot 863 & -0 \cdot 063 & -0 \cdot 164 & 0 & 0 & 0 \\
1 \cdot 489 & 0 \cdot 174 & -0 \cdot 283 & 0 & 0 & 0 \\
0 \cdot 746 & -0 \cdot 015 & 0 \cdot 816 & 0 & 0 & 0 \\
0 \cdot 743 & 0 \cdot 189 & -0 \cdot 098 & 0 & 0 & 0 \\
0 \cdot 626 & 0 \cdot 237 & -0 \cdot 119 & 0 & 0 & 0 \\
0 \cdot 746 & -0 \cdot 015 & -0 \cdot 184 & 0 & 0 & 0
\end{bmatrix}
\begin{bmatrix} P \\ Y \\ K \\ C \\ W_1 \\ I \end{bmatrix}_{t-1}
$$

$$
+
\begin{bmatrix}
-0 \cdot 224 & -1 \cdot 281 & 1 \cdot 119 & -0 \cdot 052 & 0 \cdot 063 & -0 \cdot 063 \\
0 \cdot 614 & -1 \cdot 484 & 1 \cdot 930 & 0 \cdot 143 & -0 \cdot 174 & 0 \cdot 174 \\
-0 \cdot 052 & -0 \cdot 296 & 0 \cdot 259 & -0 \cdot 012 & 0 \cdot 015 & -0 \cdot 015 \\
0 \cdot 666 & -0 \cdot 188 & 0 \cdot 671 & 0 \cdot 155 & -0 \cdot 189 & 0 \cdot 189 \\
-0 \cdot 162 & -0 \cdot 204 & 0 \cdot 811 & 0 \cdot 195 & -0 \cdot 237 & 0 \cdot 237 \\
-0 \cdot 052 & -0 \cdot 296 & 0 \cdot 259 & -0 \cdot 012 & 0 \cdot 015 & -0 \cdot 015
\end{bmatrix}
\begin{bmatrix} W_{2_t} \\ T_t \\ G_t \\ Z_t \\ W_{2_{t-1}} \\ T_{t-1} \end{bmatrix}
$$

Figure 4.5 *Reduced form coefficients for the Klein model.* Source: Adapted from Wallis (1973).

By examining the behaviour of our model over a number of time periods, we could therefore also estimate the *interim* multipliers (changes in the endogenous variables brought about by unit increases in the exogenous variables, after a number of time periods) and the *total* multipliers (changes brought about over time by sustained unit increases in the exogenous variables). The total multipliers for the Klein model are presented in Figure 4.6 where we see, for instance, that a unit increase in T_t lowers Y_t by 1·569. On the basis of our knowledge of the impact multipliers, we know that around 95 per cent of this total effect occurs during the first time period.

	P_t	Y_t	K_t	C_t	W_{1_t}	I_t
W_{2_t}	−0·192	0·536	−1·024	0·536	−0·271	0
T_t	−1·237	−1·569	−6·564	−0·569	−0·333	0
G_t	0·965	2·323	5·123	1·323	1·358	0

Figure 4.6 *Total multipliers for the Klein model.* Source: Wallis (1973).

The Klein model described is, of course, fairly simple and only includes a small number of macroaggregates and policy variables. Nevertheless, it does demonstrate one of the most important roles for econometric models from the planners' point of view, namely, the role of simulation. By developing a model of the economy, the planners may experiment with a variety of policies and may determine their likely consequences before applying them to the real-world economy. However, the models used in such simulation exercises tend to be larger than the one described above, in terms of the number of equations and variables, as increasing disaggregation tends to bring the model more into line with the complexities of the real world. The Wharton model, used by Friedman (1975) for his experiments, possesses around ninety equations and endogenous variables, whilst the Brookings model, employed by Fromm and Taubman (1968), possesses several hundred behavioural equations and identities.

Econometric simulation fits neatly into the Tinbergen methodology of economic planning; indeed, this was the original manner in which Tinbergen formulated his theory. For a one-period simulation, it is clearly the reduced-form coefficient matrix (**R**) which specifies the functional forms to determine how the policy instrument vector, P and the data vector, D, are to be multiplied. The result of this exercise will accordingly generate our range of end-state vectors, E, that is,

$$E = R(P\,D) \tag{4.14}$$

A multi-period simulation would, on the other hand, use the total dynamic multipliers instead of the simple impact relationships. For the Klein model, the P vectors will include all possible combinations of acceptable values for W_{2_t}, T_t and G_t, whilst the D vector contains the current values of the six endogenous variables.[5] Operations with the total multipliers (Figure 4.6) will provide all of the possible range of end states for these six elements. To give an example, the long-run effect of a 'balanced budget' increase of G and T of 10 units will cause a net rise in consumption of $7 \cdot 54$ units, although the capital stock will be contracted by $14 \cdot 41$ units. Clearly, a more disaggregated model would enable planners to assess the likely individual effects of different components of taxation and government expenditure. Indeed, models will be constructed to highlight the particular features with which the planner is to be concerned.

Although these simulations demonstrate the range of possible end states, they still do not provide the necessary information as to which of the possible plans is the 'best'. This search for the optimal plan forms the subject of our next chapter.

---

[5] In order to make the vectors and matrices conformable, it will be necessary to include all predetermined variables, including lagged variables, in the P vectors.

CHAPTER 5

Optimisation

STATIC OPTIMISATION

In previous chapters we have analysed the ways in which the objectives of planning may be derived and have set out methods that enable us to assemble a picture of how the economy works, from which we may in turn infer the consequences of pursuing alternative courses of action. The next stage is to illustrate the ways in which we may deduce the 'optimal' plan. The aim, then, is to choose that plan from amongst the set of possible plans that comes closest to meeting our planning objectives, given the constraints imposed by the economy. As we have seen, objectives may be expressed in different ways and, since it is also clear that the set of possible plans may be large or small it is perhaps not a great surprise to learn that there are many different types of optimisation techniques that the planner may find it expedient to use. In this chapter, we look briefly at some of the simpler techniques and give an indication of some of the difficulties that such methods may encounter. However, before discussing these techniques, we look first at some instances in which the planner does not have to concern himself explicitly with the question of optimality.

It was suggested in the previous chapter that, with the use of econometric methods, we could devise a representation of the economy which might be used to trace the effects of changes of various kinds through the economic system. In cases where the planner has such a model, and the government wishes to choose a plan from amongst a small number of alternatives, it will be possible for the planner to analyse each alternative in detail and present the government with a picture of how the economy is likely to look after the application of each alternative. Planners in this case thus have a purely informative role, all their energies being absorbed in simulation activities. It is only in such rather rare worlds that planners have no hand in either devising the set of plans that is to be subjected to analysis or in devising criteria that are used to reject plans that are known to be technically feasible. In the conditions referred to, the government applies the machinery used in society for making social choices and can, except in the unlikely event of a tie, immediately pick the 'optimal' plan and proceed from there. No optimisation techniques are employed in this case, the government simply applying a criterion of optimality derived directly from the social-choice mechanism to the alternative plans with which it finds itself confronted. The plan so chosen may still be referred to as 'optimal' since, in all cases, social preferences are the appropriate source of the optimality criterion. Often, of course, it will be convenient for the planner to explicitly use information about preferences in his calculations, but the political system is likely to include safeguards of various kinds (such as external consultants) that are designed to ensure that the planner's perceptions of preferences are accurate.

In many cases, it is likely that the government will not itself have sufficient information to assemble a small range of plans, such that it may be confident that this range contains the best conceivable plan. The planner will therefore face the task of sorting out those sets of plans to which he will devote attention. Past plans and past decisions, and presumably also details about current preferences, will generally be available for scrutiny and, provided that they exhibit a reasonably high degree of consistency, the problem of developing new plans may not be overwhelming. We will not be concerned here with the means that planners adopt in these early stages, but it is as well to be aware that there is likely to be considerable interaction between planner and government even at the very beginning of the planning process. These difficulties should not be allowed to dominate our discussion. The next stage is to look in a rather idealised way at the particular problems faced by the planner who has been asked to produce an optimal plan or a series of possible blueprints. In some of the cases, the planner will be given all the information he needs by the government before he performs any calculations at all.

Of considerable importance will be the time dimension of the analysis. In the following sections, we consider problems that differ in the degree to which the element of time has specifically to be accounted for. There are certain sorts of planning problem, notably in the allocative area, in which the time dimension can be ignored without any serious consequences. Other problems have features that demand close attention being paid to dynamic factors. Stabilisation policy, for example, is an important aspect of many economic planning problems and is, in its concern to eradicate cyclical fluctuations, essentially a question of timing and dynamics. Growth policy is another planning area in which time is of the essence, for choices are being made between outcomes that are expressed in the form of time streams. The techniques used in these different instances do, of course, vary, although the added complexity of dynamic analysis means that our treatment of stabilisation and growth policies will be relatively more sophisticated than our treatment of allocative and allied static problems. The final cautionary note involves the fact that we will be looking at planning problems that can be solved in a relatively direct way; that is, the information to be used in the calculations will always be available from the start, and we will be looking at planning as if it comprised a single level. In reality, the econometric models that planners have, and the planning tasks they face, are likely to take the form of 'modules' that may for some purposes be treated independently, but often without it being clear what values other relevant variables outside the section in question will finally take.

SIMPLE UNCONSTRAINED OPTIMISATION

As an introduction to methods of optimisation, we consider a very simple problem that may be solved by a straightforward application of basic calculus.

A planner sets out to discover the indirect tax rate, μ^*, that will maximise the government's indirect tax revenue. From a model of the economy, it has been deduced that, at a price p, demand q is given by:

$$q = (a - p)/b \qquad (5.1)$$

where a and b are positive constants. It is also known that the price that will be set by the monopolist who produces this good is $\bar{p}$ and that it will not vary as a consequence of the imposition of the tax. If we, in general, denote the tax rate as μ, then clearly government tax revenue will be given by $q\mu$ and consumers will pay a price $(\bar{p} + \mu)$ for the good. Since we have an expression for q, we may substitute to find the tax revenue function; that is,

$$q\mu = \mu(a - p)/b = a\mu/b - p\mu/b \qquad (5.2)$$

101

But we also know that the after-tax price will be $(\bar{p} + \mu)$, and thus equation 5.2 may be rewritten:

$$q\mu = a\mu/b - (\bar{p} + \mu)\mu/b = a\mu/b - \bar{p}\mu/b - \mu^2/b \quad (5.3)$$

In order to find out where tax revenue reaches a maximum, we first differentiate the tax function with respect to the tax rate to get:

$$\frac{d(q\mu)}{d\mu} = a/b - p/b - 2\mu/b \quad (5.4)$$

To maximise tax revenue, we set equation 5.4 to zero, and the appropriate tax rate, μ^*, is given as:

$$a/b - p/b - 2\mu^*/b = 0 \quad (5.5)$$

Multiplying through equation 5.5 by b and rearranging we get:

$$2\mu^* = a - p \text{ and thus, } \mu^* = (a - p)/2 \quad (5.6)$$

Deriving the second-order conditions we find that:

$$d^2(q\mu)/d\mu^2 = -2/b \quad (5.7)$$

From equation 5.1 we have $b > 0$, which will ensure that the solution of equation 5.6 will be a maximum. The planner therefore simply substitutes into equation 5.6 the appropriate values for a and p and gets the value μ^*.

There are a number of observations that we may make about this naïve example. The objective was to choose a tax rate that would give rise to the *highest possible volume* of tax revenue and *not*, for example, to choose a tax rate that would give rise to some *specified level* of revenue. We assumed implicitly that the tax rate could take any desired level, implying that it could lie anywhere between plus and minus infinity, a much wider range than the planner would ever actually consider. In order to ensure that such extreme solutions may be prevented, it is common to introduce specific constraints upon the values that the variable may assume. The example we looked at had a simple, well-behaved structure that freed us from such worries. Had, for example, the demand function taken a more complex form than a straight line, we might have had to examine a series of points in order to discover the local optima, as distinct from the global optimum being sought by the planner. We move next to a method that is appropriate if we have an input-−output model of the economy and are instructed to find a means of meeting a set of specified output levels in different sectors.

OPTIMISATION WITH FIXED TARGETS

In Chapter 4 we outline the use of an input−output matrix to summarise the nature of the inter-relationships between different sectors of an economy. The input−output table may be used to derive certain sorts of information about the response of the economy to changes in the inputs available as well as for entirely descriptive purposes. The dynamic multipliers that were derived are the medium through which the characteristics of the economy's response to changes may be expressed. In this section, we discuss in more formal terms the operations needed to derive these multipliers from the matrix of input−output coefficients and some further uses to which these multipliers may be put.

The way in which we proceed here is, in fact, to examine the problem in reverse. Rather than explore the implications for the pattern of output of changing the set of inputs, we look for the set of inputs that will be required to efficiently produce some specified pattern of outputs. 'Efficiency' in this context is in some ways related to 'optimisation', since we are using the term to mean the pattern of inputs that will be necessary and sufficient to exactly produce the particular set of outputs required.

Input−output analysis is centred around the matrix of coefficients that establish the linear relations between sectors. In the case of the three-sector economy with which we will be working for the most part in this section, the coefficient matrix X will have the form:

$$X = \begin{bmatrix} x_{11} & x_{12} & x_{13} \\ x_{21} & x_{22} & x_{23} \\ x_{31} & x_{32} & x_{33} \end{bmatrix} \tag{5.8}$$

The coefficient x_{ij} refers to the amount of good i used per unit of production of good j, and thus x_{13} refers to the amount of good 1 used in the production of a single unit of good 3. Outputs are used for two purposes: elsewhere in the economy as inputs to other sectors and, in addition, for final consumption. If we denote the output of the first good by q_1 and final demand for this good by c_1, then provided that all the output is used, we will observe that:

$$q_1 = x_{11}q_1 + x_{21}q_2 + x_{31}q_3 + c_1 \qquad (5.9)$$

In words, total output of good 1 is absorbed by its use in the production of all goods in the economy (including itself but excluding any good j for which x_{j1} is zero) as is indicated by the first three terms on the right-hand side of equation 5.9 and by its use for final-demand purposes c_1. The equation may be written in the more helpful form:

$$c_1 = (1 - x_{11})q_1 - x_{21}q_2 - x_{31}q_3 \qquad (5.10)$$

This process may be repeated for goods 2 and 3 so that our whole simple economy may be summarised as:

$$
\begin{aligned}
c_1 &= (1 - x_{11})\, q_1 - x_{21}q_2 - x_{31}q_3 \\
c_2 &= x_{12}q_1 + (1 - x_{22})q_2 - x_{32}q_3 \\
c_3 &= x_{13}q_1 - x_{23}q_2 + (1 - x_{33})q_3
\end{aligned}
\qquad (5.11)
$$

which may be rewritten in matrix form as:

$$[I - X]q = c \qquad (5.12)$$

where I is the identity matrix, q the vector of inputs, c the vector of net outputs or final demands and X is as defined in equation 5.8. We may now perform an operation on equation 5.12 which enables us to derive an expression from which we may solve the problem of finding an 'efficient' input vector. Premultiplying both sides of equation 5.12 by $[I - X]^{-1}$ we find that:

$$q = [I - X]^{-1}c \qquad (5.13)$$

Whilst from equation 5.12 we were able to determine the pattern of output obtainable from any particular set of inputs (e.g. how to determine, say $\bar{c}$, once $\bar{q}$ was known), from equation 5.13 we may work in reverse. Given any desired set of target values for final demand, $\bar{c}$, we may deduce the efficient input pattern $\bar{q}$. Thus whilst equation 5.12 enables us to deduce the effects of raising the level of production of good i, equation 5.13 enables us to deduce the pattern of production that will be needed in order to meet some specified set of final demands.

Although we are not concerned here with the details of how the inverse matrix in equation 5.13 is calculated, an important point that should be mentioned is that, as the number of sectors in the model is increased, the computational requirements multiply very rapidly indeed. These difficulties go largely unnoticed in practice because even small models pose sufficient complexity for it to be essential to delegate actual calculation to computer experts. In order to demonstrate how equation 5.13 may be used to develop an optimal plan in a particular instance, consider the case in which the matrix of coefficients X is given by:

$$X = \begin{bmatrix} 0.4 & 0.2 & 0.3 \\ 0.3 & 0.1 & 0.4 \\ 0.2 & 0.5 & 0.2 \end{bmatrix} \text{ to give } [I - X] = \begin{bmatrix} 0.6 & -0.2 & -0.3 \\ -0.3 & 0.9 & -0.4 \\ -0.2 & -0.5 & 0.8 \end{bmatrix} \quad (5.14)$$

The next stage is the inversion of the $[I - X]$ matrix in equation 5.14, which gives:

$$[I - X]^{-1} = \frac{1}{0.149} \begin{bmatrix} 0.52 & 0.31 & 0.35 \\ 0.32 & 0.42 & 0.33 \\ 0.33 & 0.34 & 0.48 \end{bmatrix} \quad (5.15)$$

Let us suppose now that the economic planner is informed that the output if the three goods is to be 100, 80 and 120 units respectively. In order to establish the complete production plan, the planner has simply to substitute into equation 5.13 these values and the inverse matrix of equation 5.15. The desired output vector, denoted c^* is thus to be multiplied by equation 5.15 in order to find the required input vector X^*:

$$\begin{bmatrix} q_1^* \\ q_2^* \\ q_3^* \end{bmatrix} = \frac{1}{0.149} \begin{bmatrix} 0.52 & 0.31 & 0.35 \\ 0.32 & 0.42 & 0.33 \\ 0.33 & 0.34 & 0.48 \end{bmatrix} \begin{bmatrix} 100 \\ 80 \\ 120 \end{bmatrix} \quad (5.16)$$

The solution may thus be written:

$$q^*_1 = \frac{1}{0 \cdot 149} \; [(0 \cdot 52 \times 100) + (0 \cdot 31 \times 80) + (0 \cdot 35 \times 120)] = 794 \cdot 0$$

$$q^*_2 = \frac{1}{0 \cdot 149} \; [(0 \cdot 32 \times 100) + (0 \cdot 42 \times 80) + (0 \cdot 33 \times 120)] = 706 \cdot 0 \quad (5.17)$$

$$q^*_3 = \frac{1}{0 \cdot 149} \; [(0 \cdot 33 \times 100) + (0 \cdot 34 \times 80) + (0 \cdot 48 \times 120)] = 790 \cdot 1$$

Clearly, any set of values for the targets q could be chosen, provided only that the economy has sufficient capacity to produce such a configuration. In each case, it is purely a matter of following the procedure that in its general form is given by equation 5.13. It is perhaps of interest to note that we have just solved an optimisation problem in which there appeared to be no objective function as such. Strictly speaking, however, we have not been dealing with an optimisation problem but simply finding the value of q associated with a particular value of C. Nevertheless, command economies tend to use precisely such procedures for deriving plans. How, therefore, then can we say that such plans are optimal? The answer to this is that the optimisation problem involved is limited to the specification of the set of net output targets. The political system in such planning situations is thus completing the task of combining information about the economy's capacity with social preferences to produce an optimal output vector, leaving the planner the relatively simple task of finding the input vector associated with the perfect attainment of the given output vector. Amongst the difficulties that such an approach is likely to encounter are the mis-specification of the 'optimal' net output and, perhaps more seriously, an absence of any indication as to priorities. For example, if the planner finds that input constraints exist preventing the simultaneous achievement of all desired output levels, he can only report the fact to the political system; there is no information about trade offs that will enable the planner to calculate which is the best of the alternatives available.

The next stage is to examine a model in which information about preferences is available to planners but in which targets remain fixed. There are two basic cases to be distinguished, the first being that in which the targets may all be simultaneously satisfied and the second in which they are not. For reasons of analytical simplicity, the latter is treated first.

All targets unattainable

The first step is to examine the case in which the set of targets that has been specified cannot be reached. To escape this *impasse*, it becomes essential to define rules or criteria that the planner may apply in order to distinguish the best amongst a set of possible plans. Typically, this will be done by the use of loss functions which specify the importance to be attached to unit deviations from the various targets in question and which have been derived from the preferences. Although, in principle, preferences and hence loss functions may take an endless variety of forms, it is convenient to use one of a very narrow range of alternatives. Three such forms will now be illustrated in the context of the familiar, if by now rather notorious, problem of a model in which there is a conflict between the achievement of price stability and low unemployment.

Suppose that the planner is advised that, ideally, the government would like low (but not necessarily zero) unemployment and complete price stability. For convenience, we will deal with the price level rather than the rate of inflation, and thus the price stability target may be written as $p^* = 1$, p referring to the price level and the asterisk denoting a particular target. In the case of unemployment, U, we choose our units in such a way that target unemployment is given by $U^* = 2$. That is to say, it is felt that, at the level 2, there is the 'right' balance between fully utilising labour resources and maintaining some flexibility in the labour market.

The next stage is to discover which policy instruments the government may use to influence the levels of prices and unemployment. For simplicity, we assume that the only policy available is government expenditure, G, which is assumed to have an effect on both target variables. From his econometric model of the economy, the planner has estimated that the relevant relationships are the following:

$$\text{price level: } p = a_1 + b_1 G$$
$$\text{unemployment: } U = a_2 - b_2 G \qquad (5.18)$$

where $b_1 > 0, b_2 > 0$. The first equation is based on the hypothesis that government expenditure puts upward pressure on demand and thus tends to be inflationary, whilst the second equation is based on the hypothesis that unemployment is reduced by increases in demand resulting from increases in government spending. From the estimated relationships in equation 5.18, it is possible to derive a linear relationship between p and U as illustrated in Figure 5.1. This diagram shows the locus of values taken by p and U as G is varied. On many occasions, we shall find that the target combination, that is, the point A, (p^*, U^*), lies off the locus of attainable points. It is in such cases that we will have recourse to preferences, since only by so doing will it be possible to determine which particular point on the locus represents the closest we can get to the unconstrained point (p^*, U^*). This next step can only take place once we have specified the form of preferences or loss function. The possibilities pursued here may be regarded as having little to recommend them for use in complicated environments, but they do have the distinct advantage of convenience, a fact that has recommended them to analysts working in a wide variety of planning situations.

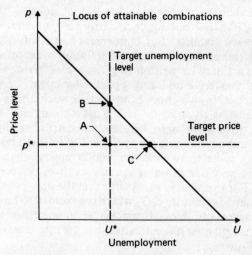

Figure 5.1 *Optimisation with fixed targets and lexicographic preferences.*

Lexicographic preferences. Preference orderings that have a hierarchical structure are known as lexicographic orderings. Their feature is that variables are listed in order of priority, and no notice whatever is taken of the levels assumed by variables 2 to n until (or unless) variable 1 meets some pre-specified target level. Once variable 1 is found to satisfy this condition, attention is switched to variable 2, holding 1 at its desired level and ignoring variables 3 to n. This procedure is continued until either we reach the nth variable successfully or find that no further targets may be reached without prejudice to the levels established for the preceeding variables.

In the case at hand, such an ordering would demand that the achievement of one or other of the targets were given absolute priority. Thus, if it is thought to be imperative that unemployment is kept at the level 2, irrespective of the consequences for the price level, then the optimal plan will be to choose the level of government expenditure that will ensure that unemployment will be 2 units. In our example, this gives rise immediately to a unique solution since there is only one level of G that will ensure that $U = 2$, although we might note that we will not be able to achieve our target of price stability.

To illustrate algebraically and denoting the target level as U^*, we use the relationships specified in equation 5.18 to find G^* as follows:

$$\text{For } U = U^*, \text{ set } G^* \text{ such that}$$
$$U^* = a_2 - b_2 G^*$$
$$\text{that is, set } G^* = (a_2 - U^*)/b_2 \qquad (5.19)$$

This will now give:

$$p = a_1 + b_1(a_2 - U^*)/b_2 \qquad (5.20)$$

Clearly, this price level will not normally satisfy the target level p^*, but nonetheless the level G^* established in equation 5.19 constitutes the optimal plan. More intuitively, we may observe that point B in Figure 5.1 represents the outcome when the unemployment target is given absolute priority. In the converse case, when the price-level target is of paramount importance, the optimal plan will be to set the level of government expenditure needed to take us to point C. We might note that the segment BC of the locus of attainable outcomes constitutes the range within which we would expect the outcomes of *all* optimal plans to lie. Thus we are led to observe that use of a lexicographic ordering gives rise to a 'polar' plan, that is to say, a plan that lies at one or other end point of the range of possible optima. We move now to consider two alterna-

109

tive criteria of optimality that may be applied and that will allow us to trade off increased deviations from one target in exchange for reduced deviations from the other target or targets.

Linear preferences. In some cases, unit deviations from one target may be directly compared with unit deviations from any other target. Normally, linear preferences will be of the general form of a weight, z_i, being attached to a unit deviation from the ith target. This will allow us to specify a loss function, L, of the form:

$$L = \sum_{i=1}^{n} z_i |x_i - x_i^*| \qquad (5.21)$$

where there are n target variables, x_i^* is the target level of the ith variable and x_i its actual level. Vertical lines are used to indicate that the modulus of the deviation is being used (that is to say, that the sign of the expression $(x_i - x_i^*)$ is treated as if it were always positive). This use of the modulus is most important because it reflects the central characteristic of the approach, namely, that positive and negative deviations are regarded with equal displeasure. The next step is to minimise the loss function equation 5.21. In order to do this, it is necessary to specify the relationships between

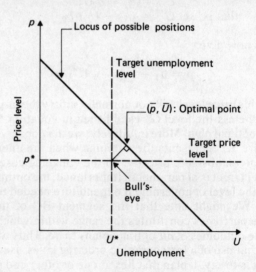

Figure 5.2 *Optimisation with fixed targets and linear preferences.*

110

the target variables x_i and the policy variables (or instruments) available to government. These are then substituted into equation 5.21. Taking the inflation–unemployment model of equation 5.18 and assuming that the weights to be applied to deviations from each target are equal, Figure 5.2 may then be constructed to illustrate the choice of plan. Since equal weight is applied in both cases, the problem reduces to one of finding the point on the straight-line locus that is closest to the target point, (p^*, U^*). Only elementary geometry is needed to demonstrate that this simply requires taking the perpendicular from the straight line that goes through the $\bar{p}$ point, giving the solution labelled $(\bar{p}, \bar{U})$. Thus, it remains only to determine directly from equation 5.18 the level of government expenditure consistent with $(\bar{p}, \bar{U})$.

Quadratic preferences. This type of trade-off function, again defined over deviations from different targets, is very widely used (Theil, 1958; Fromm and Taubman, 1968). The main feature of this approach is that the *square* of the deviation from each target is weighted by some constant. Taking any attainable combination of p and U, we measure the deviation of each from its target level, square each deviation and weight it by a constant that reflects the concern with which society regards such a deviation in relation to deviations from the target levels of other variables. The use of squared rather than absolute deviations is designed to penalise, at an increasing rate, successive increases in the size of the deviation from a target. The quadratic loss function may be written in the general form:

$$L = \sum_{i=1}^{n} z_i (x_i - x_i^*)^2 \qquad (5.22)$$

$$\text{where } 0 > z_i > 1, \quad \sum_{i=1}^{n} z_i = 1.$$

When there are only two variables (that is, $n = 2$), equation 5.22 defines an ellipse. If, further, the two weights z_1 and z_2 should be equal, we get, as a special case, a circle with centre $(\bar{p}, \bar{U})$. In either case, the choice of plan is made by finding the lowest level of loss consistent with being on the locus of possible plans and thus by finding where the loss function is tangential to the locus. Again, in the more general case in which there are more than two variables, the procedure is to minimise equation 5.22 having first

111

incorporated details about the relationships between the instruments available and the targets.

It is, however, a frequent criticism of the use of quadratic loss functions that they punish equally the overshooting and undershooting of targets, sometimes with undesirable implications. In our case, it might well be objected that a fall in the price level is not really as undesirable as a rise of the same size. The quadratic function we used is, however, unable to express such information because a deviation of size A from the ith target incurs a penalty of $z_i A^2$, regardless of whether the deviation is positive or negative. Such is the price of convenience.

All targets attainable

The second possibility with which we may be confronted is a situation in which all the targets are just attainable.[1] As a preliminary, it may be observed that the basic condition under which targets will be attainable is that there be at least as many instruments as targets. This condition was not satisfied in our earlier example in which there were two targets (stable prices and low unemployment) and one instrument (government expenditure). It is normally referred to as the 'rank' condition, usually discussed in relation to systems of linear equations (Lewis, 1969; Chiang, 1974). Should there be more targets than instruments, then there will not generally exist a solution to the set of equations with which we are concerned, whilst if there are more instruments than targets, there will generally exist multiple solutions to the problem.

To illustrate, consider the traditional IS/LM analysis. In the simple case, fiscal policy may be used to shift the IS schedule, monetary policy being used to shift the LM schedule. Suppose that we have the appropriate information about the underlying relationships (such as the investment, consumption and the demand for money functions) and that the planner is given target levels of r^* amd Y^* for the rate of interest and the level of national income respectively. Starting from an initial equilibrium $(\bar{r}, \bar{Y})$, an appropriate injection of both sorts of policy may be used to bring about the shifts in the IS and LM schedules necessary to give rise to the new equilibrium at the desired point (r^*, Y^*). Thus, in Figure 5.3 it can be seen that an expansionary fiscal policy (an increase in

---

[1] We shall not consider here the case in which all targets are met and surplus capacity is available. This state of affairs would suggest that our output targets have been mis-specified, since it is normally supposed that more of a good thing is preferred to less.

government spending) may be used to shift the IS schedule to a new position, IS_1, whilst a contractionary monetary policy (a reduction in the supply of money) may be used to shift the LM schedule to a new position LM_1, with the net result of increasing both the rate of interest and the level of income to the desired levels.

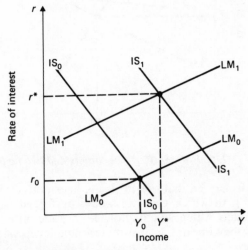

Figure 5.3 *Optimisation with two targets and two instruments.*

In the example outlined, it is clear that there is only one combination of fiscal and monetary policy that will have exactly the right effect. We might further note that there are restrictions that could be placed upon the shapes of the two schedules that would have the effect of making it impossible to reach the point (r^*, Y^*) (cf. the debate between the 'Keynesians' and the 'monetarists'). It might also be noted that the existence of a solution may be jeopardised by introducing a third target without introducing any more policy variables. Suppose, for example, it is known that the balance of payments is only in balance at certain combinations of interest rates and income levels (because of the influences of both world capital markets and world trade) and that the locus of points at which such an equilibrium occurs is described by the line FF in Figure 5.4. If it is then suggested that an equilibrium in the balance of payments is regarded as important, in addition to the two existing targets r^* and Y^*, then clearly all is not well. As indicated in

113

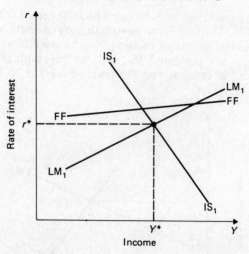

Figure 5.4 *Optimisation with three targets and two instruments.*

Figure 5.4, it may be that the FF locus does not go through the point (r^*, Y^*), in which case we would be forced back to our previous models which would allow us to trade off a balance of payments disequilibrium against undesirable levels of income or interest rates.

The need for the number of instruments and targets to coincide if all targets are to be met became well known as a result of the work of Tinbergen (1952) and Mundell (1962). The latter, however, went further, and argued that even if this primary condition is met, it is useful to examine the situation carefully to see whether certain instruments work to better effect on certain variables.

LINEAR PROGRAMMING

We have so far examined two forms of (static) optimisation, one relevant when the search is for the maximum level that a variable may reach and the other for cases when the search is for the closest to some predetermined target level that a variable may approach. The third method, to which we now turn, is designed particularly for cases where there is an open-ended objective, as in the first case already discussed, but where, in addition, a set of constraints is imposed upon the values that the system can assume. When these constraints and the objective function take a linear form, the problem is normally referred to as one of *linear programming*.[2] As an illustration of this method we consider a simple example.

A motor-vehicle assembly factory manager is faced with the problem of how to allocate his limited machine time between the production of cars and lorries. He knows that the profit he can make on each unit of output he sells is £10 per car and £20 per lorry, and thus as a profit maximiser, he will be working with an objective function:

$$\max \pi = 10x_1 + 20x_2$$

where x_1 and x_2 are the outputs of cars and lorries respectively. Further, he knows the machine-time requirements for producing a unit of each good, and is faced by an upper limit on the amount of time available on each of the three types of machinery involved. This information may be summarised as:

	hours needed per unit of:		*maximum hours available*
	car output (x_1)	*lorry output* (x_2)	
spraying	2	2	120
welding	1·5	4	120
chassis work	0	6	120
profit per unit	£10	£20	

From this information the manager may, for example, deduce the maximum possible output of each good: in the case of cars, the maximum possible output is 60 (= 120/2), because any further production would be prevented by the fact that all available spraying resources had already been used up. However, this latter fact would also mean that if 60 cars were produced, no lorries could be produced, since both types of vehicle are competing for access to the same machinery. A more helpful way of presenting the infor-

[2] In the instance where the forms are nonlinear, the more complicated methods of nonlinear programming have to be used (Kuhn and Tucker, 1951; Chiang, 1974). It might further be noted that there are other constrained optimisation methods, such as the Lagrange multiplier technique used in the discussion of growth problems later in this chapter. Such methods are applied when constraints are exactly met, a limitation that does not apply in the case of linear and non-linear programming methods.

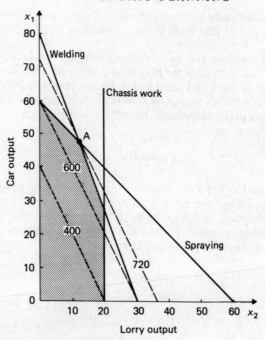

constraints ...... iso-profit levels
shaded area: set of feasible production levels

Figure 5.5 Graphical solution of a linear programming problem.

mation is in a diagram (Figure 5.5). For each process in turn we may construct a straight line representing the upper bound on the numbers of cars and lorries that may be produced. In the case of spraying we can produce 60 cars and no lorries or 60 lorries and no cars or any intermediate (linear) combination of the two. Since none of these constraints may be violated, and since production levels must also be non-negative, we may conclude that the set of possible output combinations comprises the shaded area in the diagram. The next step is to apply the objective function in order to decide which point in the opportunity set that we have just constructed is the most attractive. This is done by finding the highest iso-profit line that is consistent with the constraints upon available machine time. Given that the relative profitability of cars and

116

lorries is constant, the iso-profit lines will be straight. The sale of 10 cars would generate profits of £100, a total that could alternatively be achieved by producing 5 lorries or 3 lorries and 4 cars. Since increasing profits are represented by successive 'north-eastwards' movements in the diagram, it may be concluded that the optimal point is where the highest iso-profit line touches the opportunity set, point A in the diagram.

It is no coincidence that the optimal point lies at a 'corner', that is at a point where two constraints intersect, because unless the objective function has the same slope as one of the constraints (in which case there will be a whole set of solutions), the highest attainable iso-profit line will necessarily touch the opportunity set at a junction of two constraints. Indeed, it is this feature which gave rise to the need for methods other than the traditional calculus. The use of the latter to establish a maximum in problems of this kind is inhibited by the fact that linear functions have undefined second-order derivatives (which prevent one from distinguishing between maxima and minima) and the fact that a function composed of a succession of straight-line segments has undefined first-order derivatives at the points where the lines meet. Linear-programming methods, on the other hand, are specifically designed to handle problems in which such features are of central importance. Whilst we do not here investigate the technical methods of linear programming (such as the Simplex method of solution), it is important to remark that the method is of special relevance in a planning context because the size of the systems with which planners work is such that the simplicity of using linear rather than non linear formulations will often be at a great premium.

We have so far in this chapter been concerned with problems of an essentially static kind — the time dimension has been ignored. The next stage is to remedy this defect by looking at some problems that have an important temporal aspect. Although we will be using slightly different methods when we deal in turn with problems of growth and of stabilisation, we will continue to emphasise that the problem of planning is an essentially unitary one. In all cases, the important features are the derivation of the preferences from which objective functions may be developed and the understanding of how the economy works from which the constraints are obtained. Differences in emphasis in the treatment of apparently distinct problems should not conceal the fact that in both cases we are searching for an optimal path for the economy to follow.

GROWTH OPTIMISATION

The pursuit of high growth rates is often, but needless to say erroneously, thought of as one of the reasons for having economic planning. 'Planning', as we use the word, refers to the problem of establishing the optimal pattern of government activity (broadly defined) in the light of social preferences. As far as growth is concerned, therefore, our aim is to identify an *optimal* rate of growth — be it positive, negative or zero — and the policies that will enable us to achieve that particular rate. Growth is, of course, a most complex issue and is as yet ill-understood. Nevertheless, provided that sufficient appropriate simplification is used, it is possible to gain insights into the problem and to derive some important implications for planning. As is clear from the work of economic theorists on growth, even the simplest models are difficult, and, as a consequence, we do not here examine anything that is recognisable as a growth model in the conventional sense. Rather, we set out to show that the basic rudiments of the choice between the conflicting claims of current and future consumption for a whole economy can be analysed with the same analytical tools as the more familiar problem of the consumer who is deciding how much of his existing wealth he should save rather than spend.

All economies, whether capitalist or socialist, face the difficulty of finding an appropriate allocation of current production between consumption and investment purposes; investment increases future, but reduces current, consumption possibilities. In order to find the right balance between the two, it is necessary to define the terms upon which consumption at different dates may be traded (that is to say, the relative price of a unit of consumption at different times) and, in addition, the number of units of future consumption made possible per unit of investment today. This will involve the definition of an objective function from social preferences in which both present and future consumption levels appear and, in addition, a production function relating capital to output for the economy.

We start by supposing that, in any period t, an economy produces some level of output, Y_t, by combining labour inputs, L_t, with capital inputs, K_t. This output may be devoted either to consumption, C_t, or added to the capital stock as investment, I_t. For simplicity, it is then assumed that the level of consumption (or, more precisely, the path of consumption) is the unique determinant of the level of welfare. We justify this on the grounds that it is consumption that offers the only benefits to the consumer in the final analysis: investment is only of concern insofar as it affects the stream of consumption possibilities, offering no intrinsic satisfaction itself. With a planning horizon of T periods ($t = 1, 2, \ldots, T$), the sequence of consumption levels over time may be denoted by the vector C and the sequence of investment levels may similarly be written as I. In addition, it is assumed that there is an exogenously determined stock of capital K_0 available at the start of the first period. This stock will subsequently be augmented by additions of investment, so that if we assume that capital does not ever deteriorate, the capital stock in period $\bar{t}$ may be written as:

$$K_{\bar{t}} \equiv K_0 + \sum_{t=1}^{\bar{t}} I_t \qquad (5.23)$$

The production function relating current output to current inputs of capital and labour is assumed to display the usual characteristics of positive but non-increasing returns to both factors. If we assume that the objective function takes the form $W = W(C_t)$ then our optimisation problem may be written as:

$$\max W = W(C_1, C_2, \ldots, C_T) \qquad (5.24)$$
$$\text{subject to } Y_t = Y_t(L_t, K_t)$$

where $K_t \equiv K_{t-1} + I_{t-1}$, with $K_1 = K_0$ and $Y_t \equiv C_t + I_t$. The following restrictions will also apply to the functions in equation 5.24: $\delta W / \delta C_t > 0$, $\delta^2 W / \delta C_t^2 < 0$; $\delta Y_t / \delta L_t > 0$, $\delta Y_t / \delta K_t > 0$, $\delta^2 Y_t / \delta L_t^2 \leqslant 0$, $\delta^2 Y_t / \delta K_t^2 \leqslant 0$ (for all t).

In order to investigate this model more closely, we might start by considering the special case of $T = 2$. That is to say, our system is started at time zero and allowed to function for periods 1 and 2 before being stopped. Analysis of this simple case is both instructive in itself and, in addition, gives a solution that is susceptible of generalisation to cases in which a longer horizon is used.

In period 1, Y_1 is produced from given inputs L_1 and K_1 ($= K_0$). This output is divided between consumption, C_1, and investment, I_1. The latter is added to the capital stock so that we enter period 2 with available inputs of L_2 labour and K_2 ($\equiv K_0 + I_1$) capital units. From these is derived an output of Y_2 which is divided into consumption, C_2, and investment, I_2. Our task is to find the most appropriate values at which to set the controllable variables, namely, consumption and investment, for it is assumed that, with the exception of the constraints listed in equation 5.24, these variables may take any level the government chooses. In reality, it will very often be the case that the level of consumption must not fall below some minimum level determined by the requirements of subsistence, but such additional complications will be ignored here. Since the important variables in this system are consumption and investment, a 'plan' designed for it will consist of a list of values for each of these variables in each of the two years within the planning horizon. Let us now examine an arbitrarily chosen plan belonging to the set of plans that are possible in this context; this plan will be identified as $(\overline{C}_1, \overline{I}_1, \overline{C}_2, \overline{I}_2)$. The first observation to make is that we would expect any such plan, if it is to be optimal, to include the condition $\overline{I}_2 = 0$. This is because investment in period 2 cannot have an expansionary effect on production potential until period 3 at the earliest. Since our planning horizon has been taken to be only periods 1 and 2, our objective function will ignore any consumption that takes place (or is enabled to take place) in period 3 and onwards. Any investment in period 2 will be entirely at the expense of consumption in that period and hence can only have a negative effect on the level of welfare. Investment in period 1 will not be subject to this argument for it expands consumption possibilities in period 2. It should, however, be noted that the 'full' contribution of investment will not be registered because investment in period 1 will expand consumption possibilities in period 3 onwards as well as during period 2, increases in welfare resulting exclusively from the latter.

Having argued that any plan with a claim to be optimal in this context will have $\overline{I}_2 = 0$, we can proceed to determine any other characteristics which we might expect it to have. The next stage is to look more closely at the suggestion made earlier that this problem has important similarities to the consumer's saving problem. The latter is concerned with the consumer, in a two-period world, who is given an initial endowment of wealth which he may consume today or which he may save and spend tomorrow, such savings attracting an overnight interest payment (Green, 1976; Meade, 1966). If we call the consumer's initial lump-sum receipt that is, his initial wealth endowment) W_0, and the interest rate r, then, if the individual spends C_1 on the first day, $(C_1 \leq W_0)$, he will have $(W_0 - C_1)(1 + r)$ to spend on the second day. That is to say, he saves the wealth remaining at the end of the first day which attracts overnight an interest payment of $r(W_0 - C_1)$ leaving him an amount $(W_0 - C_1)(1 + r)$ for disposal on the second day. The individual's optimisation problem is therefore to find that level of consumption in the first period that will maximise his utility, the latter depending on consumption in both periods. This problem may be written formally as:

$$\max U = U(C_1, C_2)$$

$$\text{subject to } C_1 + C_2/(1 + r) \leq W_0 \tag{5.25}$$

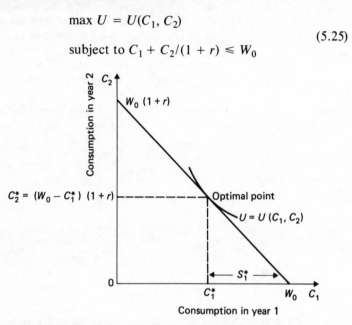

Figure 5.6 *The consumer's optimal savings plan.*

The constraint summarises the fact that the consumer must not spend more than his total wealth. Since we have assumed that utility is an increasing function of consumption in each period, we may deduce that this constraint will always be binding. In other words, we shall expect that, in any optimal plan, the constraint will hold as an equality (rather than as an inequality), the consumer spending all the wealth by the end of the second day. Figure 5.6 illustrates this situation and shows the similarity between this saving problem and the familiar analysis of a consumer allocating his limited budget between two goods. In our problem, the slope of the budget constraint, rather than being determined in the normal way by relative prices, is determined by the terms on which consumption today can be traded for consumption tomorrow, or in other words, the rate of interest. The solution of equation 5.25 is

121

achieved with the use of *Lagrange multipliers*, since it is a straight-forward constrained optimisation problem. It might be noted that our demonstration that the constraint would be binding is of relevance because the solution of problems in which the constraints are not binding is a more complex task and programming methods have to be used. Writing equation 5.25 as a Lagrangean function we get:

$$\max Z = U(C_1, C_2) + \lambda[W_0 - C_1 - C_2/(1 + r)] \quad (5.26)$$

where λ is a Lagrange multiplier. In order to determine where this function reaches a maximum, we differentiate partially to get:

$$\frac{\delta Z}{\delta C_1} = \frac{\delta U}{\delta C_1} - \lambda \quad (5.27)$$

$$\frac{\delta Z}{\delta C_2} = \frac{\delta U}{\delta C_2} - \frac{\lambda}{(1 + r)} \quad (5.28)$$

$$\frac{\delta Z}{\delta \lambda} = W_0 - C_1 - C_2 \Big/ (1 + r) \quad (5.29)$$

Setting these derivatives equal to zero, and dividing equation 5.27 by equation 5.28 we find that:

$$\frac{\delta U}{\delta C_1} \Big/ \frac{\delta U}{\delta C_2} = 1 + r \quad (5.30)$$

This is, in fact, the normal proposition that, at the optimum position, the marginal utility of a good equals its price and the marginal rate of substitution between the goods equals their relative prices.

Returning to our growth problem, we can start by arguing that the objective function will take a similar form, since the aim is still to maximise a welfare function defined over consumption levels in two successive periods. The difference arises in the form of the constraints as we now have to obey a capacity constraint in *both* periods. If the capital and labour inputs available in period 1 are such that maximum output is given as $\widetilde{Y}_1$, then clearly this will constitute a ceiling level for consumption in that period; that is, we know that the inequality $C_1 \leq \widetilde{Y}_1$ must hold. Further, we know that output must either be invested or consumed, and thus using the same line of argument as in the savings problem, we may conclude that the following inequality will, in reality, hold as an equality constraint:

$$C_1 + I_1 \leq \widetilde{Y}_1 \qquad (5.31)$$

In the second period, the capital stock will be higher by an amount I_1 and thus capacity output will have risen by an amount $Y(I_1)$, the parentheses denoting a functional relationship. This relation is derived from the production function which, for convenience, we assume to display non-increasing returns. Since we would expect an optimal plan to have output in both periods at the highest possible level, then the arbitrary plan $(\bar{C}_1, \bar{I}_1, \bar{C}_2, \bar{I}_2)$ we are considering will obey the following conditions:

$$Y_1 = \bar{C}_1 + \bar{I}_1 = \widetilde{Y}_1 \qquad (5.32)$$

$$Y_2 = \widetilde{Y}_2 = \widetilde{Y}_1 + Y(\bar{I}_1) = \bar{C}_2 + \bar{I}_2 \qquad (5.33)$$

The optimisation problem in our two-period growth model may thus be summarised:

$$\begin{aligned} &\max U = U(C_1, C_2) \\ &\text{subject to } \widetilde{Y}_1 = C_1 + I_1 \\ &\text{and } \widetilde{Y}_1 + Y(I_1) = C_2 + I_2 \end{aligned} \qquad (5.34)$$

The solution of this problem is illustrated in Figure 5.7. In order to underline the similarity with the savings problem, the special case of a linear relation between investment and future production possibilities is assumed. The major difference between Figures 5.6 and 5.7 is that, in the former, the budget line is defined over all levels of wealth, since the consumer may, if he wants to, spend all the wealth in the first period leaving nothing for period 2. In the growth case, on the other hand, if there is no investment in period 1, production capacity will remain unaffected so that consumption in period 2 would be the same as consumption in period 1, investment in both periods being zero. It is not possible to 'borrow' consumption from period 2 in period 1, and consumption in the first period therefore cannot exceed output in that period.

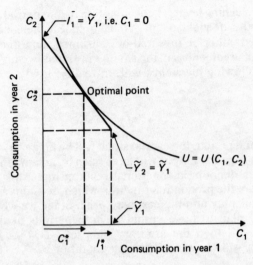

Figure 5.7 *The optimal investment plan in a two-period model with constant returns.*

The algebraic solution follows the same lines as in the savings model. Equation 5.34 may now be written as the following:

$$\max Z = U(C_1, C_2) + \lambda_1(Y_1 - C_1 - I_1) + \lambda_2(Y_1 + Y(I_1) - C_2 - I_2) \tag{5.35}$$

where λ_1 and λ_2 are Lagrange multipliers. Differentiating partially we find:

$$\frac{\delta Z}{\delta C_1} = \frac{\delta U}{\delta C_1} - \lambda_1 \; ; \; \frac{\delta Z}{\delta C_2} = \frac{\delta U}{\delta C_2} - \lambda_2$$

and

$$\frac{\delta Z}{\delta I_1} = -\lambda_1 + \frac{\lambda_2 \delta(Y(I_1))}{\delta I_1} \tag{5.36}$$

Setting the three derivatives in equation 5.36 equal to zero and, dividing the first by the second, we obtain:

$$\frac{\delta U}{\delta C_1} \bigg/ \frac{\delta U}{\delta C_2} = \frac{\lambda_1}{\lambda_2} \tag{5.37}$$

whilst rearranging the third expression gives:

$$\frac{\lambda_1}{\lambda_2} = \frac{\delta(Y(I_1))}{\delta I_1} \qquad (5.38)$$

Combining equations 5.37 and 5.38 we arrive at:

$$\frac{\delta U}{\delta C_1} \bigg/ \frac{\delta U}{\delta C_2} = \frac{\delta(Y(I_1))}{\delta I_1} \qquad (5.39)$$

Provided that we have information about the utility and production functions involved, the optimal values C_1^*, C_2^* and I_1^* may be derived by this method. Equation 5.39 is the direct analogue of equation 5.30 in the savings model which, it may be recalled, summarises the consumer's optimalility conditions. In the present case, equation 5.39 says that the marginal rate of substitution between consumption in the two periods must be equal to the rate at which consumption in period 1 may be traded, via investment, for consumption in period 2.

Expressed in more intuitive terms, equation 5.39 may be interpreted as implying that the optimal split between consumption and investment is to be found at the point at which the last unit of this year's production used for consumption adds the same amount to total welfare as the last unit devoted to investment.

The analysis is not here extended to the case of many periods because it is unlikely that the greater complexity would be compensated by the additional insight that would result. An intuitive review of such results might, however, be of some help. In the context of a many-period model, the choice between consumption and investment in period t will depend upon the contribution that current investment would make to expanded consumption opportunities in all relevant successive periods. Again, at the optimum point, the last unit of output in period t devoted to current consumption will yield as much additional welfare as the last unit of investment, the latter being given by the changes in future production it enables. If we denote the expansion of future production levels made possible by a unit of investment by $(\Delta Y_{t+1}, \Delta Y_{t+2}, \ldots)$ and assume that all this production is consumed, we get an increase in consumption of $(\Delta C_{t+1}, \Delta C_{t+2}, \ldots)$ where $\Delta C_{t+1} = \Delta Y_{t+1}$ and so on. The trade off can thus be thought of as being between current and future consumption, the optimality condition being:

$$\frac{\delta U}{\delta C_t} = \frac{\delta U}{\delta(C_{t+1}, C_{t+2}, \ldots)} \tag{5.40}$$

To the extent that more distant consumption is valued less than consumption in the immediate future, there will be less weight attached to investment than there would be in the absence of such discounting. Any strong myopic tendencies in the welfare function will thus have the same damping influence on investment as any shortening of the planning horizon.

Although we have not in this section attempted to look at the sorts of growth that may actually be used as a basis for developing economic plans, we have tried to point out the simpler sorts of methods that may be used to deduce the optimal split between consumption and investment. In devising more complex models, planners and economists have introduced a number of considerations that repay a brief glance. Most neoclassical growth models incorporate a price mechanism which acts as the medium by which the economy moves towards an optimal path. In such models, planning has much less significance since the price system makes most of the adjustments that are needed, whereas, in the model we looked at, the government was given a free hand in choosing consumption and investment levels. Thus, we were looking at a model of a directed economy rather than the essentially *laissez-faire* situation upon which many neoclassical models are based. In the intermediate case of mixed economies, planning problems related in some way to the choice of an optimal rate of investment, do often arise because of the likelihood that government, through its own expenditure programs, has a significant degree of control over the aggregate level of investment. A difficulty that is likely to arise in any economy is the existence of large variations in the relation between investment and future production in different sectors. It is as a consequence of such differences that, where feasible, model builders will try to construct disaggregated, sectoral models. All these problems are put to one side now as we move to consider the equally formidable problems that may beset the planner concerned about fluctuations in the paths of certain variables in the economic system.

OPTIMISATION IN A STABILISATION CONTEXT

The search for plans or policies that can successfully counteract the cyclical tendencies primarily found in capitalist economies has been going on for a long time. Great controversy continues to surround the findings of much of the work in this area and so we are not able to point to any single set of techniques from which optimal stabilisation plans may be derived. Instead, it is appropriate to reiterate that the problems in this area must be approached in the same kind of way as all planning problems. Thus, it is important to know which fluctuations cause the greatest *chagrin* to society and to have as accurate a picture as possible of how the economy works in order that a clear understanding of the forces giving rise to cycles is available. Without such knowledge, the planners are unlikely to be able to produce anything they might wish to term an 'optimal' plan. It will also be important to know how society values increased stability that can only be bought at the expense of damaging growth prospects — a point that serves to emphasise the essential similarity of these diverse problems.

Whilst stabilisation problems were until recently regarded as arising almost exclusively in countries with essentially capitalistic financial and other institutions, the recent reforms and proposals in the USSR seem likely to give rise to instability in what is, in most respects, a thoroughgoing socialist economy. Greater use of incentives at the worker and plant level may engender the sorts of volatility to which many Western economies are prone. Any such reductions in the importance of the central planning agencies in making allocative decisions indicate that decision makers at the plant level have more discretion, with the likely consequence that changes in incomes, output and stocks will be larger and less predictable in size and direction. In addition, expectations will start to play an important role, if not a steadying one. Further, any increase in the extent to which socialist countries rely on trade with the capitalist world will make their economies more sensitive to the fluctuations that continue to beset the Western economies. In the following sections, the focus is on problems that have received attention largely in the context of mixed economies, but as has just been indicated, the lessons may be more widely applicable.

The fluctuations with which stabilisation policy is concerned may take a variety of forms, but for the most part will be manifest as *cycles*. Thus in simple cases we may find, for example, that unemployment varies systematically with time even after allowance for a basic trend has been made. In such cases, two different sorts of questions face the analyst: first, what structural and other factors give rise to the growth or decline in what we might call the 'base' level of unemployment (that is, the trend level) and, secondly, what cyclical factors govern the pattern that the oscillations follow? The structural factors will not be discussed here — they will normally be of concern either in the context of growth problems, such as technical progress or the level of investment, or in a detailed sectoral study in which input–output models or allied methods are used to analyse the level and the pattern of production. We will, rather, concentrate on the cyclical aspect and the difficulties it poses for the planner.

Typically, but increasingly controversially, it would be suggested that, following the Keynesian prescriptions, the answer to our simple unemployment problem would be to inject government demand into the economy in those years in which unemployment was thought likely to exceed its trend level, and to finance the resulting government deficit by withdrawing demand (via taxes) in the opposite circumstances. There are, however, a number of reasons why such a policy may be inappropriate, some of which we look at below. Sometimes economists will contest such conclusions on the grounds that, if we do not understand how the system is working, we should take no action. Such arguments may be unattractive to the planner faced with the prospect of a 'null' plan (that is, no action) being implemented, since it may appear to make him redundant, despite the fact that his task is taken simply to be the identification of the optimal plan (which may well be null), and not to introduce his own predilections.

Returning to the particular case at hand, the next step is to examine two possible courses of action, plan I under which unemployment is allowed to take its 'natural' or spontaneous course and plan II, under which a judicious manipulation of demand enables all the fluctuations to be smoothed out. In addition, we assume that the desired stable level of unemployment is U^*. There is one important question surrounding the definition of stabilisation that must be answered at this point. Of the two policies we consider, it might be tempting to suppose that policy II, the smoothed path, would always be preferred since it has ironed out all the fluctuations of a cyclical nature that attend the unemployment. We have chosen, however, to reject such an argument and instead to pursue the line that stabilisation policy in such a context in fact refers to the pursuit of a stable level of unemployment, U^*. This approach seems to be much more satisfactory as it seems, intuitively at least, likely that societies tend to be concerned with keeping unemployment at some desirable level and also because use of a constant target indicates an example of how problems of growth and stabilisation will normally arise (and may be treated) in conjunction with one another. Put more informally, it is being argued that in the analysis of stabilisation planning, the secular trend of a path is important as well as whether or not it has a marked cyclical aspect.

Following the usual procedure, the first step is to argue that the welfare level associated with each of these plans will depend on deviations from the target level U^*. If we denote unemployment in period t under plan i as U_t^i, the welfare level associated with the pursuit of the ith plan over the T-period horizon will be given by a loss function L^i where:

$$L^i = L^i(U^* - U_1^i, U^* - U_2^i, \ldots, U^* - U_t^i, \ldots, U^* - U_T^i) \quad (5.41)$$

Maximum welfare is offered by the plan which gives the lowest value for this loss function, solution of this problem requiring that we specify the form of the loss function in detail. It also requires that we specify the equations from which may be derived successive values for U_t^i under each plan. Unfortunately, discussion of how cycles are to be analysed would lead us away from the important issues here and so it is avoided, although it can be seen that this problem is of the usual type in that it involves finding a way of expressing the constraints imposed on the planner by the economy's behaviour. Suffice it to say that there are well-known methods for deriving equations (for example, the introduction of time variables into our econometric model) that will enable us to compute values for the sequences U_t^i. Whilst this is sufficient for the derivation of an optimal plan, it should be noted that the choice may be sensitive to the form of the loss function.

The model just described has one particular characteristic, shared by most of the models developed for practical purposes, that deserves comment. Time enters equation 5.41 in a discrete way, that is to say, the time interval in question is broken down into a number of sub-intervals or periods. Much analysis of dynamics, on the other hand, has been developed for the case in which time is treated as a continuous variable, and since such analysis has been applied to stabilisation problems in a number of theoretical works and has implications for the optimisation techniques used, we consider it briefly now.

In a continuous version of the model, unemployment would take a particular level at every instant in time rather than being simply measured on, say, an annual basis. To denote a variable that is continuous rather than discrete, time appears within parentheses and not as a subscript; thus, at any point in time t, plan i gives rise to an unemployment level that we denote $U^i(t)$. The time horizon now becomes an interval, say 0 to T, rather than a sequence of periods. As a consequence, the loss associated with plan i must now be written in the form of an integral. The loss at a single instant, t, will be given by $W(U^* - U^i(t))$. Thus the analogue to equation 5.41 is given by:

$$L^i = \int_0^T W(U^* - U^i(t))dt \qquad (5.42)$$

In order to solve this equation for the choice between plans I and II, we clearly need a vast amount of information, since it will be necessary to be able to plot the level of unemployment associated with a plan at every instant in the time interval. This may not be as difficult as it sounds, for we are quite entitled to use a convenient form of continuous function to represent a time path. For instance, if unemployment is thought to be rising steadily, we use a linear or an exponential function, such as:

$$U(t) = a + bt \ or \ U(t) = U(0)e^{-at} \qquad (5.43)$$

where a and b are positive constants.

The introduction of cyclical paths for variables such as unemployment will complicate matters, just as it does in discrete models. Although such further complications would involve some study of differential equations, it would not necessarily give rise to any insuperable difficulties. As an intuitive illustration of how this sort of problem may be tackled, we resort to a graphical treatment. Returning to the choice between plans I and II, we next make the assumption that there is a unit welfare loss associated with a deviation of x from the target unemployment level at time t, with the consequence that a unit deviation gives rise to a welfare loss that we may denote as $\widetilde{W}$, a constant. A deviation of two units will give rise therefore to a loss of $2\widetilde{W}$, whilst more generally a deviation of n units will give rise to a loss of $n\widetilde{W}$. The loss function may now be written in the form:

$$L^i = \int_0^T \widetilde{W}[U^* - U^i(t)]dt \qquad (5.44)$$

130

where the square brackets indicate that the expression they contain is simply to be multiplied by the constant $\widetilde{W}$. This assumption allows us, in effect, to ignore the welfare function and to compare directly the integral of the deviations in each case. This in turn means that, in Figures 5.8a and 5.8b, the losses associated with the two plans will in each case be directly proportional to the area lying between the outcome that the plan would generate and the target level, as illustrated by the shaded areas in each diagram. The important conclusion to be derived from this simple example is that the perfect smoothing out of a path that would otherwise be oscillatory may give rise to welfare losses if the trend level of the variable is upwards, for clearly, losses in the null-action case of Figure 5.8b are less than those in the smoothing-action case of Figure 5.8a. A formal demonstration of such possibilities is not of concern here, it being sufficient to note that if sufficient information is available about the paths under different plans and about the welfare function, the loss function as set out in its general form in equation 5.42 may be evaluated and thus the optimal plan chosen from among the alternatives. In cases where the planner has to devise the set of plans to be examined rather than to simply choose between a small number of alternatives, more sophisticated methods such as control theory have to be used in finding the optimal plan (Fox et al., 1966; Pindyck, 1973).

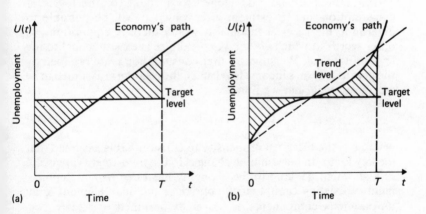

Figure 5.8 *Losses from smoothed and non-smoothed paths. Shaded areas represent losses.*
(a) policy generating a smoothed path.
(b) no-action plan generating a non-smoothed path.

Having looked at some problems of stabilisation at a rather general level, we move now to a more detailed look at the nature of the processes that gave rise to the fluctuations in the first place. It is unlikely that truly optimal plans can be devised in the absence of such understanding.

In the classic analysis of cyclical fluctuations, Samuelson (1939) showed that an interaction of the multiplier and the accelerator may give rise to various sorts of fluctuations (Rau, 1974). In order to follow this traditional line of analysis, our concern is switched from the level of unemployment to the level of real national income. This change is not a major one since we would expect an extremely close link to exist between these two variables. One further change that we make, in order to simplify, is to assume that the economy is operating somewhere near full capacity with the result that excess demand is likely to occur under some conditions just as is a deficiency of demand under other conditions.

The next step is to establish a simple model of the economy in question. In period t, aggregate demand, denoted Y_t is, by definition in our first version, equal to the sum of consumption expenditure C_t and investment expenditure I_t:

$$Y_t \equiv C_t + I_t \tag{5.45}$$

Hypotheses are now developed to account for the levels of consumption and investment after which it will be possible to determine the level of income at which there is equilibrium, in other words at which *planned* expenditure is exactly equal to the level of income. We suppose that consumption is determined by the previous year's income level and if the relation is assumed to be a proportional one, we find:

$$C_t = cY_{t-1}, \, 0 < c < 1 \tag{5.46}$$

where c is the marginal propensity to consume. It is assumed that the key factor in determining changes in the investment rate is the rate at which demand in the economy has been rising. Replacement of existing capital stock comprises the main element of an autonomous component, A_t, normally assumed to remain constant. In addition, there is a further component that depends positively on the growth in demand over the recent past. Alternatively, the formulation to be used may be interpreted as being a capital stock adjustment model in which anticipated output or desired

132

output in the period is calculated on the basis of output or demand over the past couple of periods, investment then taking place in the light of the change in the level of the capital stock computed to be the optimum level at which to produce the planned output. In either event, the hypothesis may be written as:

$$I_t = A_t + v(Y_{t-1} - Y_{t-2}), v > 0 \qquad (5.47)$$

where v is a parameter. In order that the economy be in equilibrium, it is clear that planned expenditure given by equations 5.46 and 5.47 will have to be equal to the level of income equation 5.45. This equilibrium condition may be written as:

$$Y_t = cY_{t-1} + A_t + v(Y_{t-1} - Y_{t-2}) \qquad (5.48)$$

which may be rearranged to give:

$$Y_t = A_t + (c + v)Y_{t-1} - vY_{t-2} \qquad (5.49)$$

Equation 5.49 describes the relation between income in successive periods. Provided that the parameters c, v and A_t remain constant, we should expect the economy to eventually settle at some particular level of income at which the economy was in equlilibrium, Y_t. In order to ascertain this income level, we have simply to observe that, in an equilibrium, income will be unchanging, as a consequence of which we may set $Y_t = Y_{t-1} = Y_{t-2}$. Substituting these values into equation 5.48 we find that the condition becomes:

$$Y_t = A_t + cY_t \qquad (5.50)$$

and therefore the equilibrium level may be written:

$$\bar{Y}_t = A_t/(1 - c) \qquad (5.51)$$

In words, the equilibrium level of income is given by the product of the level of replacement investment and the familiar Keynesian multiplier, $1/(1 - c)$. If, however, for some reason, the system is moved temporarily away from $\bar{Y}$, we are interested in whether it will return to its equilibrium level or not— more formally, whether the equilibrium is stable or not (Quirk and Saposnik, 1968). We may well also be concerned with the path the economy follows in returning to equilibrium, that is, its disequilibrium behaviour.

133

There are two major sorts of disturbance that may throw the economy out of equilibrium. In the first of these, the level of autonomous investment changes and remains then at its new level indefinitely. It may be deduced directly from equation 5.51 that, if the level of autonomous investment increases by an amount ΔA_t, then the level of equilibrium income will rise by an amount $\Delta \overline{Y}_t = \Delta A_t/(1 - c)$. In the second case, autonomous investment rises in year t by an amount ΔA_t but returns to its previous level the following year where it remains, and thus the level of equilibrium is only different for a single period. In both cases, the economy will take some time to return to equilibrium because, even if the change is temporary, the initial disturbance sets in motion forces that operate through the accelerator to retard a return to equilibrium.

In order to simplify matters as much as possible, we limit our attention here to the case of a temporary change in the level of autonomous investment. As in our earlier stabilisation models, it will be assumed that there is a target level, in this case an income level Y^*. Further, it will be supposed that the economy is in equilibrium at precisely this level initially. The economy is then subjected in period 1 to a fall in investment of ΔA that lasts just one period. If the system contained no lags, this would simply give rise to a fall in income of $-\Delta A$ in period 1 but a resumption in period 2 of its initial equilibrium level $\overline{Y}$. The existence of lags makes the adjustment path much more complex because it generates a reaction through the dependence of investment and consumption on past levels of income.

Inquiry into the time path of income in response to the change in autonomous investment is greatly facilitated by noting that equation 5.49 is a standard second-order difference equation. Without going into technical details, we may simply observe that this implies that the time path of Y_t may take various forms, some of which are explosive, that is, cause Y_t to move ever further from the equilibrium level $\overline{Y}$ rather than back towards it, and some of which are cyclical, that is, cause Y_t to take an oscillatory path. These latter oscillations may themselves be explosive, that is, have an ever-increasing amplitude, or be damped, having an ever-reducing amplitude. There is also an intermediate case in which the amplitude remains constant, meaning that the same cycle is repeated indefinitely. None of the explosive solutions is of further interest here since they would only arise in conditions that implied that the economy suffered from serious structural instability, a finding that would signal that a rather different approach would be needed. A detailed investigation of the various aggregates concerned would, in such circumstances, be essential and any planning would have to be geared to stop the appearance of even the slightest signs of a disequilibrium.

As the model has so far been developed, there is no scope for government action at all since past income levels are the only determinants of planned expenditure. Whilst there are many ways in which this defect could be rectified, we concentrate here on two possibilities, the choice in part being designed to illustrate that government planning may not involve explicit action at the time the problem arises. In the first formulation, the government uses a 'discretionary' policy or plan under which it decides at the beginning of each period whether to inject public expenditure into the economy (and if so, how much) or not.

Since we have been dealing so far with a model that contains no government expenditure, the introduction of such additional spending will only be of help when expansion is needed; spending must be non-negative. The optimal plan for the government to adopt in situations in which there is a sudden temporary fall in investment, will be to inject an amount of demand that is sufficient to restore aggregate demand to the level at which equilibrium between income and expenditure will continue. This optimal policy may be derived algebraically. Since the fall in investment has been taken to be $-\Delta A$ in period 1, then, clearly, the government can keep the level of total demand consistent with equilibrium by injecting an amount of the same size. Denoting the level of optimal public expenditure in period one by G_1^* we may write:

$$G_1^* = Y^* - C_1 - I_1, \qquad (5.52)$$

where Y^* is the target income level. We may, however, substitute into equation 5.52 values for planned consumption and investment expenditure to get:

$$G_1^* = Y^* - cY_0 - (A - \Delta A) - v(Y_0 - Y_{-1}) \qquad (5.53)$$

But from equation 5.51, and the knowledge that the system started in equilibrium, we know that $Y_1 = Y_0 = Y_{-1} = Y^*$ and $Y^* = A/(1 - c)$; therefore:

$$G_1^* = Y^*(1 - c) - A + \Delta A = \Delta A \qquad (5.54)$$

135

This ensures that expenditure in period 1 remains at the level Y^* and hence leaves the economy ostensibly unaffected by the change in investment: when investment returns to its previous level in period 2, the economy will proceed smoothly as if nothing had happened, government expenditure returning to zero. The conclusion to be drawn from this simple example is that, provided that the government has sufficient information and control variables, it can with relative ease, prevent cycles from occurring. It is interesting to note that the government would have been powerless in the case of a rise in investment, because of the lack of a variable with which to inhibit demand. This shortcoming is, however, avoided if government expenditure is in excess of ΔA in the pre-existing equilibrium.

We now move to a second formulation in which the government operates a stabilisation policy that does not require calculation each time a disequilibrium is predicted but that is built into the economy. 'Automatic' stabilisation as this is called is normally introduced through the medium of the tax system. To illustrate, we introduce a proportional income tax that is levied at the rate B on all incomes. This has the effect of inhibiting planned consumption expenditure since it reduces the disposable income available to consumers. The consumption function of equation 5.46 has thus to be respecified as:

$$C_t = c(Y_{t-1} - T_{t-1}), 0 < c \leqslant 1 \tag{5.55}$$

where T_t is income tax revenue in period t. Since however we have taken a proportional tax function,

$$T_{t-1} = BY_{t-1}, 0 < B < 1, \tag{5.56}$$

equation 5.55 may be rewritten as:

$$C_t = c(Y_{t-1} - BY_{t-1}) = cY_{t-1}(1 - B) \tag{5.57}$$

As a result, the level of income previously given by equation 5.48 now becomes:

$$Y_t = c(1 - B)Y_{t-1} + A_t + v(Y_{t-1} - Y_{t-2}) \tag{5.58}$$

This again is a second-order difference equation since Y_t still depends upon Y_{t-1} and Y_{t-2}. The important point is that the cycles, be they steady or damped, will now have a reduced amplitude as compared to the case where no government action was taken. The reason for this can be seen intuitively by comparing equations 5.49 and 5.58. In the former, the coefficient of the term Y_{t-1} is given by $(c + v)$ whilst in the latter it will be given by $[v + c(1 - B)]$. Since $0 < B < 1$, the second expression will be smaller than the first. This suggests, first, that, in the presence of a tax rate B, the cycles will have a lesser amplitude (since Y_t is now less sensitive to Y_{t-1}) and, secondly, that as B is increased towards unity, so this effect is enhanced: as the tax rate is increased, so its dampening powers are increased; as the economy booms, an enormous amount of potential consumer demand is diverted into the government's tax receipts whilst, in times of relative depression, abnormally low tax bills will encourage consumption. The impact of such measures on the level of total planned expenditure and income will of course depend upon the assumptions made about the relation between tax revenue and the level of government expenditure, for, if the additional revenue is all spent by the government, then the deflationary effects will be offset at least in part.

It has already become clear that the existence of lags is a key factor in the models of cyclical behaviour that we have so far examined. The next stage is to determine whether changes in the lag structure may have a significant influence on the results that we obtain. The question of which lags may be most profitably investigated is one for the econometrician rather than the economic theorist, since at the theoretical level, one lag has no greater or lesser claim to validity than any other. Econometric models are concerned with the empirical problems of how variables seem to be related and thus are likely to concentrate on phenomena such as the lags that operate within an economy. Rather than discuss the primarily empirical issue of the choice of a lag structure, we look first at the role that lags play in planning problems (chiefly in the context of stabilisation) and then at some of the implications that some of these lags might have.

In the preceding paragraphs, it was assumed that the government could predict with certainty when cycles would occur, how large they would be, how much they could be affected by the available control variables, and so on. Implicitly, it was assumed that once the government became aware that, at time t, it would be necessary to execute action x, then all that was required was a bit of patience. Is it not, however, likely that the government will have doubts about its ability to forecast when any undesirable fluctuations are going to take place? The answer is, of course, yes, because just as the strength of relationships (in terms of estimated coefficients) is not known with certainty, neither is the lag structure. It can, therefore, be seen that a knowledge of the form of the lag structure is of the same order of importance as a knowledge of how different aggregates are related, and that optimal economic planning cannot effectively proceed if either is absent. It will be shown in the following paragraphs that, amongst the difficulties associated with the existence of lags, is a breakdown of the proposition derived in the previous section, namely, that automatic and discretionary types of policy can be simply and unequivocally compared. In addition, it will be shown that the lags entering the relationships between variables are not the only sort that may be encountered. Rather, three different types of lag will be identified, namely, lags in recognition, implementation and impact (although the avid reader may be interested to know that other authors (for example Shaw, 1972) have managed to identify more than these).

The first of these problems that the planner faces is predicting when a deviation is likely to occur. It was for example, slightly curious in our investment example that a change in autonomous investment should have been predicted before the event: there is nothing in the model we set up that would be capable of signalling that such a change might be the case, since an autonomous component by definition is something that is independent of the other variables in the system. Accordingly, it is difficult to imagine that the planner will discover such an aberration until after it has occurred. Until he knows what the problem is, he cannot devise a solution, with the consequence that it will be too late to take evasive action, at least in the case of discretionary policy. Thus, in the case of our investment problem, it is unlikely that the change taking place in period 1 will be observed until the end of that period and so the preventive measure of an injection of government expenditure will not be possible at the time when it is needed. In the case of the built-in stabiliser (the tax rate B), there would be no need for the planner to spot the problem since it is automatically picked up in the income level.

The second of the problems is that, once the planner has observed (or predicted with sufficient confidence) that some destablilising event is going to occur (or has possibly already occurred), he has to come to a decision about the optimal plan to adopt. In the simple case we looked at, the fact that the autonomous investment change is going to take place may not be sufficient information. As it happened, we were in a situation in which the existing level of income was regarded as optimal, leaving the planner the relatively trivial task of returning to it as quickly as possible. Suppose, however, that income had been running at a sub-optimal level and that there took place a sudden increase in autonomous investment that showed signs of being permanent. The planner would have to predict whether in fact such permanence was likely and whether the change could be used as a vehicle for moving the economy to the optimal level. Decisions of this kind would involve both a considerable amount of computation to discover the consequences of injecting different amounts of expenditure into the economy at different times, and in addition, consultation with the political process in order that the assumptions being made about preferences were still the correct ones and were being properly reflected. This difficulty would not occur in the case of an automatic policy since all the necessary calculation and consultation would have taken place before the implementation of the policy. It would still, however, be important to be sure that the objectives embodied in the automatic mechanism were still the appropriate ones. Thus it is that, especially where there is some possibility of a change in preferences, there may be significant delays as the planners compute the optimal action to be taken.

The third of the problems is that there may be lags between decisions about policies and the plans being implemented, and their becoming fully effective. A delay in the implementation of policies may result from a statutory requirement that changes in tax rates have to be announced in advance of their imposition or can only be altered at specific intervals such as six months or a year. Further delays may accompany the process by which political decisions are translated into the enactment of legislation, although this is obviously an area in which the precise details of institutional structure will be the important factor. Further, taxes may be collected in arrears or the link between the policy change and the variable in which alterations are to be effected may be such that transmission of the desired effects takes time.

We now look at the implications that the existence of lags may have for the choice between automatic and discretionary policy. Although we will not be concerned with analysis of which of the different sorts of lags are involved, we might note that it may well be of help for the planner to know which sort they are because he may be able to economise on time if he is careful. The simple deterministic model we looked at above incorporated only lags in the relations between variables in the system; it did not include the kinds of lag we have just been discussing. In this earlier model, we found that discretionary policy was effective because it allowed the planner sufficient freedom to maintain the level of income undisturbed. The next step is to examine the consequences of depriving the planner of the ability to predict the change in autonomous investment. Instead, we assume that he observes the discrepancy during the period in which it occurs and is able to devise a policy very quickly, ready for application in the following period. Generously perhaps, we assume that the planner can correctly predict that, in period 2, investment will return to its original level. Thus the planner is searching for an optimal pattern of government expenditure in a world that has been in an optimal equilibrium at Y^* for some time, that is, $Y_{-1} = Y_0 = Y^*$, but which is disturbed by a sudden, unsustained and, in this case, unpredicted fall in investment of $-\Delta A$ in period 1. Planned expenditure in this economy is again given by the multiplier–accelerator formulation of equation 5.48. Given that investment falls by $-\Delta A$ in period 1, the level of income in period 1 will this time be given by:

$$Y_1 = (A - \Delta A) + cY_0 + v(Y_0 - Y_{-1}) \tag{5.59}$$

which may be simplified to give:

$$Y_1 = \Delta A + cY^* \tag{5.60}$$

The planner observes this income level and, finding that $Y_1 < Y^*$, decides that action is needed. In order to restore equilibrium, the planner first has to compute the level that income would reach in period 2 in the absence of any such action. Using the assumption that autonomous investment will resume its original level, we may deduce that income in the absence of action will be given by calculating equation 5.48 for $t = 2$, with the level of Y_1 given by equation 5.60:

$$Y_2 = A + cY_1 + v(Y_1 - Y_0) \tag{5.61}$$

and also since $Y_0 = Y^*$, we may write equation 5.61 as:

$$Y_2 = A + c(A - \Delta A + cY^*) + v(A - \Delta A + cY^* - Y^*) \tag{5.62}$$

This expression may be simplified to give:

$$Y_2 = A(1 + c + v) + Y^*(c^2 + vc - v) - \Delta A(c + v) \quad (5.63)$$

The planner will want to set the level of government expenditure in period 2 at the deficiency indicated by $(Y^* - Y_2)$, and thus by substituting equation 5.63 for Y_2, he will choose to set his control variable at:

$$
\begin{aligned}
G_2^* &= Y^* - Y_2 \\
&= Y^* - A(1 + c + v) - Y^*(c^2 + cv - v) + \Delta A(c + v) \\
&= Y^*(1 - c^2 - cv + v) - A(1 + c + v) + \Delta A(c + v) \quad (5.64)
\end{aligned}
$$

Provided that the system is sufficiently flexible and fast acting to permit the calculation and implementation of the solution indicated by equation 5.64, then we will have managed to restore income in period 2 to its optimal level. A similar sort of calculation is then needed to determine the apropriate level of government expenditure in period 3, because the low income level of period 1 will have an influence on planned investment in period 3. By period 4, however, all is back to normal provided that the calculations of G_2^* and G_3^* were correct, since the level of income will have been at its optimal level for the requisite two periods, thus satisfying the equilibrium condition $Y_t = Y_{t-1} = Y_{t-2}$.

As well as indicating that a very simple lag in observation slows down the process of correction, this example shows that the nature of the optimal policy is now more complex and sensitive to the parameters of the system. The solution for the optimal government expenditure pattern has, as a result of the introduction of the lag, changed from $G_1^* = \Delta A$ as in equation 5.54 to the expression for G_2^* in equation 5.64 and a similar expression for G_3^*. In other words, it has become crucial that the planner has correct information about c and v.

It is this finding that may affect the choice between discretionary and automatic types of policy. From equation 5.58, it is possible to derive the path that the economy would take in the event of a disturbance, this path being normally a cyclical one but of relatively low amplitude. This outcome in the case of automatic policy may be compared to the outcome under the use of discretionary policy as we have just derived it. Clearly, as the lags become longer and the inaccuracy of the estimate of c grows, so the case for using an automatic policy is strengthened, an imperfect but predictable return to equilibrium being preferred to the more complex method that may give rise to quicker but potentially erratic adjustments. In the final section concerned with optimality, we move from the relatively specific problem of lags to the much wider area of the general problem of uncertainty and how it may be incorporated into the process of determining the optimal plan.

OPTIMISATION UNDER UNCERTAINTY

In the preceding analysis of lags, we investigated the consequences of the planner discovering an unanticipated change too late. Errors of this kind are very easy to make because planners are working with imperfect models and data. This is not to say, however, that attempts are not made to improve matters. In addition to the obvious step of continually trying to improve the quality of the information and the econometric models with which they work, planners have looked to developments in economic theory to help in their treatment of different forms of uncertainty. Progress in this field is difficult and we present here nothing more than a glimpse of the kind of approach that is used. Nevertheless, this is clearly an area that is of considerable significance for the planner in problems both of stabilisation and of growth, although clearly the emphasis will be slightly different in the two cases.

The basic method of analysis typically applied to problems of uncertainty is straightforward. To illustrate, we consider an example in which two plans are being compared and in which there is uncertainty about the course of future events and hence about the consequences for welfare. The policies are labelled I and II and we make the assumption that there is a simple welfare function that depends solely on the level of aggregate income. In addition, we define two states of the world, 1 and 2, which summarise the two possible paths that future events beyond the planner's control may take. It is assumed that the probability that state of the world 1 will apply is estimated to be π_1 and that the two states are mutually exclusive, with the implication that the probability of the second state of the world applying is given as $\pi_2 = 1 - \pi_1$. The next step is to assume that, associated with each combination of policy and state of the world, is a single level of aggregate consumption denoted C_{ij}, where i is the policy adopted and j the state of the world. Combining the latter information with our welfare indicator, it becomes possible to associate with each policy the welfare level generated in the event that either state of the world prevails.

Summarising, we find that the welfare levels pertaining to the different possible regimes are as follows.

		state of the world	
		1	2
plan adopted	I	$W(C_{11})$	$W(C_{12})$
	II	$W(C_{21})$	$W(C_{22})$

where C_{ij} refers to aggregate consumption and $W(C_{ij})$ refers to the level of welfare.

The next stage is to determine which of the two available plans is to be regarded as optimal. Whilst it will sometimes be the case that one plan out-performs the other regardless of which state of the world prevails, on other occasions we may find one policy doing better under one state of the world but worse under the other. In order to resolve such conflicts, it is necessary to introduce further information about social preferences. One method of doing so — the expected utility hypothesis — is based on the assumption that the welfare of a plan may be derived by weighting each outcome by the probability of its occurrence. That is to say, in choosing between the two plans, we consider the average pay-off that would be associated with each if we were to take such a decision very many times. As a consequence, we may compute the expected welfare associated with any plan imaginable, and thus the search for an optimal plan will involve searching for the plan offering the highest level of expected welfare. In the simple case at hand, we calculate the expected welfare level:

$$\left. \begin{array}{l} \text{Plan I: } E[W(\text{I})] = \pi_1 \cdot W(C_{11}) + (1 - \pi_1) \cdot W(C_{12}) \\ \text{Plan II: } E[W(\text{II})] = \pi_2 \cdot W(C_{21}) + (1 - \pi_1) \cdot W(C_{22}) \end{array} \right\} \quad (5.65)$$

where $E[W(i)]$ in the expected welfare level associated with plan i and π_1, π_2 are the probabilities of the alternative outcomes. Extension of this analysis to cases in which there are many policies and many possible states of the world is simply a matter of introducing more probabilities and more aggregate consumption levels, the principle remaining the same.

As is normally the case in planning problems, the form taken by the welfare function will have important implications for the choice of plan. Restricting ourselves to an intuitive explanation, we may see that, if the function displays rapidly diminishing returns, then in a choice between plans that offer the same level of

143

expected aggregate consumption, the plan showing less dispersion about the mean will be preferred to its competitor. Consider the simple case in which the two states of the world are equally likely (that is, both have a probability of $0 \cdot 5$) and that plan I is associated with consumption levels of 10 in state 1 and 40 in state 2, whilst plan II gives consumption levels of 20 and 30 in the respective states. Both plans offer the same level of expected consumption:

$$\left. \begin{array}{l} E[C_I] = {}^{1}/_{2} \cdot 10 + {}^{1}/_{2} \cdot 40 = 25 \\ E[C_{II}] = {}^{1}/_{2} \cdot 20 + {}^{1}/_{2} \cdot 30 = 25 \end{array} \right\} \quad (5.66)$$

Suppose next that the welfare function is diminishing and more specifically that it tells us that associated with different levels of aggregate consumption are the following welfare levels:

$$W(10) = 5, W(20) = 8, W(30) = 11, W(40) = 12.$$

Substituting these values into equation 5.65, we find that plan II is strictly preferred to plan I since:

$$\left. \begin{array}{l} E[W(I)] = {}^{1}/_{2} \cdot W(10) + {}^{1}/_{2} \cdot W(40) = {}^{1}/_{2} \cdot 5 + {}^{1}/_{2} \cdot 12 = 8{}^{1}/_{2} \\ \text{whilst} \\ E[W(II)] = {}^{1}/_{2} \cdot W(20) + {}^{1}/_{2} \cdot W(30) = {}^{1}/_{2} \cdot 8 + {}^{1}/_{2} \cdot 11 = 9{}^{1}/_{2} \end{array} \right\} (5.67)$$

The use of a welfare function that features diminishing returns is commonplace and is normally referred to as indicating the presence of *risk aversion*, that is to say that, *ceteris paribus*, an outcome offering lower variability about the expected level is preferred to one offering higher variability. It should, however, be emphasised that the planner is only entitled to incorporate notions of this kind if they constitute the preferences of society as expressed through the extant political process. There is nothing intrinsic to economic analysis that endows this hypothesis with validity — it is simply a convenience.

There are variants on this basic analytical approach to incorporating uncertainty (Green, 1976). One of these is the mean-variance approach, the seminal treatment of which is to be found in Markowitz (1959). In some respects, this approach bears a close relation to the expected utility hypothesis. The various possible outcomes associated with a plan may be measured in terms of their mean, just as in equation 5.66 and, in addition, in terms of their variance, the latter simply being one way of summarising the degree of variability. A welfare function defined on these two parameters may then be applied in order to discover which of two plans is preferred. An alternative approach is to use a rule such as the maximin criterion. Such an approach involves making a choice between plans on the basis of the worst possible outcome. The optimal plan is the one that offers the most attractive outcome under the least favourable state of the world, irrespective of how low the probability of this state of the world occurring may be. The most widespread application of this particular approach is to situations in which different agents are playing a game against each other, for, in such circumstances, it is often difficult to assign meaningful probabilities to particular outcomes for these are normally dependent upon the actions taken by other players. Rawls (1973), whose work was discussed in an earlier chapter, made extensive use of this particular criterion in analysing decisions under uncertainty.

It was suggested in the section on stabilisation planning that the centrally planned economy might be less susceptible to fluctuations than the capitalist economy because decisions were directly co-ordinated in the former but not in the latter. To the extent that this is the case, there will be a narrower range within which uncertainty may operate in centrally planned systems. The reforms taking place in the USSR, however, are introducing a greater degree of decentralisation, with the consequence that uncertainty is a problem that Soviet planners are having to take more seriously. This point is very clearly made by Siroyezhin who remarks:

'At the present stage of socialistic development, the policy of decentralising gives the manager of a firm a broader range in which he can choose his decisions. This broadening of the range of possible decisions, as well as the appearance of a greater number of alternatives available to management, imply that risk and uncertainty become important elements in decision-making.' (Siroyezhin, 1968)

It is important at this point to note that the introduction of uncertainty into planning contexts may cause confusion about precisely what is meant by 'optimality'. We choose plan A rather than plan B if, in overall terms, taking account of uncertainties and so on, it offers a more attractive prospective outcome according to the criteria we are applying. If, however, plan A does less well than plan B under some circumstances, then we will not expect to do better using plan A on *all* occasions. Bad luck may mean that we would have done better on a particular occasion had we adopted plan B. This is quite different, of course, from arguing that the choice of plan A was inappropriate or sub-optimal. Taking an example, suppose that an individual is offered the chance to join a game in which a fair (that is, unbiased) coin is tossed once only, the would-be entrant being told that if the coin lands 'heads' he wins £1 and if it lands 'tails' he pays 50 pence. Clearly, unless he is very averse to risk — or extremely poor — the individual is likely to find this an attractive proposition. Having gone ahead, however, he may be unlucky and lose, but that is not to say that he should feel that he acted wrongly or pursued the wrong plan. Planning takes place before the relevant events start to happen, the problem of optimisation being to make sure we choose the plan that offers the most attractive *prospect*, since uncertainty may make it impossible to choose a plan that out-performs all available alternatives under each and every one of the possible sequences of events that nature (or even unpredictable human behaviour) may happen to bestow.

In addition to this traditional distinction between luck and judgement, it is also useful to note that plans themselves may be state-contingent, that is to say, dependent upon the course of events. Plan X may not simply entail an instruction to sow corn in year t; it may further specify that the crop should be sold on the home market if the domestic crop, because of unfavourable weather, is poor but on the foreign market otherwise. An alternative to using plans that follow the form 'if i happens then do z' is to adopt the approach to uncertainty outlined earlier (Chapter 2) where we discussed the role of the Walrasian Auctioneer in an uncertain world. This would involve defining one plan, say x_1, that would apply under one set of circumstances and another plan x_2 that would be appropriate otherwise. In this sort of framework, the particular action to be taken at harvest time would be found by consulting the plan that came into action when it became known how good the harvest was going to be. Whilst both approaches to the definition of planning in uncertain conditions are equally valid, it is as well to be clear which is being used.

In the final section of our discussion of uncertainty, we deal with a problem that has been receiving an increasing amount of attention recently — the possibility that the planning horizon is itself uncertain. Our analysis so far has been confined to the case in which a single measure of future prospects in the form of an aggregate consumption level is available. Often, however, there may be doubt about the distance of the planning horizon that is relevant when plans are being devised, and it may sometimes be desirable to investigate the optimality criteria (if any) to apply in such cases.

For an example of this type of uncertainty, we might think of the cost-benefit analyst engaged in drawing up information about the desirability or otherwise of building a canal that has a projected 'economic' life of 200 years. A key element in his calculations will be the weight he assigns to the consumption benefits to be derived from the canal in all future time periods. In this case, should he restrict his attention to the lifetime of the existing government, can he find some other means of articulating the relevant social preferences or should he simply choose some arbitrary time horizon? The frequent absence of guidance on this point has had the consequence that, when information on large-scale long-term projects is being assembled, it is quite common to use sensitivity tests (Flowerdew, 1972). Thus, if it is thought that there will be controversy about whether benefits over 200 years or over fifty years are the relevant measure of gains, then the net present value of the project would be computed using the different assumptions in turn. This practice makes explicit the differences and allows analysis of how sensitive the final conclusion is to the choice of horizon. Sensitivity analysis can, of course, be appplied in a great variety of planning problems, since examination of whether the optimality of a plan is sensitive or insensitive to changes in the assumptions underlying its selection in the first instance may throw important light on the quality and the robustness of the plan. It has for example, been recently argued by Matthews and King (1977) that proposed stabilisation policies be subjected to a more thorough scrutiny to see how well they would fare under relatively unfavourable assumptions about future events. Discussing UK economic policy in recent times they say:

'A justifiable criticism of much past macro-economic policy making has been that it has not incorporated enough contingency planning: a single scenario has been set out, and not enough provision has been made about what will be done if things turn out otherwise than expected (as they are bound to in some respects) ...An important part of the appraisal of a policy package must therefore be the quality of the contingency planning it incorporates.'

147

Thorough scrutiny of competing alternatives under a variety of assumptions is not without costs in terms both of time and effort, but is nevertheless certainly worth some attention, especially in situations where there is a wide range of possible future events.

Important but difficult work on a related problem has produced some interesting findings. In the growth problem analysed earlier in this chapter, it was seen that, once the choice of a horizon, say T, for planning has been made, it is likely that investment will fall off over the last few periods of the horizon because of the continually reducing contribution to future relevant consumption possibilities made by a unit of investment. Since this phenomenon is clearly undesirable, it has become common practice in growth models to impose a terminal capital stock constraint; that is, the capital stock in period T, K_T, must be not less than some specified level $\bar{K}$. If, however, we are not sure how long the horizon is to be, it is unlikely that we will be able to devise an optimal plan, or put another way, the optimal plan is likely to be sensitive to the length of the horizon. Provided that we are constructing a plan that will only be in operation for a few years then there may be several plans, each of which is optimal for a different horizon, that would lead us along paths that are close together. The implication of this is that any such plan may be chosen provided that it is only to be implemented over the early stages of the horizon, for little improvement would be possible at that time even if we knew for sure what the horizon was to be (Hammond and Mirrlees, 1973; Heal, 1973). The use of 'rolling' plans, in which decisions are formulated notionally for a long period but continuously revised in the light of experience, seems to make good sense when looked at with the aid of such analysis. Work of this kind is, however, very much in its infancy and cannot really at this stage be readily utilised in the devising of optimal or approximately optimal plans in real-world planning contexts.

A good deal of ground has been covered in this chapter. In most cases, however, the basic problem has been the same, namely, to find the plan that maximises a welfare function within the constraints imposed by the structure of the economy and the kinds of policy instruments available. The bulk of the effort has been directed towards examining various common themes that underlie the constraints encountered in different circumstances. This should not, however, be allowed to distract attention from the functions. Thus, for example, we have often taken welfare to be a function of aggregate consumption without regard to how the aggregate is distributed. In some cases, it will be possible to introduce constraints that encapsulate some of our desires in this area, but clearly there are often explicit redistributive ends that are to be incorporated into economic plans. A lexicographic welfare function could be used for example, plans not satisfying the specified pattern of distribution being ruled out irrespective of any other merits they may have. Particularly in capitalist economies, however, it may well be that society, recognising that redistribution may adversely affect the pursuit of allocative efficiency, will specify terms upon which redistribution is to be traded against the latter. Provided that sufficient is known about the operation of the economic system, the relevant objectives and about the consequences for both distribution and allocation of different plans, then ordinary optimisation techniques may be used to choose the plan that offers the better balance of the two. To give a simple example, we consider the case of choosing an optimal income-tax rate in a world in which higher tax rates have disincentive effects (that is, give rise to a reduction in the supply of labour) but do generate higher tax revenue, thus allowing greater scope for redistribution (Atkinson, 1973; Mirrlees, 1971). Provided that we have enough information about objectives, we may establish a social-welfare function that is sensitive to both types of effect. This function may then be differentiated with respect to the tax rate set and its optimal level ascertained. Straightforward as such analysis appears on the surface, we might note that the optimisation techniques required become rapidly more sophisticated as the model of labour supply or the welfare function becomes more complex.

The later sections were concerned with a demonstration of some of the ways in which the problems of optimisation may be increased. The introduction of lags into the planning process at different stages and of uncertainty into the prognoses of the economy's path under different policies serve to increase the difficulties of specifying the objective function to be maximised or the constraints to which the economy is subject, or sometimes both. These central issues have been dealt with at the expense of discussion of the sorts of optimisation methods actually employed by planners who work with large-scale, sophisticated, econometric models. This has meant that the sorts of optimisation problems examined have had simple basic structures that have enabled us to concentrate on the conceptual rather than computational aspects of the central questions.

CHAPTER 6

Planning in Practice

The discussion up to this stage of the argument has been largely abstract, an approach which we have justified in terms of our belief in the fundamental unity of the planning process. However, we have now come to the point where the perpetuation of the theoretical perspective is less profitable, and this is the area of practical plan construction and implementation. In this chapter, we therefore examine the methods by which a specific macroeconomic plan might be drawn up and put into operation, and we conclude with a review of the planning experiences of France and the Soviet Union.

PLAN CONSTRUCTION AND IMPLEMENTATION

Because of the political and economic peculiarities of the planning machinery in individual nations, it is impossible to deal with plan construction in general terms; we shall accordingly examine one particular case, although mention will be made of others during the course of the discussion. The plan with which we shall be concerned is the Fourth French Plan (1962–65) which, despite the fact that it was developed about fifteen years ago, has much to recommend it as a case study — it is well documented and it clearly demonstrates the linkages between all the planning elements which we have examined in previous chapters. As we shall see, the process described has much in common with the more refined system currently employed.

After the end of the Second World War, in a political climate favourable to the establishment of a planned economy, the French took the first steps in developing institutions necessary for a more centralised control over economic resources. In 1946, the General Planning Commissariat was set up, charged with the overall responsibility for the implementation of national blueprints for the postwar reconstruction and development. The first formal plan appeared in 1947, to be followed by a second (1954–57) and a third (1958–61), and, over this period, the institutional and administrative structure of the planning machinery became more refined, eventually developing into the form which we shall now examine.

Like children, plans do not suddenly appear — they are conceived, born and finally develop to maturity. The conception of the Fourth Plan occurred in late 1959 (midway through the course of the Third Plan) when the Commissariat, in association with the French Statistical Office, undertook some preliminary work on forecasting and feasability. Projections of the major macroaggregates were made — production, consumption, manpower, international trade etc. — which, coupled with more detailed analyses for particular industries, resulted in a seventeen-sector projection for 1965, on the basis of the attainment of three possible growth rates.

This projection provided the basic broad alternatives available to the French economy; what was now required was further guidance as to which of these general directions was the 'correct' one. As a first step in determining the appropriate objective function, the projection was next submitted (November 1959) to a body entitled the Economic and Social Council, which occupied a key role in the decision-making structure as its composition indicated. This Council, which had existed in some form or another since 1946, had a consultative role and was essentially composed of two groups of members. First, there existed specialists in the fields of economic, social and cultural matters, who were able to comment authoritatively on the implications of the Commissariat's projections and, secondly, members were also appointed in order to reflect aspects of public opinion. In addition to the specialists, the Council embodied representatives of particular interest groups — trades unionists, employers, agriculture, the nationalised industries, family associations, and so forth — who could comment on the implications of the projections for their particular area of the economy. Together, these two groups developed the initial projection, by producing both a consumption and a general growth study. These studies differed from the previous exercise in that they contained recommendations for policies and highlighted foreseeable problems.

The next stage of the process was the submission of the Council's reports to the government for debate. Here, for the first time, the plan entered the political arena in a formal way, and parliamentary debate (the constitutional public choice process) determined the basic objectives of the plan. On the basis of these discussions, the Government directives were issued (June 1960).

'The issue by the Government of its directives to the General Planning Commissariat represents a watershed in the process of elaborating the Plan. Before that, work is essentially one of forecasting and of facilitating the choice of ends and means by the competent bodies who have either to advise on the choice or to make the final decisions. Afterwards, the technicians have a specific set of objectives to which they must work ...' (Hackett and Hackett, 1963)

These directives spelled out the major tasks facing the economy during the planning period (modernisation, growth and the expansion of trade) and mentioned areas for special attention (regional imbalances, housing, and so forth). The target rate of growth was set at a 5 per cent increase in gross national product per annum, but flexibility was also deemed to be an important requirement.

Given these guidelines, planning could now begin in earnest. Under the auspices of the Commissariat, twenty-seven Planning Commissions began work on detailed analyses of planning requirements and possibilities. Twenty-two of these Commissions were 'vertical', specialising in particular sectors of economic activity such as agriculture, transport, steel and housing, whilst the remainder were 'horizontal', concentrating on general issues such as manpower growth and regional problems. In composition, the Commissions were similar to the Economic and Social Council, being made up of a combination of specialists and interested parties. Taking responsibility for the coordination and collation of these twenty-seven reports, the Commissariat was finally in a position to present a more detailed proposal to the government (March 1961). From this, it appeared that the projected 5 per cent growth target was unduly pessimistic, and a decision was made to aim at 5·5 per cent. Having established the final figure, the government was now able to provide the planning bodies with a detailed breakdown of its own required public expenditure and investments. From this additional information, the Commissariat could now perform the final synthesis and it accordingly presented the first draft of the plan to parliament (May 1961).

Although this draft was formally approved by parliament (September 1961), there were still further checks required to ensure viability and general acceptability. The Economic and Social Council and the High Planning Council (a body of ministers and senior officials from political and economic agencies) both debated the document, pointing out a number of reservations, before returning it to the government for formal ratification (December 1961). The debates of mid-1962 led to a number of modifications, but a substantially unaltered Fourth Plan was eventually presented to the nation in August 1962.

From this review of the evolution of the Fourth French Plan, we may derive a number of observations:

(1) The length of time elapsing between the initial projections of the Commissariat and the final publication of the planning document was almost exactly three years. The implication of this is that the planning agencies of France will be permanently occupied since, as soon as one Plan is operationalised, projections will commence for the next. In an economy which relies even more heavily on the planning process, such as the Soviet Union, it is clear that this pressure will be even greater. For nations such as these, therefore, planning will be a continuous activity.

(2) The French experience demonstrates the high degree of interaction between the technical aspects of planning and the social-choice mechanisms at all levels. The primary articulator of preferences, the government, was responsible for establishing the basic objectives of the Plan at an early stage and, as we have seen, interfered in the process when it felt that a new target was more appropriate. It also determined the important parameters of public spending and ultimately decided the form in which the plan was actually implemented. Furthermore, some central functions in the plan's construction were partially performed by representatives from society at large, to ensure the closest possible correspondence between that which was desired and that which finally resulted.

(3) The practical planning process does not follow the neat logic of a theoretical argument. Neither social decisions nor technical plans can be developed in isolation, without recognition of one another's requirements. As we have seen, the social-decision process had to be presented with a range of possibilities from which a choice was to be made, just as the planners themselves had to be set an objective function before detailed work could begin.

It would be incorrect to think that the social-decision process ends once a plan is ratified and operationalised. This was certainly not the case with the Fourth French Plan, where public debate continued with a view to the bringing about of reforms in the system. Whilst there was substantial agreement over the basic objectives of the Plan itself, much criticism was levelled at the planning machinery, and account was taken of this during subsequent plans. The left-wing parties in France, whose political support was then growing, attacked the planning institutions for giving insufficient voice to the views of labour. Others argued that the degree of planning was such that free competition in the economy was precluded and that decisions had become over-centralised. Some preferences, whilst not being particularly relevant to the operations of the Fourth Plan, would clearly have implications for any subsequent planning decisions. In the same way, economic developments during the planning period will inevitably lead to some modification in social preferences: one does not have to be particularly Marxist to suggest that the operations of the economy will exert some influence upon social choice.

In a highly centralised economy, such as that of the Soviet Union, these inter-relationships between social preferences and technical calculations are more nebulous, for the simple reason that the implicit 'social contract' of such a society endows the planning body with much more sovereignty over the choice of goals. Nevertheless, the technical problems of relating social demands to the feasible combinations of production will be conceptually similar to the case described above, although presumably more complex owing to the larger number of sectors to be directly planned.

Having examined the political and economic relationships which serve to produce the final planning document, we now turn to a discussion of the possible methods of putting the policy recommendations into operation, that is, the 'realisation' of the plan. Naturally, these procedures will depend upon both the plan's specific proposals and the structure of the economy concerned, although we shall confine our remarks to three possibilities in the range of planning strategies.

The implementation of a plan can be seen essentially in terms of the nature and degree of control exerted over the operations of the economy by the central government or planning authorities. For our first case, let us therefore pose the question — what is the role of a plan when the degree of central control is zero? In such a situation, the plan's task is the provision of a detailed overall forecast of undirected economic evolution, whilst realisation remains strictly in the hands of the individual microeconomic agents. These agents are free to develop in any direction they wish but, with the aid of the plan, they now become aware of additional information regarding the likely activities of all other agents within the economy and outside. Each agent should therefore have prior notice of possible economic problems pertaining to itself (shortages in inputs, price changes etc.) which permits it to make arrangements for pre-emptive action. The liberal philosophy behind this 'forecasting' planning variant was best expressed by Pierre Massé (1962, 1965), a major influence on French planning in the early 1960s, and this form of methodology was explicitly incorporated into the rubric of the Fourth French Plan (the closing statement has been emphasised by the authors):

'The first reason for the success of the plan is its coherence. The very methods by which the forecasts are drawn up means that they prefigure a general equilibrium of exchanges of goods and services at the end of the plan. This prospective equilibrium does not become a reality unless all the economic agents conform to the recommendations of the plan, *but it is obviously a powerful factor inducing them to move in this direction.*' (Quoted in Lutz, 1969)

Under this regime, therefore, it is merely necessary for the planners to forecast the economy, and common sense will then step in to make the prophecy self-fulfilling, by the 'natural tendencies' of the market mechanism.

This form of planning is conceptually rooted in the free-market model of the economy. However, despite the apparent incorporation of this planning ideology into the earlier French plans, it is not difficult to prove that the zero-control position is inappropriate to a planned mixed economy for two main reasons. First, some proportion of economic activity is, by definition, always under direct central control — to our knowledge, in all modern societies the state retains responsibility for the provision of defence, for example. As some activity is accordingly outside the free-market influence, it possesses no 'natural tendency' which could be forecast, in the same manner as the market-determined output of a private steel industry might. Furthermore, as we have seen from our discussion of policy instruments, where a government has the power to tax and spend, it also possesses the implicit power to control. Secondly, as we have seen from Chapter 2, it is generally

155

recognised that the free reign of the capitalist system produces effects which are not necessarily in the best interests of society as a whole, and it is therefore likely that the plan will incorporate measures to modify such 'natural tendencies'. The characteristic methodology of planning in the mixed economy accordingly takes the form of a combination of the direct allocation of central expenditure and the modification of market tendencies to meet the requirements of the specified objective function. This methodology is generally termed *indicative* planning.

The responsibility for the implementation of the indicative plan falls squarely upon the state, and not upon the individual economic agents. In our second variant, therefore, the state possesses a degree of control which exceeds zero but is less than complete. In order to meet the plan's objectives, the state will be required to perform two operations:

(1) It must allocate its public expenditure with a view to providing the planned level of publicly provided goods and services, and also to provide those necessities such as the infrastructure to enable the private sector to fulfil its targets, and

(2) by means of the policy instruments and direct controls which society has placed at its disposal, it must attempt to direct the semi-autonomous private sector along the lines indicated in the planning document.

How will such implementation occur in practice? The public sector, being under the direct control of the state, will generally be the area in which the operations of the plan first appear. Indeed, as we have seen, the state will already have made its preliminary assessment of public-sector developments, owing to their importance in plan formulation. The general state budget will be allocated to local authorities and nationalised industries according to the criteria laid down for them; this represents the state's commitment to the creation of output. In addition, steps will also be taken to fulful the plan's targets by making policies for application in the private sector; these may be both positive (to encourage individual agents to develop further in the direction in which they are already going) or negative (to discourage particular forms of economic activity). Examples of the former class might be investment subsidies to stimulate further growth or increases in the money supply to encourage consumer expenditure, whilst examples of the latter could be a licensing system to prevent exports or a discriminatory tax adjustment to modify consumption patterns.

The indicative approach naturally embodies the forecasting aspect of the previous planning strategy, and its proponents argue for its effectiveness in terms of the provision of co-ordinated output decisions. The indicative format does, however, potentially give rise to a number of problems during implementation. First, by virtue of the fact that public-sector resources are under direct control, it is generally true that the state-expenditure area of the plan always comes up to expectations. However, because the private sector has been left largely to its own devices, with some government influence, no such guarantee can be made in its case. Historically, most Western economies have found that their private sectors never quite reach their required objectives, with the result that there has been a progressive imbalance in such systems in favour of the relative growth of the public sector. Secondly, the publication of the plan might well create an air of expectation in the economy (indeed, this is one of its functions), with the result that economic agents could well act on the basis of what they *think* will happen, as specified by the planning document, rather than on the basis of events in the real world. Trades unions could well bid for wage rises in anticipation of the planned, but unrealised, productivity increases, a situation which would clearly be inflationary; again, some firms might undertake their planned investments only to discover that, owing to shortfalls in interacting firms, this capacity is surplus to requirements.

A third class of problems involved in plan implementation derives from the technical basis of the plan's construction. As we have seen, the skeleton of any plan which suggests the economic possibilities open to society, is derived from an analysis of the data and functional relationships which characterise the particular economy. During implementation, we run the risk of discovering a number of possible errors in our analysis. At the simplest level, data might have been wrong — firms might have told us what they *hoped* to produce rather than that which they were *actually capable* of producing. Again, our estimation of the functional forms might not have been sufficiently accurate — if taxation only cuts consumption by 5 per cent, instead of the 7 per cent which we might have estimated, we have many millions of pounds, francs etc. in unanticipated consumption expenditure to generate unexpected inflation.

Because of problems such as these, it is clear that we cannot

157

really think of simply creating a plan and then applying it; the world will be changing daily, both in terms of the social preferences of society and in terms of the nature of the economy which we are attempting to plan. The implication of this is that, once the initial stages of the plan have been put into operation, the workings of the economy must be continuously monitored to ensure that events are taking their planned course.

This monitoring process may take one of two forms, and it will be appreciated that a monitoring facility will be a partial determinant of whether or not a particular form of policy is to be used. In the first place, we could have a policy which actually monitors itself and we have discussed examples of such automatic mechanisms in the previous chapter. In the case of such automatic monitoring, the planners will play a minimal role, as any imperfection in the plan's operation will naturally tend to cancel itself out. A commonplace example in a mixed economy is *fiscal drag* — given a progressive taxation system, increased consumer income results in individuals moving into higher tax brackets such that more income is withdrawn in the form of tax; the inflationary tendency is accordingly alleviated. In all fairness, this example does not depict a 'pure' mechanism, as some side effects will be induced, such as an increase in the size of the public sector, but it serves to demonstrate the point that the field of economics is not as fortunate as that of mechanics, in having the neat example of Watt's steam-engine governor!

The second, and more common, method of control takes the form of the feedback of information. As the economy develops during the progress of the plan, additional values for the data vector will be obtained and, from these, the re-estimation of the functional relationships can take place to provide a continuously reviewed, up-to-date picture of the economy at the current time. From this information, the planners can inform the state of any changes in policy which might be necessary to maintain the economy on course, policies again determined by the simulation and optimisation techniques used in the original plan. The success of discretionary implementation of the plan therefore depends upon a number of factors — the accuracy and speed in processing the information and, ultimately, the rapidity of the translation of decisions into action.

Our third planning variant, *imperative* planning, is the polar opposite of our first case. In this situation, the central authority has total direct command over all controllable economic parameters.

(We should therefore exclude at present such factors as the weather!) The influence of unforeseen actions by individuals is therefore minimised and, accordingly, plan implementation should be much simpler than in the previous case. Problems will arise, however, owing to general uncertainty and the effort involved in the resultant necessary recalculation of targets. The same continuous monitoring process must therefore operate although, in a totally controlled economy, all action will be discretionary rather than automatic. Nevertheless, we could reasonably believe that imperative planning should be more successful in the strict sense of meeting targets, than planning under an indicative regime, as resources can be directly allocated at the will of the social decision maker, no reliance being placed upon the uncertain effects of inducements.

Plan implementation is therefore about control. No practical economy will exist at the extreme ends of our dimension with zero or total control; rather, economies lie somewhere in between, their exact position being a function of the amount of direct state control regarded as optimal by their societies. Very broadly, we should wish to say that the socialist economies tend to be somewhat more 'imperative' than capitalist systems, although individual positions depend upon individual circumstances.

PLANNING IN FRANCE

Planning in France has evolved through three fairly distinct stages since its first formal adoption in 1946, from the initial postwar reconstruction, through the target-orientated plans of the 1950s and 1960s, to the highly sophisticated planning models developed over the past decade. In this section, we shall consider the development of French planning in some detail.

The First Plan (1947–1952/3) was initially prepared in 1946 under the guidance of Jean Monnet. Intended primarily as a postwar reconstruction programme, it attracted a considerable amount of international attention for a number of reasons. First, this was the first time that any capitalist nation had overtly adopted any form of macroplanning on a large scale. Secondly, substantial interest was generated in the USA, where the plan was seen as an effective way of intelligently allocating the resources provided by Marshall Aid. Finally, the French reconstruction attempt provided interesting contrasts with other Western developments, in particular the return to the free-market capitalism adopted by the Germany of Adenauer and Erhard.

The First Plan did not set a required overall growth rate but established a number of 'imperative targets' for basic sectors — coal, electricity, steel, oil — and 'indicative forecasts' for other industries such as manufacturing and agriculture. The planning process was significantly facilitated in this respect, as a number of these key industries were state monopolies under direct central control with, in many cases, already completed draft-investment programmes. The original plan targets were over-optimistic and were continuously revised downwards, although this is hardly surprising in view of the fact that (1) the data base was extremely poor — there were no national accounts and the most recent production census had been made some fifteen years previously — and, (2) the plan was drafted and operationalised in a period when the rate of inflation was extremely high — prices almost quadrupled between 1946 and 1949 (Liggins, 1975) — leading the planners into a conflict between stabilisation and growth policies. In itself, the First Plan cannot be considered as a unit, as its targets, objectives and content varied considerably over the planning period. Additional basic sectors were added to the range of 'imperative targets', and even the time horizon was extended from the original termination date of 1950, to coincide with the arrangements of the Marshall Aid agreement.

The general aim of the Plan was an overall doubling of industrial production over the 7–8 year period, athough the basic sectors had widely differentiated targets — coal output was to expand by 22 per cent, steel by 28 per cent and oil-refining by 670 per cent (Lutz, 1969) — and the realisation of these figures also varied; by 1953, coal output had reached 90 per cent of its target, whilst oil had over-run by 20 per cent. Of more importance, however, was the fact that, whilst some of the basic sectors had not met their targets for output, they had generally undertaken a considerable expansion of capacity which could render such output possible given the appropriate demand conditions. In this sense, the Plan did actually achieve something, despite the poor performance of the 'indicative forecast' sectors, as it seems likely that this expansion of productive capacity would not have occurred in the absence of a degree of central direction in the economy.

The Second Plan (1954–7) departed from the methods of the First in a number of ways and heralded the second period of planning in France which exended into the mid-1960s. For the first time, an overall growth target was set, accompanied by a wide range of individual targets and forecasts for the major industrial sectors. The economy was required to expand by 25 per cent from its 1952 level, with a heavier emphasis being given to investment rather than consumption, and this Plan may be seen as the first to be concerned with the co-ordination of all sectors of the economy. In terms of realisation, the Second Plan achieved a greater degree of success than the First. Because of the extensive modernisation which had taken place in the basic sectors of the economy under the First Plan, these industries were invariably able to fulfil their planned targets. Moreover, and in spite of their poor performances under the First Plan, manufacturing industries such as textiles and chemicals exceeded their target figures, although agriculture suffered owing to a period of bad weather.

The area in which the Plan manifestly failed was the financial sector. The rapid growth of the economy during the planning period was accompanied by the reappearance of inflationary tendencies and a growing imbalance of payments. These problems had certainly not been foreseen by the planners whose operations had been made inceasingly difficult by the government's decision to take discretionary stabilisation measures. The political climate had, in fact, undergone a considerable change: nonmilitary Marshall Aid had been terminated and, in many cases, the government appeared openly hostile to the principle of planning, preferring instead a series of its own *ad hoc* programs.

These economic and political problems which appeared at the end of the Second Plan meant that the Third (1958−61) inevitably started off under the most unfavourable of conditions. Conceptually, the Third Plan was no different from the Second; it was simply based upon more accurate data and it included a much more detailed industrial and sectoral breakdown. Even during the period of its introduction, it became clear that the economy could not possibly respond in the manner predicted and the government was immediately obliged to take emergency measures (credit control and devaluation) to control the economy. The Third Plan was officially abandoned in 1960 and was replaced by an 'Interim Plan'. In the latter, the growth targets for output, consumption and investment were much more modest, and an increasing inflow of imports was also anticipated. As it happened, however, the French economy experienced a slight recovery at the end of the planning period and, in terms of performance, finished with a set of target achievements midway between the Third and Interim predictions.

The Fourth Plan (1962−5) brought to an end the comprehensive, target-orientated period of French planning. Again, it was of the same basic structure as its two predecessors and, like the Third Plan, ran into the same problems of underestimating the rate of inflation which was to occur and the extent to which imports would exceed exports. It too was abandoned, in 1963, in favour of a government-directed stabilisation policy. Its fundamental problems were common to all the plans of the 1950s — it was only effective in the basic production sectors, it paid little attention to the financial areas of the economy, and it made no allowances for the application of short-term economic policies in the context of medium-term planning. However, the Fourth Plan is particularly important as it marks the transition to the third stage of French planning, a stage at which French planning currently finds itself. It was during the development of the Fourth Plan that the technical aspects of plan construction really became sophisticated, and the degree of detail on which projections were based assumed much higher levels than had been previously attained. In addition, the administrative machinery for plan construction (which we examined earlier) was finally formalised into an embryonic permutation of its present form.

Whilst interest in the French planning experience had waned considerably during the 1950s, it was substantially revived by the Fourth Plan, both at home and abroad. First, the French economy in the early 1960s was much healthier than ever before and France was becoming an important competitor in international markets. In contrast, a number of other Western countries were experiencing increasing economic difficulties after their postwar booms, and they naturally felt that it might be possible to learn from the French planning system. Secondly, the continued development of planning techniques suggested that it might indeed be possible for the economy to be understood and controlled in a fairly precise manner. By the early 1960s, in other words, it seemed that planning in a mixed economy was reaching the status of an exact science, and both these reasons go a long way towards explaining the growing interest in planning which the United Kingdom experienced at the time.

In France too, the volatile political cimate, which had earlier been inimical to the success of plans, was now such that the Fourth Plan came into the limelight, this being partially due to its personal endorsement by De Gaulle.

' "The Plan" now became the subject of almost daily references in the press. It began to be treated as one of the major issues of national economic and political life, and struck a large part of French intellectual opinion with the force of a new religion.' (Lutz, 1969)

It was during the construction and implementation of the Fourth Plan that debate ensued over the requirements for the third stage of French planning. In particular, it was observed that the second-stage plans had generated a number of problems and the resolution of these was to be the framework for the evolution of current French practice. First, it was seen that, whilst the plans invariably performed well when it came to the prediction of the performances of the basic sectors of the economy, such areas as manufacturing and agriculture rarely expanded in the manner anticipated. These were, of course, generally the areas under the least direct central control and their erratic behaviour was exacerbated by the fact that the earlier plans had been essentially supply orientated. The second-stage plans had incorporated few details of demand and consumption patterns and this goes a long way towards explaining their apparent inability to deal with inflation and rising imports. The possibilities of inflation were further disguised by the severely limited account taken of the financial sectors — second-stage French planning had been primarily physical.

Secondly, the Third and Fourth Plans had also foundered because of their inability to come to terms with the possibility of short-term measures being applied in the context of the medium-term plan. A requirement for the third stage of French planning was therefore the incorporation of the inter-relationship of both the short and the long term within the medium-term planning structure.

Thirdly, if the plans were to be integrated development programmes for France, they would have to pay far more attention to the regional and social aspects of the economy. Finally, there was some doubt thrown upon the logic of the planning process as it then stood, and it was here that the influence of Massé (who had been heavily involved in second-stage planning) was particularly felt. There had been growing confusion as to the precise role of 'targets', 'forecasts' and 'predictions' and Massé now attempted to resolve this issue for the benefit of the constructors of the Fifth Plan. Under Massé's 'new look' at French planning (developed in 1963–4), the emphasis on the targets which had been so important in the second-stage plans was played down. Massé emphasised that the Plan should not be considered as a collection of targets but as a totality, which tolerated a variety of deviations from the target figures, on the understanding that the overall trend and balance of economic evolution was maintained. Depending upon priorities, the government might, or might not, undertake corrective action during the plan's operation to maintain particular sectors on their planned path, and this possibility could extend to the public as well as the private sector. Although this point of view was not completely adopted by the French planning bodies, the third stage of planning in France was to be significantly 'softer' than those which preceded it — much less emphasis was placed on the production of single-value targets, and relatively more was placed on the generation of accurate forecasts given a variety of eventualities.

Whilst the Fifth Plan (1966–70) made significant moves in the direction indicated earlier, it is really the Sixth Plan (1971–5) which demonstrates the French planning system in its most up-to-date form, and we shall accordingly review the latter in some detail.

In the same way as we observed in the case of the Fourth Plan, the Sixth began with a review of the long-term developments of the French economy, although the degree of detail and scope of the exercise was beyond comparison with anything previously undertaken. An initial set of projections was made to provide a general indication of the likely expansion of ouput over the next two decades, under a variety of assumptions relating to productivity and population growth. Based upon this, a number of specialised groups were set up to examine possible developments in particular sectors, such as agriculture, housing, energy and consumption.

Whilst the Fourth Plan had gone some way towards the introduction of social and regional variables, the Sixth Plan established formal channels for the incorporation of such material. Within the areas of demography, health, education, standard of living, social costs of growth, and participation in social and economic life, over 400 separate indices were incorporated into the planning framework, On the regional side the SESAME project had been established in 1968 to investigate the operations of the central plan in a regional context. Although SESAME's original brief had been simply the development of implications of the long- and medium-term projects from a regional point of view, it rapidly expanded its role to present a set of 'alternative futures' for the French economy, as far ahead as the year 2000. The project went on to consider all aspects of French evolution — social, economic and political — with the eventual intention of developing a large-scale model for the purpose of computer simulation.

If these innovations of data collection and widening of scope were merely extensions of trends that were inherent in the Fourth Plan, developments from a technical point of view were truly revolutionary. On the one hand, a new methodology of planning — value planning — was introduced and, on the other, a new model of the economy was devised to produce, for the first time, a simulation and forecasting model of the French economy.

Value planning made a brief appearance during the construction of the Fifth Plan, engendered by the failures of the previous plans to come to terms with inflation. The basic idea of value planning was to relate the equilibria in the physical economy with financial flows, largely in a short-run context. As far as the Fifth Plan was concerned, all that was deemed necessary was the inclusion of price forecasts over the short and medium term, but value planning took on an extra dimension with the widespread acceptance of Courbis's theory of the 'competitioned economy'.

Courbis effectively argued that the simple incorporation of a monetary sector into the physical-planning process was insufficient to generate a viable planning model. The key point at issue was whether or not the French economy could be described in a traditional Keynesian manner as the previous generations of planners had believed. Courbis argued that the French economy did not possess Keynesian-type properties and outlined a new theory based upon the following main assumptions (Liggins. 1975).

First, as far as the international sector is concerned, France is a 'competitioned' economy, that is, it contains some industrial sectors which are exposed to international competition and some which, for a variety of reasons, are protected from it. Given the existence of a fixed exchange rate, the behaviour of competitive firms in the exposed sectors is therefore conditioned by the activities of foreign competitors.

Secondly, Courbis assumes that retained profits are the major source of funds for reinvestment, and he justifies this on the basis of empirical research. Thirdly, the growth of wage rises is determined by a Phillips-type relationship and this assumption is necessary to prevent the elimination of an exposed sector by strong competition. With such competition, output will fall, bringing down employment and slowing down wage rises. As labour becomes progressively cheaper, costs and prices can fall and output should expand.

Using Courbis's theory, the French planners were in a better position to understand the balance of payments problems which had beset the second-stage plans, in the same way in which the introduction of general value planning had allowed them to come to grips with the problem of inflation. The main implications of the Courbis theory are as follows: In an exposed sector suffering from increasing foreign competition, we should, at one level, anticipate increased demand for imports owing to their favourable relative price. However, this demand will also be sustained in the medium term as, with competition, the exposed sector's profits and hence reinvestment will also fall. The resulting decline in capacity will make firms unable to meet the buoyant domestic demand with a result that imports will increase over and above the level which the relative price difference would lead us to expect. A stabilisation policy which boosts demand will therefore not increase the output of the exposed sectors of the economy; rather, it will increase the import bill and could even bring about a long-term decline in the exposed sectors. As a corollary, Courbis also noted that protected firms, which are more likely to be oligopolistic price-makers than price-takers, would produce less overall economic benefit from an investment programme, than would the competitive firms in the exposed sectors.

Although a simple Keynesian model had been developed in 1966, its scale and scope were greatly enchanced by the adoption and programming of the Courbis model. By 1968, the final macroplanning model, FIFI, was set to work to construct the Sixth Plan, and consisted of some forty simultaneous equations of the household, production and international sectors.

Whilst the employment of a central model was an innovation to French planning, it was clearly not yet sufficiently sophisticated to serve as the only planning tool. Indeed, even some of its con-structors had some reservations about particular functional forms (in particular, the wage—price—unemployment functions), and the pattern of trade evolving with the EEC made the concept of 'exposed sectors' less clear than it had been when France was to be considered in isolation. The simulations made with FIFI were therefore complemented by retrospective studies and sectoral models.

The forecasts, derived in 1969 using this FIFI class of simula-tions, produced a particularly bleak outlook for France by 1975. It appeared that the balance of payments' deficit would increase, inflation would be maintained (particularly in the protected sec-tors), and the growth rate would not be sufficient to absorb the increase in the available labour force. This information led the

166

planners to undertaking a wide range of policy variant analyses, concentrating particularly upon sensitivity and uncertainty. Whilst the former type of analysis is concerned with the incremental effect of changes in particular control variables, such as the tax rate and the rate of interest, the latter is more concerned with the impact of unforeseen eventualities which could modify not only the variables but also the functional relationships themselves; examples of the latter might be the possibility of more aggressive competitive behaviour on the part of foreign exporters or a change in the distribution of income. From these analyses, it was discovered that the plan was capable of making available the required corrective action to prevent the predicted deterioration of the economy in the absence of such measures.

Having constructed the Plan, the final class of innovations was the development of an extended monitoring and revision system. The Fifth Plan had established a system of 'flashing indicators' which consisted of the monthly analysis of key indices relating to the economy. If, for example, the change in the price level, the excess of imports over exports, or the unemployment rate exceeded certain values for three consecutive months, then this was an indication that corrective action was required. The Sixth Plan, however, made a number of modifications to the original system. First, a distinction was made between those indicators which monitored the attainment of objectives and those indicators which demonstrated changes in the basic assumptions of the model. Secondly, indicators were now to be regarded as passive; that is, certain changes over certain periods were no longer deemed automatically to necessitate corrective action. Finally, the indicators were now calculated quarterly rather than monthly, as the latter were found to be too sensitive for medium-term planning. For practical purposes, it was found that twelve classes of indices could serve the required purposes, including figures for competitive prices, industrial growth, productivity and wage costs.

The role of the indicators as a guide to target revision was taken over in the Sixth Plan by the institutionalisation of annual reviews and economic budgets and, by this means, France went a long way towards resolving the perennial conflict between short-term policies and the medium-term plan. The passive indicators now became incorporated within the general review of the plan's performance with revised forecasts, and the whole was presented annually to the government (in time for the regular Finance Act) which was thereby enabled to take the appropriate action. The new planning structure therefore possessed a high degree of flexibility — policies could be monitored or even modified on a year-to-year basis — and this was an additional reason for the incorporation of sensitivity and uncertainty analyses.

Most of the planning research currently being undertaken in France is orientated towards the expansion and elaboration of the basic models of the economy. FIFI is still insufficiently detailed to describe the economy adequately for the purposes of macroplanning and it is hoped that its successor, FIFITOF, which includes still more relationships from the monetary and social fields, will make the necessary improvements to permit complete value planning. In turn, this project is to be integrated with the REGINA programme (a derivative of SESAME), a macromodel concerned with the regional and social aspects of French economic activity. The ultimate aim of these lines of research is clearly the development of a complex, integrated model of the French economy. Furthermore, work has already commenced on a second generation of macromodels which concentrate their attention on the dynamic short-run effects of economic budgeting.

In conclusion, we therefore see that the French planning process, from the technical point of view, has evolved from the elementary establishment of production targets for basic sectors towards a fully integrated macroplanning model. French planners currently employ all the analytical techniques described in this text (in addition to several which are not!). Whilst the techniques of planning have become increasingly rigorous, the logic of the planning process, if anything, has moved in the opposite direction. With the influence of Massé in the mid-1960s, the French plans have been seen less as a blueprint for economic development and more as a guidebook, and it is possibly in this area of the role of the planning that the planning debate in France is the most protracted. At the opposite extremes are opposed the 'soft' planners who, wishing to return to the liberal, free-enterprise economy, regard their role as the employment of the models to generate collective forecasts of increasing accuracy, and these are arrayed against the 'authentic' planners who wish to see far more centralised control of the economy in order for the plan's targets to be fully realised. Naturally, there exist many shades of opinion in between. At the present time, it is the former school of thought which appears to wield the greater influence, and this position seems likely to be maintained during the development of French planning for the remainder of the 1970s.

PLANNING IN THE SOVIET UNION

The nations of the Eastern communist bloc and, in particular, the Soviet Union, form the sole examples of countries whose long-term economic evolution has been directly managed by macroeconomic planning. If only for this reason, therefore, an appraisal of the historical planning record of an economy such as that of the USSR is particularly interesting when contemplating the practical implications of the more theoretical approach developed in the present text. The Soviet economy is, of course, highly sophisticated and we have already referred to it on numerous occasions. In this section, we simply concentrate upon the most important features of the development of modern Soviet planning methods.

An increased role for the state in the direction of the economy was a major theme in the Bolshevik political programme, and, immediately after the 1917 Revolution, steps were taken to attain this end. Land was nationalised with the right of ownership being conferred upon the peasantry; in a similar manner, industrial enterprises came under the control of their workforces. The free-market system was to be superseded by a form of planning and the Supreme Council of National Economy (*Vesenkha*) was therefore quickly established. *Vesenkha* was to be responsible for the co-ordination of the decisions of individual economic agents, and it was also empowered to impose upon the latter very broad production norms in line with the requirements of centrally determined economic policy.

It is stretching a point, however, to see *Vesenkha* as the first Soviet planning authority as, in truth, there was very little to plan. The First World War, in conjunction with the radical structural changes in the economy effected by the revolution, had left the Soviet Union in a state of devastation, whilst the extreme winter of 1918 brought it to the point of collapse. To complicate these problems, the political situation was to remain fluid for a number of years and recurrent attempts were made to wrest power from the Bolsheviks. Nove (1972) provides us with a graphic sketch of the 1917–21 period, a period usually termed 'war communism':

'A seige economy with a communist ideology. A partly-organised chaos. Sleepless, leather-jacketed commissars working round the clock in a vain effort to replace the free market'.

By 1921, Lenin and the Bolsheviks had established themselves as the new rulers of the Soviet Union. Their power base, however, was exceedingly frail. The rapid drive towards full communism had imposed severe economic and social costs — industrial output was less than one-third, and agricultural output less than two-thirds, of the 1913 figure (Nove 1972). Furthermore, these conditions were producing rumblings of discontent amongst the populace, rumblings which were beginning to take the form of active revolt.

Lenin's 'New Economic Policy' (NEP), which was introduced in 1921, therefore relaxed the commitment to the rapid attainment of full communism; indeed, in many ways, it was a reversal of former economic policy. Under NEP, the role of the market was developed in a number of respects. During the period of 'war communism', the agricultural surpluses of the peasants had been confiscated, but this system was now replaced by taxation, firstly in kind but later in monetary terms. The reintroduction of the money economy was, in fact, another result of NEP. During the immediate post-revolutionary period, resources had been allocated centrally and the workers had been paid in kind. However, production without consideration of costs had brought many industries to a standstill for want of material inputs, and money was now employed as a means of ensuring economic efficiency.

The USSR under NEP was basically a form of mixed economy, with private agricultural and small-scale industrial sectors, large-scale manufacturing being taken over by central control, and this fact is reflected by the planning techniques of the period. *Vesenkha* still retained formal control over the general direction of industry, but it began to find its role being paralleled by *Gosplan*, a body directly responsible to the political leadership. Planning was rudimentary under NEP, if only because economic data were virtually non-existent. Nevertheless, the planners did attempt to construct a broad framework for the analysis of economic structure revolving around forecasts for the major sectors and serving as a guide for investment decisions.

The death of Lenin in 1924 left the Soviet economy at a crossroads. By any form of reckoning, NEP had represented a retreat from communist ideals and Lenin's successors were undecided as to how long this apparent transition period should be allowed to continue. That which took place in the years after Lenin's death is often referred to as the 'Great Debate' as, during this period, the Soviet leaders discussed a wide range of possibilities for future economic prospects (Erlich, 1960). These years of ideological debate (and the concomitant political struggle for the succession to power) are significant for they represent the first major attempt at the rational discussion of the appropriate form of a nation's socio-economic development. All shades of political and economic opinion were represented in the discussions, which centred around the appropriate rate of industrialisation. To mention just four of the principal views: on the one hand, Bukharin favoured the retention of NEP to permit the establishment of a strong agricultural base whilst, on the other, Preobrazhensky argued for high-speed industrialisation under central control, agriculture and private industry being heavily exploited to attain this end; Shanin believed that progress was only possible by the expansion of trade links with the capitalist world, whilst Trotsky was equally concerned with the possibilities of international socialist development.

Within the general debate over strategy, there also rose a discussion regarding the appropriate form of economic planning. In this area, more than any other, the Soviet analysts were working completely in the dark. As the Soviet Union was the first nation to undertake macroplanning in its present form, no external guidance was available and methods had to be developed from first principles. In particular, these principles resolved themselves into two schools of thought, which became know as 'genetic' and 'teleological'. The former was much the more conservative, laying stress upon the prevailing conditions of the economy and making use of NEP-type economic characteristics, such as market forces and relative profitability as an indication of the appropriate distribution of investable resources. The economy was therefore to 'grow naturally', and the plan was to provide a collective forecast and a guide for economic policy. The 'genetic' variant clearly had much in common with the Massé methodology for French planning. In contrast, 'teleological' planning was a much more radical departure; it was forward-looking by its emphasis on the necessity of reconstruction and general structural change, to bring the economy into closer harmony with the prevailing political objective function.

The ideological debates of the 1920s were resolved by the rise to power of Stalin, who was strongly committed to high-speed industrialisation accompanied by the eventual nationalisation of all those means of production which remained in private hands. Such a radical departure from the gradual evolution of the Soviet economy necessitated a commitment to the 'teleological' planning variant which, in itself, implied the development of new planning methods.

The principal techniques formerly employed by *Vesenkha* were now abandoned. These had included the analysis of comparative data from nations in the West, and also the extrapolation of time series; clearly, such studies were more appropriate to the 'genetic' methodology. In their place, decisions about the pattern of economic activity in the 1920s were largely guided by two factors, the 'control figures' and the 'operational plans'. The former were annual target rates of growth for the major industrial sectors, developed by *Gosplan* on the basis of the increasing volume of statistical material which was being collected and, not surprisingly, the highest targets for growth were allocated to capital goods' production. These control figures were, however, simply general guides to development, and short-term policy was effected by the operational plans. These plans were constructed by a two-way consultation process, in theory if not in fact. Plans for the individual plants would be drawn up by the local planning committee and then passed on to *Vesenkha* for co-ordination into an aggregate framework. Each plant's output was therefore determined by the interaction of feasibility (at the local level) and national requirements (at the central level). It must be borne in mind that the administrative machinery of planning was, at this stage, much more impressive than planning performance. Much of the mid-1920s economy was still beyond central control, and there existed little possibility of enforcing targets in any but the basic industrial sectors which had been nationalised at an earlier stage.

In spite of the progressive modification of the planning methods, planning in the Soviet Union was still not 'macroeconomic' at this point in time. True, an aggregate fifteen-year programme had been drawn up in 1920, followed by a 1934 five-year scenario devised by *Gosplan*, although neither had been accepted as official policy by the political leadership. With the entrenchment of Stalin, however, the whole operation of a planned economy was reappraised and this led to the formulation of the consolidated First Five-Year Plan (Carr and Davies, 1974).

Discussions relating to the nature of the First Plan began in 1926 and continued until the acceptance of the final version in 1929. Considering that macroplanning was a relatively new innovation, the planning document was remarkably sophisticated. Comprising some 1,700 pages, the Plan was divided into a number of major sections. In a sense, it was 'two plans in one' as it began with a review of two alternative strategies. In simple terms, these might be described as the 'optimum' variant (developed on the assumptions that the vagaries of fortune were favourable, such as good harvests, industrial cost reductions and trade expansion), and the 'basic' variant, a more modest proposal. The actual plan to be followed therefore depended upon historical circumstances. After this general survey, more detail was devoted to particular problems, such as labour productivity, consumption, pricing policy and trade.

The core of the Plan was composed of three elements. First, there was a detailed breakdown of economic activity by sector, to indicate the particular performances required by each individual agent. Secondly, plans were outlined for social development (education, health etc.) and the desirable distribution of economic rewards amongst members of the population. Finally, the entire Plan was restructured on a regional basis, to indicate the expected contribution of each particular geographical area of the Soviet Union.

The policy measures which went hand in hand with the First Plan during its period of implementation are nowadays regarded by most commentators as so extreme as to preclude consideration when discussing modern planning methods. History, nevertheless, suggests that they did occur. The major measure applied to agriculture was forced collectivisation and the anguish imposed upon the peasantry is legendary (Lewin, 1968). Similarly, in the industrial sectors, forced savings and extensive limitations of the social goods and consumption sectors (both necessary to finance the massive investment drive) imposed tremendous human costs. Against this has to be placed the considerable achievements of the Plan. National income almost doubled within five years, and gross industrial output increased by two and one-half times, although these totals conceal wide disparities amongst individual sectors. Agricultural performance, not surprisingly, fell far below the planned level, although substantial inroads were made into unemployment. Nove (1966) ascribes this latter success to 'accident' rather than planning; as targets had been set at an unrealistically high level, plant managers were obliged to employ more and more labour in order to attempt Plan fulfilment.

The Second Plan (1933–37) was constructed along similar lines to the First, although its approach was a little less austere — the costs of the former extreme policies had been appreciated and more care was now taken to avoid going 'too far, too fast'.

173

Notwithstanding, income and output again doubled, with an improved performance being registered by the agricultural sector. It is from this period that we observe the establishment of the 'command' economy, which was to become the primary method of economic organisation for the next three decades.

Although we have already discussed the central features of the command economy in Chapter 2, it is as well to re-emphasise one or two salient features of the system in view of its importance.

	$T-2$	$T-1$	T	$T+1$	$T+2$	$T+3$ etc.
SOURCES OF INPUTS						
For *each* of the firm's inputs, volumes are recorded by origins:	Recorded figures		Expected figures		Target levels	
(i) From other producers						
(ii) Imports						
(iii) Stocks already held						
(iv) Other sources						
DISTRIBUTION OF OUTPUT	All entities measured in *physical* units, e.g. weight of coal, lengths of pipe, volume of oil.					
(i) To other producers						
(ii) Capital construction						
(iii) Exports						
(iv) Market sales						
(v) Accumulation of stocks						
(vi) To state reserves						
(vii) Other users						

Figure 6.1   *Material balance for a firm producing a given commodity in year T*. Adapted from Ellman (1971).

First, the allocation mechanism of the command economy was that of 'material balances' and Figure 6.1 presents a hypothetical balance in schematic form. Balances were clearly accounting devices, measuring the required inputs and outputs of particular industries or plants in terms of physical resources, the national planning framework being developed from these individual balances.

The material-balance approach always possessed a number of potential disadvantages: it did not provide a complete picture of the economy as many forms of activity were not appropriate to quantification in such a manner; problems of integration and consistency would occur when individual balances were aggregated; the influences of technological and productivity advances were not made explicit. Nevertheless, material-balance planning *was* extremely effective in developing the production-goods sector, whose outputs and inputs *could* be accurately described in such a manner, and this, of course, was the goal with the highest priority in the range of policy objectives at the time. The planning mechanism was, in other words, largely appropriate to the desired policy outcomes.

Secondly, and following from the above, the command economy in the USSR during this period is remarkable for its explicit and firm statement of the objective function with which to operate; as we have seen, coherent planning can only occur in a situation where aims are unequivocally stated and supported. The monolithic social preference for high-speed industrialisation was undoubtedly due to the extraordinary personal power of Stalin.

Between the 1920s and the 1950s, the methods of Soviet planning altered little. Material balances provided the mainstay of the development and fulfilment of objectives and targets, and the economy continued to grow at an unprecedented rate. After the death of Stalin, however, significant changes occurred in Soviet economic thinking. The economy was becoming exceedingly complex, which meant that the centralised planning agencies were becoming unwieldy and progressively less receptive to variations in patterns of demand and supply. As the growth priority became relatively less important, an interest in consumption goods began to evolve, although the forecasting of these was difficult to incorporate into the material-balance framework. In addition, the increasing liberality of the social and political regime, coupled with exposure to Western ideas, permitted Soviet planners to explore two major areas in order to improve the existing planning process. It is interesting to note, by the way, that these ideas had been conceived many years before their official introduction, an illustration of the belief that innovations only take place 'when the time is right'.

The first reform of planning to be considered occurred in the field of economic management. Although the command system had proved itself effective in producing high rates of growth, its limitations were becoming increasingly manifest. The material-balances approach emphasised gross physical production and used physical indicators as a guide to the success of enterprises. This had led to a lack of pressure on producers to provide the appropriate range of commodities actually demanded by the market. In addition, no account was taken of quality, and, furthermore, it was clearly in the interests of enterprise managers to conceal productive capacity in order to be allocated easier targets to fulfil. Finally, the system ignored the desirability of the efficient use of intermediate inputs; all that mattered was the ultimate physical output.

Evsai Liberman had first put forward proposals for the introduction of a new management system in the late-1940s, but he did not succeed in arousing significant interest until the publication of a paper in *Pravda* in 1962 (Nove and Nuti, 1972). Within three years, the principles of Liberman's proposals had been accepted as official Soviet planning policy.

Quite simply, the Liberman reforms required the reintroduction of a form of profit as a motivation for efficient economic management. Whilst the overall economic strategy was to remain the province of the central planning authorities, the individual enterprise was now to be given much greater freedom in many spheres of activity, such as the purchase of inputs and the use of resources. Success was now to be measured, not by physical output, but by profitability — total revenue less total cost as a proportion of fixed and working capital. To encourage efficiency, an incentive payment scheme was to be applied, the size of the payment being an increasing function of profitability.

Liberman believed that such a system would significantly ease the problems of the central planners in ensuring efficient production:

'In order to achieve a high level of profitability, an enterprise must strive to place the fullest load on equipment and capacity when working out plans under our conditions and at plan prices (after all, profits will be computed as a percentage of capital!). This means it will be in the enterprises' interests to increase the number of shifts and the load on existing equipment, to stop asking for excess capital investments and machine tools and creating unneeded reserves. While all these surpluses now serve the enterprises almost as a free reserve, under the new system they would 'drain the pockets' by cutting down the size of the incentive payments.

Consequently, the 'struggle' waged by an enterprise to obtain lower plan figures would disappear. After all, such plan figures would never give the enterprise a sufficiently high level of profitability.' (Nove and Nuti, 1972)

As Liberman recognised, a major requirement for the successful implementation of the profits scheme was the rationalisation of pricing. Without centrally planned prices, firms could potentially exploit the consumers in the same way, it was argued, as they did under a monopoly capitalist regime. In addition, prices must permit profitability in all areas of production, to discourage firms from concentrating their efforts on the most profitable of commodities at the neglect of others. In practice, the pricing problem was solved by the 'two-tier' pricing system: At the first level, all enterprises operate under the criterion of 'producer prices'. These are centrally determined on the basis of planned industrial requirements and it is these prices which are a determinant of the firm's total revenue. Clearly, if the planners wish to encourage production of a particular commodity, they need only increase the producer price and profitability is raised. Under the incentive system, expansion should follow automatically. 'Retail prices', on the other hand, are again centrally determined, but this time with regard to the appropriate market-clearing conditions of supply and demand; the difference between these two price levels is made up of a 'turnover tax' which could, of course, be negative.

The direct control of the price level has therefore become a key policy instrument in the Soviet Union. By the setting of prices for producers, the planners should ensure that the desired level and range of commodities are produced. In addition, the setting of the retail price levels should ensure the clearance of the market, the difference between the two providing revenue for central government. Note that the Soviet Union has therefore made a conscious decision to substitute an indirect control (output expansion via incentives) for a direct one (the central fixing of production targets) such that the system has become a little less 'imperative'. As in all cases of the choice of controls, the decision to make this change rested partially on an assessment of the relative efficiency of the two methods, a constituent of which is the cost of information inputs (high in the direct control case).

The second major area of reform is that of planning techniques although, again, the basic concepts had been in existence for a long time.

177

Gosplan had constructed a prototype input–output table in 1926, but the prevailing political climate was antagonistic towards mathematical techniques. As Treml *et al.* (1972) have observed:

'In a 1929 speech, Stalin contemptuously dismissed the Gosplan exercise as "not a balance of the national economy but a game with figures", and soon thereafter many statisticians and planners associated with the balance studies disappeared in the Gosplan purge.'

After the death of Stalin, input–output analysis re-emerged as a vital technical tool, in its modern form as developed in the USA by Leontief. The first Soviet tables were constructed for 1959 and development has continued to date. In a sense, input–output is a logical progression of the material-balance approach, although it now provides an integrated portrait of the economy rather than a review of loosely related sectors. In addition, value-accounting techniques and the 'final-demand' sector are embodied, factors which are particularly relevant to the contemporary Soviet system. The Soviet tables are not only impressive in terms of the degree of detail provided by disaggregation, but also in terms of the additional analyses carried out on the basic matrix, such as the estimation of technical coefficients and sensitivity variants for dynamic programming.

The Stalinist reliance upon the Five-Year Plans has now been superseded by an integrated structure of plans for a variety of periods. Long-range plans and projections for fifteen to twenty years have been constructed, which are particularly concerned with demographic patterns and the prediction of changes in the world economy. The medium-term Five-Year Plans are now embodied within this framework, giving matters a more concrete form and specifying in detail the planned course of domestic economic events in much the same way as before. Such plans now provide the essential guidelines for One-Year Plans, the central government's immediate plan of action. It is this level at which economic control is applied and such plans therefore perform a similar role to the French annual budgets. Of crucial importance is the fact that all these forms of planning are not mutually exclusive, but operate in concert to chart the course of development.

The culmination of Soviet planning methodology is to be found in the work of the Central Economic Mathematical Institute and, in particular, in the theories of Kantorovich (Ellman, 1971). These ideas have come into prominence over the past ten to fifteen years and are still the subject of debate. On the basis of the institutional reforms which have been carried out in the Soviet Union, Kantorovich believes that it is now possible to generate an optimally functioning economy by the general application of optimising techniques (essentially linear programming) to a partially decentralised system, the functional relationships of which are well understood by virtue of input–output and other statistical techniques.

To conclude, we see that the technical apparatus of the Soviet planning machinery bears a remarkable resemblance to its French counterpart which we reviewed in the previous section, and both nations have clearly learned from one another. As in the French case, Soviet planning makes use of all the techniques with which we have dealt, although we can detect some difference in relative emphasis; Soviet planning generally makes less use of econometric models as there is less probabilistic individual action occurring within the economy. The main data base is therefore the input–output table and its dynamic extensions, whilst the opposite tends to be true of the current French situation.

Our belief in the unity of planning is therefore reaffirmed by a consideration of the practical methods of the two most advanced nations — advanced in the sense of their possessing highly sophisticated planning procedures. Neither, however, has yet taken the final step towards complete optimal planning as we have envisaged it (as, indeed, has Kantorovich), and it remains to be seen whether total, integrated planning will ever become a reality, particularly in the Soviet Union whose economic and political structure is so well suited to it.

CHAPTER 7

Conclusions

Once a particular plan has been constructed and implemented, it might appear at first sight to be reasonable to ask — how successful was the plan? We believe that, in this context, the interpretation of the word 'success' is of crucial importance.

First, it seems eminently sensible to ask — how close was the correspondence between the actual outcomes of the policies implemented, and their predicted outcomes, based upon simulations and extrapolation? For example, if the particular target level for unemployment was 3 per cent and this was realised, then the plan must be counted as a 'success'; conversely, realised levels of 10 or even 1 per cent must be viewed as various degrees of 'failure'. Given the complexities of modern economies and the imperfections in data and models with which real-world planners are obliged to work, we should not really expect to see any one plan fulfil its targets exactly: as we have observed, even the sophisticated methods of France and the Soviet Union have yet to achieve total success in this respect. Nevertheless, the reasons for the possible 'failures' of particular areas of a plan are, in themselves, of great relevance to the planners' calculations for subsequent planning attempts, as they represent an increase in knowledge as regards the actual functioning of the economy. An essential element in the construction of the new plan is therefore a post-mortem of the old, in order to highlight false assumptions, incorrect equation specifications, inaccurate data, and so forth.

In a second sense, however, we regard it as unreasonable to judge a plan's success *vis-à-vis* alternative strategies which could have been implemented at that particular point in time. Whilst it might sometimes be clear, with the benefit of hindsight, that the pursuit of a different plan would have produced a 'better' state of affairs, this possibility does not entitle us to say that the chosen plan was sub-optimal. To illustrate with a rural example, consider the choice between planting a variety of corn, A, which yields 100 tonnes/ha in good weather, but is completely ruined by frost, and a second variety, B, which yields 75 tonnes/ha whether frost occurs

180

or not. Since we are unlikely to be able to do more than assign probabilities to the occurrence of different possible weather conditions, then however elaborate our analysis of attitudes towards risk and our knowledge of welfare levels engendered by crops of different volumes, it is quite conceivable that our outcome will be inferior to that of a different plan. If we had assigned a 99 per cent probability to frost occurring, variety B would probably have been planted, although this does not preclude the one-in-one-hundred chance from paying off; 1 per cent of the time there will be no frost and it will appear that we have planted the wrong corn. As optimal planning is a quesion of making the best possible policy in a given situation at that point in time, a plan cannot be blamed for an *ex post* failure if it were potentially the most successful *ex ante*. Conceiving of success in these terms, it is not a question of whether or not frost occurred, but rather one of whether or not our chosen plan embodied the best available information about crops and weather conditions. Given that this was the case, then clearly the correct variant was chosen although, as we have seen, the selection of the potentially most successful plan does not preclude the possibility of its failure in its own terms.

To summarise, given the maximum available information, under optimal planning a 'best' plan can always be chosen although it need not inevitably fuflfil its targets. Statements to the effect that, in the light of subsequent events, an alternative strategy would have been more successful than the one actually chosen are simple applications of retrospection and counter-factual history which, although entertaining are of dubious intellectual validity.

Figure 7.1 presents a theoretical synthesis of the concepts and inter-relationships which we have explored during the course of the text, and it accordingly forms a summary of the planning process as we see it. For the sake of simplicity, this model considers only a discrete plan, although it is clear that dynamic planning involves the continual consolidation of such individual plans.

As may be seen, the 'prime movers' of the model are a set of properties of the economy which constitutes *economic reality* and a corresponding set which constitutes *individual preferences*. Each member of society will assess the likely evolution of the contemporary economy in the light of his own subjective preferences. An aspect of a particular individual's thinking might therefore be represented as follows: 'On the basis of the present progress of the economy, per capita output will be £X in 1990, whilst I

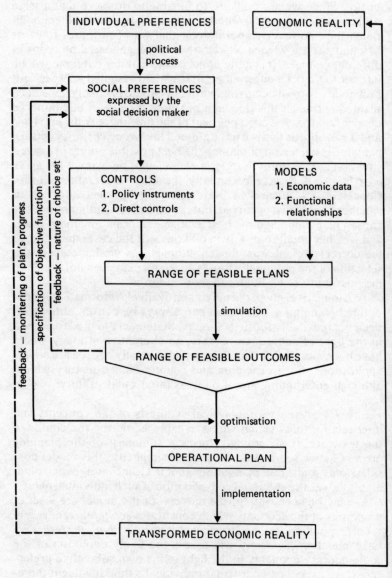

Figure 7.1 *A model of the planning process.*

should prefer a higher figure of £Y; steps should therefore be taken to assess the feasibility of such an increase and, if possible, the direction of economic evolution should be correspondingly altered'. Note that, in the real world, each individual's preferences are not articulated directly but are manifested via the medium of a corporate body such as the state or the government; individual choices are aggregated into *social preferences* by a means of a particular form of political process, such as a social contract or a voting system. It is these social preferences which will dictate whether purposeful redirection of the economy is desirable.

In the planning context, a primary function of social preferences is the specification of the acceptable scope, range and values of economic *controls* with which to influence economic reality. Again from the planning point of view, the practical aspects of the process will not concern themselves with reality as such but with *models* of that reality, in terms of the data relating to particular variables and the functional relationships which explain their interaction. Taken together, models and controls can be combined to produce a *range of feasible plans*, the attainment of which is technically possible given the constraints of current economic reality.

From this range, simulation exercises may be performed to produce a *range of feasible outcomes*, each outcome being logically derived from its plan counterpart. At this stage, this range must be 'fed back' to the social decision maker who will provide guidance to the planners as to which of the general outcomes is the most desirable. Given the objective function, the planners may narrow down their range of plans and, by optimisation techniques, produce the ultimate *operational plan*.

During the implementation of the final plan, information feedback will occur continuously to permit the authorities to monitor the plan's progress; control measures can therefore be applied to maintain the plan on target or even to modify its performance if social preferences or external influences so dictate. The eventual implication of the operational plan is the creation of a *transformed economic reality* which becomes, of course, a new economic reality and we may therefore see the process as beginning again. Again, a comparison will be made between the direction being followed by the new economic reality and social preferences to establish whether further planning is required; having observed what was and is happening, society might again decide to redirect the course of its future.

As we have envisaged it, the mechanisms of macroeconomic planning appear to be a particularly sensible way of ensuring the rational allocation of economic resources. Indeed, as we have seen, a number of nations already make extensive use of such a system in the management of their economies. The fact remains, however, that several major countries do not appear to be at all keen to undertake macroeconomic planning, and the United Kingdom is one of these. In many ways, this is surprising. After the Second World War, the conditions for planning in the UK were most favourable — there was a high degree of political consensus, state control of the economy was expanding, a socialist government was in power and the French were also developing their early planning experiments — yet no consolidated plan appeared until 1965. As this attempt appeared to be a total failure, it was abandoned within one year of inauguration and we have since seen no desire on the part of any major political party to repeat the exercise. The final question to be answered is therefore — if planning is such a good idea, why do the United Kingdom and other countries not use it more extensively?

A possible reason for the apparent distrust of planning might be found in the area of what could be termed 'planning technology'. A major advantage claimed for the free-market system by its proponents is the fact that it requires only a minimum amount of information on which to operate, that which flows between the individual parties involved in the transactions of the Walrasian auction. In contrast, centralised planning will require a tremendous volume of detailed knowledge about economic variables and their inter-relationships in order to allocate resources on a discretionary, rather than an automatic, basis. For many of the earlier theorists, this particular problem was sufficient to prove a conclusive case against operational planning, In the first place, it was argued, the necessary information simply did not exist and, secondly, even if it did, processing techniques were not available to rapidly translate data into policies — by the time all the production decisions had been collected, for example, the world would have changed and these responses would therefore be inappropriate. Finally, there exists the problem of the 'curse of dimensionality' which, put crudely, suggests that the problems of consolidation and management of data increase more than proportionately with the quantity of data collected.

In recent years, advances in the techniques of data processing have largely invalidated such objections. In terms of the data themselves, the planning bodies of most modern economies now have a large volume of statistics at their disposal and this quantity is growing all the time, for information agencies are being continuously created. Furthermore, the methods by which such data are translated into models have been revolutionised by developments in computer technology; modern machines can now perform policy simulations on large-scale econometric models in a matter of seconds, whilst detailed input–output matrices can be inverted in minutes. This resultant speed of analysis and degree of detail is certainly an important contributory factor towards the belief of those analysts such as Kantorovich who argue that sufficient information currently exists, and the economy is so structured, that an optimally functioning economic system can be designed and managed.

Given the accelerating progress of economic method, we feel it unlikely that those imperfections in data processing which must still exist are the principal factor mitigating against the more widespread adoption of macroeconomic planning. The real key to the problem seems to lie in the following observation by Myrdal (1960):

'While in the Western countries the trend towards planning is certainly not a danger for democracy, there is more truth in the converse proposition. A democracy . . . can, in certain of its manifestations, endanger, or at least postpone, the fullest rationality of planning.'

To our minds, it is this inter-relationship between planning and democracy which provides the answer to our question and we therefore turn our attention to an examination of (1) those features of the democratic political process which raise problems for the planners, and (2) those features of the planning process which could be seen as incompatible with the ideology of democracy.

The choice of an optimal plan has been characterised in previous chapters as a process in which 'neutral' technicians apply knowledge of social preferences to discriminate between alternative feasible plans. Whilst it was suggested that the range of plans to be considered may well be influenced by the ideological tenets of the society in question, little mention has so far been made of the very serious difficulties that may attend the choice of plan in a country with a 'democratic' political system. In order to examine these difficulties, it is necessary to abstract somewhat from the details of particular political systems, for 'democratic' is a widely used adjective. The economic theorists, notably Downs, who have concerned themselves with the investigation of political structures, have in most instances developed models of democracy in which periodic voting establishes which party is to rule for the following period. The other central assumption usually made is that the political parties that inhabit these democracies act purely on the basis of their own self-interest.

The main problem in this context is that voting systems based upon simple majorities may give rise to the possibility of significant periodic changes in the social-welfare function with which the planner is to work. Even very small changes in the proportion of votes attracted by different parties in successive elections may mean a change of ruling party and thus a change in the declared ends of economic policy. This issue may be approached in a number of ways. In the following paragraphs, we concentrate first on the implications of significant changes in effective preferences for the choice of plan and, secondly, on the suggestion that a key element of democracy is the dialogue that takes place between government and individual citizens (or groups of citizens) *after* the election. This element is ignored by the normal social-choice models from which social preferences are derived, and, to a lesser extent, by the Downsian-type economic theory of democracy. In the idealised context with which we have been dealing, these essentially dynamic elements were ignored; we were considering a world in which preferences were expressed once and for all, and in which the government acted purely in the light of these preferences. Moving from the idealised world to the more pragmatic one provides a set of reasons for the relative scarcity of serious attempts at planning in democracies. After the discussion of the relation between democratic political structures and the choice of plan, the final stage will be concerned with the more general controversy that surrounds the postulate of there being a basic conflict between state and individual. First, however, there are the two more technical issues that may complicate the role of the planner.

It has been assumed that the planner is given a clear idea of what social preferences are, and that from these he is able to construct a criterion with which to judge alternative available plans. Social preferences do, however, change through time in most societies, and, particularly in countries that have more than one party, it is likely that such changes will occur as spasmodic, discrete shifts in the goals being pursued by government. Whilst individual preferences may change gradually, political institutions are likely to be such that the pattern of *aggregate* preferences is only ascertained from time to time. In the UK, for example, elections are scheduled to occur once every five years, although there are provisions for the ruling party to be brought down within this period or for it to call an election should it so wish before the term has elapsed. This may be interpreted as a situation in which the social-welfare function proposed by the winning party in an election will form the basis for decisions made in the subsequent five years, irrespective of changes in the structure of individual preferences. A different function (proposed by either the ruling party or an opposition party) will be substituted five years later, after the next election. If, however, it is assumed that the central objective of political parties is to be in power for as much of the time as possible, it may be found that the ruling party will superimpose some additional values of its own upon its professed aims and inform the planner of the new, modified pattern of objectives rather than simply the package it purported to be offering to the electorate. Since the winning party at an election will only really be concerned with the following five years, it may be expected that this will, for example, make it more myopic than it would be if it were to be elected for a longer period. The longer-term consequences of different plans are thus likely to be ignored or at least undervalued, and in addition, unduly favourable weight may well be assigned to events or consequences that occur shortly before the next election.

In the case of stabilisation policy, lags may assume a particular importance because policies that offer a smoother path today may well offer a much more volatile path tomorrow and vice versa. Thus if a reduction in unemployment does not lead to an immediate rise in the price level but rather to a rise in the price level at some later stage, then it is most likely that one would find expansionary policies being implemented in the latter part of a government's life, since the impending costs are neglected but the immediate improvement is exploited. In the case of growth policy, unless the government is already confident of winning the next election or of getting credit for pursuing a particular growth strategy, it might be expected that government will give less weight to growth than stabilisation simply because the latter is likely to offer more spectacular opportunities for government action. In the case of both types of policy, the structure of the political system will be expressed through the objective function; if governments are short lived, then greatest weight will be assigned to events in the near future whilst, if governments are longer lived, then a longer-term view is likely to even out the pattern of weights to be assigned. Analytical investigation of the case in which governments are deliberately myopic have only recently begun in earnest (Nordhaus, 1975), although more intuitive discussion about cycles in which there is a pre-electoral expansion has been going on for a long time. It is the nature of political institutions that leads to these difficulties, the choice of an optimal plan being constrained by these exigencies but otherwise proceeding in precisely the same way as before.

Rather than argue that social preferences are adjusted for the inclinations of the ruling party and then used as a consistent criterion, some authors (for example, Buchanan, 1954) have argued that it is important to examine the ways in which government policy comes to be modified as a result of pressures put upon government *between* elections. The key element in this different approach is the suggestion that the notion of deriving a social preference ordering from time to time and acting accordingly runs counter to the ways in which democracies may be seen to work. Compromise, discussion and the formation of interest groups to press for particular policies are advanced as the important constituents of models in which government is viewed as a device for enabling a whole series of individual decisions to be made or issues to be resolved; emphasis is put on the processes by which decisions during the life of a government are made, the more grandiose attempts of theorists such as Arrow (1951) being rejected as unhelpful. Economic planning cannot play much of a role in Buchanan's democratic world because, at least implicitly, it is assumed that large-scale systematic government activity will be absent.

Much of the work by economists on democracy suggests very little scope for planning of the kind that has been outlined in the previous chapters. This could be taken to imply either that the models of democracy are mis-specified, in that they give too much prominence to the forces of compromise or to the degree of myopia with which governments operate, or that democracy is intrinsically incompatible with planning. The implications for our analysis of planning are that we should either abandon any attempt to apply the methodology in a Western context or otherwise look more closely at the decision-making processes that are actually used in the construction of plans. The suggestion that there is something fundamental to democracy that makes planning an unacceptable activity is hardly a recent one. Liberal theorists have been arguing for a very long time that planning may be in conflict with the freedom of the individual and is thus to be resisted.

Our second line of enquiry into the failure of a number of countries to wholeheartedly adopt the strategy of planning is therefore via their underlying political philosophies. We have already seen (Chapter 3) that some theorists believe that the only valid role which may be deduced for the state is a minimalist one, being restricted to the provision of public goods and the correction of market imperfections. We may term this philosophy 'economic liberalism' and, from the planning point of view, it raises two related problems.

The first axiom of such liberalism may be taken to be the belief that the function of society is the maximisation of the individual's liberty, subject to the constraint of the non-restriction of similar liberties on the part of other members of society:

'This fundamental notion that the essence of humanity is the capacity to choose, and not simply the ability to reason clearly, implies that individuals must be granted the widest possible freedom of choice (and with it a corresponding responsibility) if they are to develop their capacities. Coercion of some individuals by others can only be justified as a means of resolving conflicts between the choices of individuals and even then must be minimised in the process of conflict resolution. The essence of liberalism is freedom, therefore, not as an instrument, or even as a human preference, but as an ethical value in itself.' (Rowley and Peacock, 1975)

Society must accordingly provide its members with an unrestricted range of options from which to choose in terms of, say, nature of occupation, contract and consumption. Furthermore, the second axiom of this ideology is the non-existence of objective truth and it is therefore left to the individual's rationality and conscience to determine the appropriate course of action.

'For liberals ...believe that a good society is one that is uncertain of its truths and dedicates itself, not to an ideal, but to an eternal search.' (ibid)

This, in turn, implies that society must allow its members to run the

189

risk of making the 'wrong' decision for, by definition, it is preferable to permit this state of affairs rather than to force individuals to
take the 'right' action.

'For liberals, fallibility and the right to err are viewed as
necesssary corollaries to the capacity for self-improvement;
symmetry and finality are mistrusted as enemies of freedom, and
truth is viewed as many-sided.' (ibid.)

In its extreme form, liberalism deals two body-blows to our
methodology of planning. In the first place, because no objective
truth can be defined and because we possess no method of comparing one individual's preferences with those of another, we must
immediately rule out the possibility of being able to generate a
social objective function which is the cornerstone of plan construction. Secondly, we must also exclude the possibility of government
control of the economy for a similar reason; the state has no
objective criteria upon which to base its operations, operations
which could, furthermore, inhibit the primary objective of individual liberty.

In the real world, such extreme liberalism is really a non-starter.
Most theorists, and all modern societies, permit some role for
collective action and, as we have seen (Chapter 2), there are good
grounds for believing that such a system gives rise to a preferable
form of economic organisation. Similarly, societies do make rules
which they take to be criteria for the 'right' choices to be made by
individuals such that freedom of action becomes limited — people
are therefore generally discouraged from slaughtering one another
or from filling their bodies with debilitating drugs. The real point at
issue is therefore the amount of individual liberty to be sacrificed,
because macroeconomic planning is sure to demand a sacrifice of
some sort. It would clearly be a gross oversimplification to generalise at this juncture as each social system will differ on its conception of the 'proper' degree of liberty (and, indeed, on its appropriate definition of the term). Taking a few examples from the UK, we
find that, whilst members of society are happy to have their marginal consumption decisions affected by government policy, they do
not wish to see the output mix being totally determined by state
institutions as in the USSR. Again, whilst they do not mind being
induced to migrate, they appear to resent the idea of being forced
into a particular region or type of employment.

Human liberty is such an important and enormous subject that it might appear presumptuous to treat it in just a few paragraphs. Whilst we accept that political philosophers will undoubtedly inform us that we have not come to grips with the concept at all, let us simply reaffirm our point — given that planning involves collective action, the existence of individual welfare functions which contain a significant element of individual freedom of action must precipitate a potential conflict which is only reconcilable in terms of the particular social system concerned.

In our conclusions, we have suggested that the major obstacles to macroeconomic planning are political and philosophical. We have not attempted to resolve them for, as was observed before, this is a text on planning principles and not a treatise on political morality. With respect to these latter problems, which we accept are of the utmost significance, might it be suggested that the reader draws his own conclusions, thereby relieving the authors of a terrible responsibility.

ADDITIONAL READING

As the persevering reader will by now have realised, this text is somewhat eclectic, having attempted to force what is a very large subject into a fairly small space. The great diversity of the aspects of the planning problem has made a selective approach unavoidable. In an effort to provide a partial remedy, we append a number of representative works which deal with particular areas in more depth.

General. There exist a number of books which cover the same general area as the present text, although they naturally differ in the degree of emphasis placed upon particular issues: Cole (1937), Myrdal (1960), Mitchell (1966), Faber and Seers (1972). For an advanced treatment, see Heal (1973).

Planning is, of course, very much a 'live' political issue and has attracted a great deal of attention from polemicists. The debate has included the contributions of von Hayek (1935, 1944), Lange and Taylor (1938), Wootton (1945), Meade (1948), Jewkes (1948), Durbin (1949), Lewis (1949) and Rowley and Peacock (1975). The early planning debates in the Soviet Union are covered by Erlich (1960).

Planning theory. Many formative ideas on the theory of planning are presented in Tinbergen (1952) and Theil (1958). Such ideas have been developed by Meade (1970) and Friedman (1975), whilst

Ward (1967), Ellman (1971) and Nove and Nuti (1972) are particularly concerned with planning theory in a socialist context.

Theory of markets. A central building-block of our work was the analysis of market failure in capitalist economies. The functioning of the market system is most elegantly discussed in Debreu (1959) and Arrow and Hahn (1971). The allied analyses of welfare economics and general equilibrium may be found in such texts as Winch (1971), Weintraub (1973) and Green (1976), whilst Quirk and Saposnik (1968) provides a significantly more advanced treatment.

Social choice and preferences. The volume of papers edited by Phelps (1973) provides a coverage of many of the central issues. Arrow (1951), Sen (1970) and Mayston (1974) are particularly concerned with the relationships between individual preferences and social choice. Barry (1970) and Breton (1974) explore the relations between individual preferences and social decision making in a more practical context. Mueller (1976) also surveys a number of the relevant issues.

Techniques. Many of the basic mathematical techniques used in planning may be found in a standard mathematical economics text, such as Black and Bradley (1973) or Chiang (1974) which is more comprehensive. More sophisticated methods are discussed by Gale (1960) and Lancaster (1968).

For a discussion of the problems of economic data, Stone (1951) and Morgenstern (1963) may be profitably consulted.

Standard texts on the methods of input−output analysis include Miernyk (1965) and Cameron (1968). For particular applications, refer to Gossling (1970) on the United Kingdom, Treml *et al*. (1972) on the Soviet Union, and Richardson (1972) for regional analysis.

The basic theory of econometrics is covered by Wonnacott and Wonnacott (1970) or Allard (1974), whilst Wallis (1973) and Wynn and Holden (1974) develop a more applied approach. Macroeconomic models are discussed at length in Fromm and Taubman (1968), Worswick and Blackaby (1974) and Renton (1975). For criticism of the econometric approach, refer to Renton (1975) and Streissler (1970).

The central set of mathematical techniques used in optimisation is discussed at length in Theil (1964), Chiang (1974), Friedman (1975), Baumol (1977) and Dorfman, Samuelson and Solow (1958).

The particular problems of growth optimisation are discussed in Solow (1970) and Phelps (1966), whilst stabilisation is covered by Shaw (1972). Optimisation under uncertainty is dealt with by Luce and Raiffa (1957) and Green (1976).

Planning practice. For a discussion of planning experiences in France, the principal sources are Lutz (1969) and Liggins (1975), whilst for the United Kingdom see Brunner (1965), Polanyi (1967), Leruez (1975) and, of course, the Department of Economic Affairs (1965, 1969). For methods of economic policy and control, which are generally applicable to most capitalist economies, refer to Shaw (1971), Rowan (1974) or Peston (1974).

Economic policy and planning in the Soviet Union is dealt with by Kaser (1970), Csikós-Nagy (1973), Nove (1972) and Wilczynski (1970, 1973).

Although we have not formally discussed planning in 'Third World' countries, there is a substantial literature devoted to their particular problems: a basic text is Tinbergen (1967). Amongst such nations, India has a long planning history, described by Hanson (1966), Myrdal (1968), Streeten and Lipton (1968) and Shenoy (1971).

BIBLIOGRAPHY

Ackley, G. (1961) *Macroeconomic Theory* (London: Macmillan).

Alchian, A. A. (1950) 'Uncertainty, evolution and economic theory', *Journal of Political Economy*, vol. 58, pp. 211–21.

Allard, R. J. (1974) *An Approach to Econometrics* (Oxford: Philip Allan).

Arrow, K. J. (1951) *Social Choice and Individual Values* (New York: Wiley).

Arrow, K. J. (1959) 'Toward a theory of price adjustment' in M. Abramowitz (ed.), *The Allocation of Economic Resources* (Stanford, Calif.: Stanford University Press).

Arrow, K. J. (1962) 'Economic welfare and the allocation of resources for invention' in R. R. Nelson (ed.), *The Rate and Direction of Inventive Activity*, pp. 609–26. (Princeton, NJ: Princeton University Press).

Arrow, K. J. (1967) 'Values and collective decision-making' in P. Laslett and W. G. Runciman (eds), *Philosophy, Politics and Society*, vol. 3, pp. 215–32 (London: Blackwell).

Arrow, K. J. (1971) 'The firm in general equilibrium theory' in R. Marris and A. Wood (eds), *The Corporate Economy: Growth, Competition and Innovative Potential*, pp. 68–110 (London: Macmillan).

Arrow, K. J. and Hahn, F. H. (1971) *General Competitive Analysis* (Edinburgh: Oliver & Boyd).

Atkinson, A. B. (1973) 'How progressive should income tax be?' in M. Parkin (ed.), *Essays in Modern Economics*, pp. 90–109 (London: Longman).

Barry, B. (1970) *Sociologists, Economists and Democracy* (London: Collier–Macmillan).

Baumol, W. J. (1977) *Economic Theory and Operations Analysis*, 4th edn (London: Prentice-Hall International).

Bentham, J. (1961) *Principles of Morals and Legislation* (London: Doubleday). (First published in 1789.)

Bergson, A. (1938) 'A reformulation of certain aspects of welfare economics', *Quarterly Journal of Economics*, vol. 52, pp. 314–44.

Bergson, A. (1966) *Essays in Normative Economics* (Harvard: Harvard University Press).

Black, J. and Bradley, J. F. (1973) *Essential Mathematics for Economists* (London: Wiley).

Borch, K. and Mossin, J. (eds) (1968) *Risk and Uncertainty* (London: Macmillan).

Breton, A. (1974) *The Economic Theory of Representative Government* (Chicago: Aldine).

Brunner, J. (1965) *The National Plan*, IEA Eaton Paper 4.

Buchanan, J. M. (1954) 'Individual choice in voting and the market', *Journal of Political Economy*, vol. 62, pp. 334–43.

Buchanan, J. M. (1968) *The Demand and Supply of Public Goods* (Chicago: Rand McNally).

Burn, D., Seale, J. R. and Ratcliff, A. R. N. (1965) *Lessons from Central Forecasting*, IEA Eaton Paper 6.

Cameron, B. (1968) *Input–Output Analysis and Resource Allocation* (Cambridge: CUP).

Carr, E. H. and Davies, R. W. (1974) *Foundations of a Planned Economy 1926–1929*, vol. 1 (Harmondsworth: Penguin).

194

BIBLIOGRAPHY

Cazes, B (1962) 'La planification française: esprit et méthods', *Problèmes de l'Europe*, vol. 18, pp. 31–9.

Chalmers, J. A. and Fischel, W. (1967) 'An analysis of automatic stabilisers in a small econometric model', *National Tax Journal*.

Chiang, A. (1974) *Fundamental Methods of Mathematical Economics*, 2nd edn (London: McGraw-Hill).

Christ, C. F. (1966) *Econometric Models and Methods* (New York: Wiley).

Clower, R. W. (1965) 'The Keynesian counter-revolution: a theoretical appraisal' in R. W. Clower (ed.) *Readings in Monetary Theory*, pp. 270–98 (Harmondsworth: Penguin, 1969).

Coase, R. H. (1960) 'The problem of social cost', *Journal of Law and Economics*, vol. 3, pp. 1–41.

Cole, G. D. H. (1937) *Practical Economics* (Harmondsworth: Penguin).

Csikós-Nagy, B. (1973) *Socialist Economic Policy* (London: Longman).

Culyer, A. J. (1974) *Economic Policies and Social Goals: Aspects of Public Choice* (London: Martin Robertson).

Department of Economic Affairs (1965) *The National Plan*, Cmnd 2764 (London: HMSO).

Department of Economic Affairs (1969) *The Task Ahead: An Economic Assessment to 1972*, (London: HMSO).

Debreu, G. (1959) *Theory of Value* (New York: John H. Wiley).

Demsetz, H. (1967) 'Toward a theory of property rights', *American Economic Review*, vol. 57, pp. 1347–59.

Demsetz, H. (1969) 'Information and efficiency: another viewpoint', *Journal of Law and Economics*, vol. 12, pp. 1–22.

Dobb, M. (1960) *An Essay on Economic Growth and Planning* (London: Routledge & Kegan Paul).

Dorfman, R., Samuelson, P. A. and Solow, R. (1958) *Linear Programming and Economic Analysis* (New York: McGraw-Hill,).

Downs, A. (1957) *An Economic Theory of Democracy* (New York: Harper & Row).

Durbin, E. F. M. (1949) *Problems of Economic Planning* (London: Routledge & Kegan Paul).

Edey, H. C., Peacock, A. T. and Cooper, R. A. (1967) *National Income and Social Accounting*, 3rd edn (London: Hutchinson).

Ellman, M. (1971) *Soviet Planning Today*, Department of Applied Economics, Occasional Paper 25 (Cambridge: CUP).

Erlich, A. (1960) *The Soviet Industrialisation Debate 1924–1928*, Russian Research Center Studies 41 (Harvard: Harvard University Press).

Evans, M. K. (1969) *Macroeconomic Activity* (New York: Harper & Row).

Faber, M. and Seers, D. (eds) (1972) *The Crisis in Planning* (London: Chatto & Windus).

Flowerdew, A. D. J. (1972) 'Choosing a site for the Third London Airport: the Roskill Commission's approach' in R. Layard, (ed.) *Cost-Benefit Analysis*, pp. 431–51 (Harmondsworth: Penguin).

Fox, K. A., Sengupta, J. and Thorbecke, E. (1966) *The Theory of Quantitative Economic Policy with Applications to Economic Growth and Stabilisation* (Amsterdam: North-Holland).

Fried, C. (1970) *An Anatomy of Values* (Harvard: Harvard University Press).

Friedman, B. M. (1975) *Economic Stabilization Policy: Methods in Optimization* (Amsterdam: North-Holland).

Friedman, M. (ed.) (1956) *Studies in the Quantity Theory of Money* (Chicago: Chicago University Press).

Friedman, M. (1957) *A Theory of the Consumption Function* (Princeton, NJ: Princeton University Press).

Friedman, M. (1961) 'The lag in effect in monetary policy', *Journal of Political Economy*, vol. 69, pp. 447–77.

Friedman, M. (1964) 'Note on the lag in effect of monetary policy', *American Economic Review*, vol. 54, pp. 759–61.

Friedman, M. (1970) *The Counter Revolution in Monetary Theory*, IEA Occasional Paper 33.

Fromm, G. and Taubman, P. (1968) *Policy Simulations with an Econometric Model* (Amsterdam: North-Holland)

Gale, D. (1960) *The Theory of Linear Economic Models* (New York: McGraw-Hill).

Gordon, B. (1975) *Economic Analysis before Adam Smith* (London: Macmillan).

Gossling, W. F. (ed.) (1970) *Input –Output in the United Kingdom* (London: Frank Cass).

Green, H. A. J. (1976) *Consumer Theory*, 2nd edn (London: Macmillan).

Hackett, J. and Hackett, A. M. (1963) *Economic Planning in France* (London: Allen & Unwin).

Hammond, P. and Mirrlees, J. A. (1973) 'Agreeable plans' in J. A. Mirrlees and N. Stern (eds), *The Theory of Economic Growth*, pp. 283–99 (London: Macmillan).

Hanson, A. H. (1966) *The Process of Planning* (London: OUP).

Hardin, R. (1971) 'Collective action as an agreeable n-prisoners' dilemma', *Behavioural Science*, vol. 16, pp. 472–81.

Hart, P. E., Mills, G. and Whitaker, J. K. (eds) (1964) *Econometric Analysis for National Economic Planning* (London: Butterworth).

Heal, G. M. (1973) *The Theory of Economic Planning* (Amsterdam: North-Holland).

Henderson, J. M. and Quandt, R. E. (1971) *Microeconomic Theory: a Mathematical Approach*, 2nd edn (London: McGraw-Hill).

Hicks, J. (1939) 'The foundations of welfare economics', *Economic Journal*, vol. 49, pp. 696–712.

Intriligator, M. M. (ed.) (1971) *Frontiers of Quantitative Economics* (Amsterdam: North-Holland).

Jewkes, J. (1948) *Ordeal by Planning* (London: Macmillan).

Johnston, J. (1963) *Econometric Methods* (London: McGraw-Hill).

Kaldor, N. (1939) 'Welfare propositions of economic and interpersonal comparisons of utility', *Economic Journal*, vol. 49, pp. 549–51.

Kaser, M. (1970) *Soviet Economics* (London: Weidenfeld & Nicolson).

Keynes, J. M. (1936) *The General Theory of Employment, Interest and Money* (London: Macmillan).

Klein, L. R. (1950) *Economic Fluctuations in the United States, 1921–1941*, Cowles Commission Monograph 11 (New York: John Wiley).

Klein, L. R. (1953) *A Textbook of Econometrics* (New York: Row, Peterson & Co.).

Kuhn, H. W. and Tucker, A. W. (1951) 'Nonlinear programming' in Neyman (ed.), *Proceedings of the Second Berkeley Symposium on Mathematical Statistics and Probability*, pp. 481–92 (Berkeley, Calif.: University of California Press).

Laidler, D. E. W. (1969) *The Demand for Money* (Scranton, Pa.: International Textbook).

Lancaster, K. (1968) *Mathematical Economics* (New York: Macmillan).

BIBLIOGRAPHY

Lange, O. and Taylor, F. M. (1938) *On the Economic Theory of Socialism* (Minneapolis, Minn.: Minnesota University Press).

Layard, R. (ed.) (1972) *Cost-Benefit Analysis: Selected Readings* (Harmondsworth: Penguin).

Leruez, J. (1975) *Economic Planning and politics in Britain* (London: Martin Robertson).

Lewin, M. (1968) *Russian Peasants and Soviet Economic Power* (London: Allen & Unwin).

Lewis, J. P. (1969) *An Introduction to Mathematics for Students of Economics*, 2nd edn (London: Macmillan).

Lewis, W. A. (1949) *The Principles of Economic Planning* (London: Allen & Unwin).

Liggins, D. (1975) *National Economic Planning in France* (Farnborough: Saxon House).

Lipsey, R. G. and Lancaster, K. (1956–57) 'The general theory of second best', *Review of Economic Studies*, vol. 24, pp. 11–32.

Little, I. M. D. (1950) *A Critique of Welfare Economics* (London: OUP).

Luce, R. D. and Raiffa, H. (1957) *Games and Decisions* (New York: Wiley).

Lutz, V. (1969) *Central Planning for the Market Economy* (London: Longman).

Markowitz, H. W. (1959) *Portfolio Selection* (New York: Wiley).

Massé, P. (1962) 'French methods of planning', *Journal of Industrial Economics*, vol. 11, pp. 1–17.

Massé, P. (1965) 'The French Plan and economic theory', *Econometrica*, vol. 33, pp. 265–76.

Matthews, R. C. O. and King, M. A. (1977) 'The British economy: problems and policies in the late 1970s', *Midland Bank Review*, February, pp. 1–10.

Mayston, D. J. (1974) *The Idea of Social Choice* (London: Macmillan).

Meade, J. E. (1948) *Planning and the Price Mechanism: The Liberal Socialist Solution* (London: Allen & Unwin).

Meade, J. E. (1966) 'Life-cycle savings, inheritance and economic growth', *Review of Economic Studies*, vol. 33, pp. 61–78.

Meade, J. E. (1970) The Theory of Indicative Planning (Manchester: Manchester University Press).

Miernyk, W. J. (1965) *The Elements of Input–Output Analysis* (New York: Random House).

Mirrlees, J. A. (1971) 'An exploration in the theory of optimum income taxation', *Review of Economic Studies*, vol. 38, pp. 175–208.

Mishan, E. (1971) *Cost–Benefit Analysis* (London: Allen & Unwin).

Mitchell, J. (1966) *Groundwork to Economic Planning* (London: Secker & Warburg).

Modigliani, F. and Brumberg, R. (1964) 'Utility analysis and the consumption function' in K. Kuriha (ed.), *Post Keynesian Economics* (New Brunswick: Rutgers University Press).

Morgenstern, O. (1963) *On the Accuracy of Economic Observations*, 2nd edn (Princeton, NJ: Princeton University Press).

Mueller, D. C. (1976) 'Public choice: a survey', *Journal of Economic Literative*, pp. 395–433.

Mundell, R. A. (1962) 'The appropriate use of monetary and fiscal policy for internal and external stability', *International Monetary Fund Staff Papers*.

Myrdal, G. (1960) *Beyond the Welfare State* (London: Duckworth).

Myrdal, G. (1968) *Asian Drama*, vol. 2 (Harmondsworth: Pelican).

Newbold, P. (1975) 'The principles of the Box–Jenkins approach', *Operational Research Quarterly*, vol. 26, pp. 397–412.

Nordhaus, W. D. (1975) 'The political business cycle', *Review of Economic Studies*, vol. 42, pp. 169–90.

Nove, A. (1966) 'The explosive model', *Journal of Development Studies*, vol. 3, pp. 2-13.

Nove, A. (1972) *An Economic History of the USSR* (Harmondsworth: Penguin).

Nove, A. and Nuti D. M. (eds) (1972) *Socialist Economics* (Harmondsworth: Penguin).

Nozick, R. (1974) *Anarchy, State and Utopia* (Oxford: Blackwell).

Olsen, M. (1965) *The Logic of Collective Action* (Harvard: Harvard University Press).

Pattanaik, P. K. (1968) 'Risk, impersonality and the social welfare function', *Journal of Political Economy*, vol. 76, pp. 1152–69.

Pearce, D. W. (1971) *Cost–Benefit Analysis* (London: Macmillan).

Peston, M. H. (1974) *Theory of Macroeconomic Policy* (Oxford: Philip Allan).

Phelps, E. S. (1966) *Golden Rules of Economic Growth* (New York: Norton).

Phelps, E. S. (ed.) (1971) *Microeconomic Foundations of Employment and Inflation Theory* (London: Macmillan).

Phelps, E. S. (ed.) (1973) *Economic Justice: Selected Readings* (Harmondsworth: Penguin).

Pigou, A. (1920) *The Economics of Welfare* (London: Macmillan).

Pindyck, R. S. (1973) *Optimal Planning for Economic Stabilization: The Application of Control Theory to Stabilization Policy* (Amsterdam: North-Holland).

Polanyi, G. (1967) *Planning in Britain: The Experience of the 1960s*, IEA Research Monograph 18.

Pollack, R. A. (1968) 'Consistent planning', *Review of Economic Studies*, vol. 35, pp. 201–08.

Prest, A. R. (1968) *The UK Economy – A Manual of Applied Economics*, 2nd edn (London: Weidenfeld & Nicolson).

Quirk J. and Saposnik, R. (1968) *Introduction to General Equilibrium Theory and Welfare Economics* (New York: McGraw-Hill).

Ramsey, F. P. (1928) 'A mathematical theory of saving', *Economic Journal*, vol. 38, pp. 543–59.

Rau, N. (1974) *Trade Cycles: Theory and Evidence* (London: Macmillan).

Rawls, J. (1973) *A Theory of Justice* (London: OUP).

Renton, G. A. (ed.) (1975) *Modelling the Economy* (London: Heinemann).

Richardson, H. W. (1972) *Input–Output and Regional Economics* (London: Weidenfeld & Nicolson).

Rowan, D. C. (1974) *Output, Inflation and Growth*, 2nd edn (London: Macmillan).

Rowley, C. K. (ed.) (1972) *Readings in Industrial Economics*, vol. 2 (London: Macmillan).

Rowley, C. K. (1973) *Antitrust and Economic Efficiency* (London: Macmillan).

Rowley, C. K. and Peacock, A. T. (1975) *Welfare Economics: A Liberal Restatement* (London: Martin Robertson).

Samuelson, P. A. (1939) 'Interactions between the multiplier analysis and the principle of acceleration', *Review of Economic Statistics*, vol. 21, pp. 75–8.

Samuelson, P. A. (1947) *Foundations of Economic Analysis* (Harvard: Harvard University Press).

Samuelson, P. A. (1954) 'The pure theory of public expenditures', *Review of Economics and Statistics*, vol. 36, pp. 387–9.

BIBLIOGRAPHY

Samuelson, P. A. (1955) 'Diagrammatic exposition of a theory of public expenditure', *Review of Economics and Statistics*, vol. 37, pp. 350–6.

Sen, A. K. (1970) *Collective Choice and Social Welfare* (Edinburgh: Oliver & Boyd).

Shaw, G. K. (1971) *Fiscal Policy* (London: Macmillan)

Shenoy, S. R. (1971) *India: Progress or Poverty?* IEA Research Monograph 27.

Shubik, M. (1959) *Strategy and Market Structure: Competition, Oligopoly and the Theory of Games* (New York: Wiley).

Siroyezhin, I. M. (1968) 'Risk and uncertainty in the management of Soviet firms' in Borch and Mossin (eds), *Risk and Uncertainty*, pp. 359–63 (London: Macmillan).

Smyth, D. J. (1963) 'Can automatic stabilisers be destabilising?', *Public Finance*.

Solow, R. M. (1970) *Growth Theory – An Exposition* (Oxford: Clarendon Press).

Stone, R. (1951) *The Role of Measurement in Economics*, Department of Applied Economics Monograph 3 (Cambridge: CUP).

Streeten, P. and Lipton, M. (eds) (1968) *The Crisis in Indian Planning* (London: OUP).

Streissler, E. W. (1970) *Pitfalls in Econometric Forecasting*, IEA Research Monograph 23.

Strotz, R. H. (1955–56) 'Myopia and inconsistency in dynamic utility maximisation', *Review of Economic Studies*, vol. 23, pp. 165–80.

Taylor, A. J. (1972) *Laissez-Faire and State Intervention in Nineteenth Century Britain* (London: Macmillan).

Taylor, M. (1976) *Anarchy and Co-operation* (New York: Wiley).

Theil, H. (1958) *Economic Forecasts and Policy* (Amsterdam: North-Holland).

Theil, H. (1964) *Optimal Decision Rules for Government and Industry* (Amsterdam: North-Holland).

Theil, H. and Boot, J. C. G. (1962) 'The final form of econometric equation systems', *Review of International Statistical Institute*, vol. 30, pp. 136–52.

Thomas, D. (ed.) (1970) *The Mind of Economic Man (London: Quadrangle Books)*.

Thomson, D. *(1957) Europe since Napoleon* (London: Longman).

Tinbergen, J. (1952) *On the Theory of Economic Policy* (Amsterdam: North-Holland).

Timbergen, J. (1961) 'Do communist and free economies show a converging pattern?', *Soviet Studies*, vol. 12, pp. 333–41.

Tinbergen, J. (1967) *Development Planning* (London: Weidenfeld Nicolson).

Treml, V. G., Gallik, D. M., Kostinsky, B. L. and Kruger, K. W. (1972) *The Structure of the Soviet Economy* (New York: Praeger).

Victor, P. A. (1972) *Economics of Pollution* (London: Macmillan).

von Hayek, F. A. (ed.) (1935) *Collectivist Economic Planning* (London: Routledge & Kegan Paul).

von Hayek, F. A. (1944) *The Road to Serfdom* (London: reprinted by Routledge & Kegan Paul).

Wallis, K. F. (1973) *Topics in Applied Econometrics* (London: Gray-Mills).

Walras, L. (1874) *Elements d'économie politique pure* (Lausanne: L. Corbaz). English translation by W. Jaffe (1954) *Elements of Pure Economics* (London: Allen & Unwin).

Ward, B. N. (1967) *The Socialist Economy* (New York: Random House).

Weintraub, E. Roy (1973) *General Equilibrium Theory* (London: Macmillan).

Weintraub, E. R. (1975) *Conflict and Co-operation in Economics* (London: Macmillan).

Weisbrod, B. A. (1968) 'Income redistribution effects and benefit-cost analysis' in R. Layard (ed.) (1972) *Cost-Benefit Analysis: Selected Readings*, pp. 395–426 (Harmondsworth: Penguin).

Wilczynski, J. (1970) *The Economics of Socialism* (London: Allen & Unwin).

Wilczynski, J. (1973) *Profit, Risk and Incentives under Socialist Economic Planning* (London: Macmillan).

Wilde, D. J. (1964) *Optimum Seeking Methods* (Englewood Cliffs, NJ: Prentice-Hall).

Wiles, P. J. D. (ed.) (1971) *The Prediction of Communist Economic Performance* (Cambridge: CUP).

Wilson, C. (1965) *England's Apprenticeship 1603–1763* (London: Longman).

Winch, D. M. (1971) *Analytical Welfare Economics* (Harmondsworth: Penguin).

Wonnacott, R. J. and Wonnacott, T. H. (1970) *Econometrics* (New York: Wiley).

Wootton, B. (1945) *Freedom and Planning* (London: Allen & Unwin).

Worswick, G. D. N. and Blackaby, F. T. (1974) *The Medium Term* (London: Heinemann).

Wynn, R. F. and Holden, K. (1974) *An Introduction to Applied Econometric Analysis* (London: Macmillan).

Yeomans, K. A. (1968) *Statistics for the Social Scientist*, vols 1 and 2 (Harmondsworth: Penguin).

INDEX